In Two Minds

In Two Minds

Stories of Murder, Justice and Recovery
from a Forensic Psychiatrist

Dr Sohom Das

SPHERE

SPHERE

First published in Great Britain in 2022 by Sphere
This paperback edition published in 2023 by Sphere

3 5 7 9 10 8 6 4 2

A CIP catalogue record for this book
is available from the British Library.

ISBN 978-0-7515-8379-3

Typeset in Dante by M Rules
Printed and bound in Great Britain by Clays Ltd, Elcograf S.p.A.

Papers used by Sphere are from well-managed forests
and other responsible sources.

Sphere
An imprint of
Little, Brown Book Group
Carmelite House
50 Victoria Embankment
London EC4Y 0DZ

An Hachette UK Company
www.hachette.co.uk

www.littlebrown.co.uk

For my wife and confidante, Rizma, and my two little homies,
Kamran and Rayaan.

Contents

Author's Note

Aside from the cases that are already out in the public domain, the people in this book, including patients and colleagues, are anonymised. I have intentionally changed their names, some demographic details and sometimes the dates and locations of our interactions to make them less recognisable. On occasion, I have merged cases into one presentation. This is all in order to maintain patient confidentiality and also out of respect for the victims and their family members. Nevertheless, the essence of all my stories is 100 per cent genuine. (My wife and kids are very real!)

I think it is important to explain **why** I've written this book. My aim is to throw open the doors to the secure psychiatric units, prisons and criminal courts where I have assessed and helped rehabilitate mentally disordered offenders. I hope I have shone some light on these dark corners that the public are otherwise shielded from. My intention is to expose the brutal realities and struggles of the extremely vulnerable, damaged and often misunderstood individuals. How else can we demystify forensic psychiatry and truly tackle the stigma attached to those within its system? I sincerely I hope that I have managed to straddle the fine line between writing about my patients as sensitively as possible, yet simultaneously not pulling any punches.

Prologue

It was an exceptionally windy day. A flurry of police officers in uniforms, solicitors in suits and barristers in gowns and wigs were ambushed by gales the moment they stepped out of the Old Bailey. I had arrived almost two hours early, and spent the morning pacing up and down the street outside. I re-read my court report obsessively, trying to distract myself from the sense of dread, while chain-smoking – giving evidence in a murder trial seemed as good a reason as any for a relapse. Forget butterflies, I felt like I had bats in my stomach, amplified by the pompous grandiosity of the Old Bailey – the pillars, the statues, the stone carvings and the Latin inscriptions.

When I finally took the witness stand in my shiny new suit, ignoring the sweat trickling down my back, I read out the affirmation. 'I do solemnly, sincerely and truly declare and affirm that the evidence I shall give shall be the truth, the whole truth and nothing but the truth.' I took a deep breath. As I waited for the barrage of cross-examination from the barristers and the judge, I took sips of water, feeling like a gazelle at a watering hole, drinking trepidatiously, wary of lions creeping closer.

At the time, as a junior doctor, I had to pass all major decisions through the consultant who led our team. However, my boss recognised that this case would undoubtedly be a goldmine of knowledge of the intricacies of the medico-legal world and so he had passed it on to me. A few weeks after submitting my court report, I was summoned to give oral evidence at a murder trial. Acting as an expert witness is my specialism now, but I was wet behind the ears back then.

On the witness stand I was acutely aware of how important it is for forensic psychiatrists to get it right. Although our advice to the court is not binding, our opinions heavily influence judges. A poor performance backing up that evidence under cross-examination can have critical repercussions. Our words can change the lives of those in the dock. We can steer the incapacitated, the vulnerable and the voiceless away from a lifetime of incarceration, towards recovery. Get it wrong, and we can be instrumental in the guilty literally getting away with murder.

The vast majority of psychiatric patients are not violent. The vast majority of violent offenders are not mentally ill. But when the two worlds collide, the results can be catastrophic. In this case at the Old Bailey, a promising young schoolgirl of previously good character with no history of antisocial behaviour could kill a toddler in a flash of psychosis, ripping the very fabric of the family apart for ever. Those tasked with assessing, treating and rehabilitating patients whose symptoms cause violence are also tasked with preventing future atrocities and protecting the public from harm. I am one of them.

My duty is to evaluate, risk-assess, treat and rehabilitate people whom we in the business call 'mentally disordered offenders' but tabloids might call 'the criminally insane'. My clients typically assault, rob, stab, set fires and rape. Some kill. They are often driven by paranoia and delusions of grandeur. Some hear voices commanding them to commit these atrocities. The majority also have co-morbid issues, which may include drug and alcohol addiction or severe and pervasive character flaws such as a lack of remorse, morality, or empathy. This can lead them to habitually offend, attack, lie, manipulate and treat others with callous indifference. Collectively, these traits are known as personality disorder.

Forensic psychiatry is also a world of compassion. My patients are some of the most damaged, vulnerable people, once victims themselves. Abuse has reared one or more of its ugly heads throughout their childhoods. Plus, they are doubly stigmatised: for their mental illness and for their crimes. After identifying these individuals, we forensic psychiatrists are responsible for rehabilitating them inside secure psychiatric units; we analyse their lives in depth and try to understand the exact circumstances and reasons for their offending, thus ascertaining their risk factors. We eliminate the eliminable, over years and sometimes even decades. We strive to give them the best chance to be re-integrated into a society that wishes at best to ignore them, and at worst to lock them up and throw away the key.

Her name was Yasmin Khan. She killed her two-year-old nephew by smothering him with a pillow. She believed she was removing demons from him and that he would wake up. She was one of my first criminal cases and her trial was the first time I set foot inside the Old Bailey. Since then, I have undertaken hundreds of assessments and treated a plethora of mentally ill offenders. After being exposed to a huge range of felonies, and details of brutality, it is easy to become inured. Yet some cases will always be etched on my mind. Sometimes, the act of violence is exceptionally shocking or senseless. Sometimes, the victim is particularly vulnerable or unsullied. Sometimes, the perpetrator is too. Sometimes, the diagnosis is ambiguous or elusive. Yasmin's case incorporated all of the above.

There are four natural habitats of the forensic psychiatrist, and we tend to work across one or two of these at any one time. We are most often found within secure psychiatric units, behind large, escape-proof, fingerprint-scanner-activated, industrial-strength, magnetic doors, and surrounded by tall wire-mesh fences. These are hospitals reserved for the most high-risk clientele, where security is paramount and staff are on high alert for the possibility of aggression or agitation. A smaller group of us work in Community Mental Health Teams, following up patients once they have been released from secure hospitals to help reintegrate them into society. By doing this, we are unique among psychiatrists (and among all other doctors) in that we are also tasked with ensuring the safety of those around them: friends, family, strangers. Potential future victims.

Another common environment of the forensic psychiatrist is inside the bowels of prisons across the country, where blood-curdling screams and dirty protests are not uncommon, and where mental health issues are rampant. Here, we are usually part of a Mental Health In-Reach Team and we typically run psychiatric clinics and oversee patients within the healthcare unit – like a hospital ward inside prison – for those wretched souls who are tortured with psychosis and require the highest level of treatment and observation.

Our other place of work is within criminal courts, either as part of a Liaison and Diversion Team or independently. Our task here is to assess the defendants who come into court on any given day: from police stations (if they have just been arrested), from the community (if they are on bail) or from prison (if they are on remand), ahead of their tête-à-tête with the judge. We identify those with serious mental health issues, or other vulnerabilities such as learning disabilities or substance misuse, and align them with the appropriate health or social care services. In the rare cases of floridly unwell defendants, who are too disturbed to unleash on to society, we divert them away to secure psychiatric hospitals by sectioning them.

Some forensic psychiatrists also undertake expert witness work. This is mostly private work, distinct from the above duties. As expert witnesses, our role is to advise the criminal court on a range of medico-legal issues, from whether an individual's mental state would fully absolve them from criminal responsibility (not guilty by reason of insanity), to down-grading their murder charge to manslaughter (diminished responsibility). We determine who needs to be urgently sectioned to specialist psychiatric hospitals, for the most dangerous mentally ill offenders, where spaces are limited and rehabilitation is probing, intense and prolonged. All of these medico-legal issues and more were pertinent to Yasmin's exceptionally sticky and complex case.

That day at the Old Bailey, the barrister for the prosecution argued against my recommendations, for both the psychiatric defences and also the disposal of Yasmin's case (i.e. prison or hospital). She pushed for a custodial life sentence, but not by arguing the nuances of mental health law or questioning the validity of Yasmin's admittedly uncertain diagnosis. Instead she tried to attack my credibility as an expert witness, by commenting repeatedly on my limited experience. If my ears were serving me correctly, she was emphasising the 'junior' in 'junior doctor' and kept using this term long after my job title was established. She aggressively tried to fluster me by deliberately making tenuous and tangential inferences from what I said to make me contradict myself, and by frequently interrupting me. But that was her job. I knew that. As the Godfather once said, 'it's not personal, it's strictly business'. I had the advantage of having spent months assessing Yasmin and developing familiarity with her case. It made sense that the barrister would go for the jugular by trying to discredit me. I stood my ground. She asked leading, convoluted questions. I answered them logically and neutrally. She made misleading inferences. I parried them, as per my training. It was a prolonged, repetitive, passive-aggressive, formal, intellectual argument. Overseen by a judge with a deadpan, unflinching facial expression. As per his training, I would imagine. Something occurred to me on the witness stand: not only had my initial anxiety dissipated, but, perversely, I was actually *enjoying* this. The suit, the wigs and gowns, the unnecessary Latin, the grandiosity of it all. Plus, I was winning the argument.

I can still picture Yasmin perfectly. Her mousey face,

plaited hair and precarious eyebrows. Her eerily vacant smile. Her case remains one of the most harrowing of my career and one of the most emotionally charged experiences of my life. It left me with so many questions. At the time, my wife and I were considering starting our own family in the next couple of years. Could something so precious that takes so long to build really be annihilated in an instant? Once her psychotic fog had lifted, could Yasmin ever come to terms with what she'd done? Could her family ever forgive her? Could she rebuild her life? To find the answers, I knew I would have to dive into pursuing a career within this niche specialty that I had only dipped my toe into thus far. But this was also a huge learning opportunity for me as a junior doctor and I am grateful to my consultant for having the confidence in me to hand over the reins.

My experience at the Old Bailey taught me something. The butterflies and the cigarettes weren't necessary. I would make a pretty decent expert witness. The very prospect of being cross-examined strikes fear in the heart of some of my peers, but I relished the exhilaration of it all. Before this case, I had some doubts about whether forensic psychiatry was a suitable career for me. But my experience on the witness stand woke something inside me. This was what I wanted to do. I also learnt that I had a lot to learn. And learn I did. It just took hundreds of cases, assessments and cross-examinations, untangling a litany of violent assaults, murders and rapes to get there.

Part One

Secure Hospitals

Chapter 1

The Origin Story

I became interested in crime long before psychiatry. Actually, it was more like rap, then crime, then psychiatry. From my early teenage years in the nineties, I would sit in awe listening to Cypress Hill, House of Pain, and the Wu-Tang Clan openly and shamelessly rap about dealing drugs, beating people up or even killing them. These artists tickled my fascination with crime but Snoop Doggy Dogg blew my mind (he has since dropped the 'Doggy', perhaps sensing his moniker was excessively canine). Not only was Dr Dre's production incredibly bold and funky, but Snoop's message was clear. That same man who now appears in cameos in Hollywood films and prances around in Just Eat adverts unequivocally rapped about drinking gin and juice, smoking cannabis, killing for little or no reason, and having carnal relationships with a variety of impressionable women, without having the courtesy to call them the next day. Of course, I cannot now condone these hugely misogynistic and violent views but at the time it was the *audacity* of his message rather than the content that had me glued to the stereo (volume down, when my parents were at home, as they would not tolerate the profanity).

The sheer nerve of it all fascinated me. I grew up in a sheltered and strict household in a boring if idyllic village named Poynton in Cheshire, where danger was represented by a particularly high rope swing. Police sirens, gang rivalry and prison stabbings were all elements of a surreal fantasy world.

My mother was a secretary for a company that made earplugs, then later on a secretary for a university lecturer. My father was a chemical engineer, whose job was, bizarrely, to formulate less carcinogenic and quicker-drying glues for cigarettes. They had come over from India to London in the early sixties separately and were unique among their many siblings in having had a love marriage, as opposed to an arranged one. They suffered blatant racism and discrimination. After facing a number of doors being slammed in their faces (figuratively and literally) their dreams of integration and acceptance were replaced by domination and success, an approach that we have different perspectives on to this day. As is the Indian way, my parents were obsessively invested in my and my older sister's futures. As I was intelligent and had an affinity for science subjects, they pushed me to go to medical school, even though I was immature and frankly indifferent. They came from a country with no welfare state, so education was paramount. It could be the difference between a comfortable life and literally starving to death on the street. They would make me do extra studying for several hours most days to stay ahead of my peers and the school curriculum. Of course, I now appreciate it was their support and encouragement, more than my tepid motivation, that propelled me to medical school and beyond, but at the time I resented the enforced studying. I only cared about riding my bike, then later about martial arts and video games, then eventually about buying booze with fake IDs and going to parties.

Like many of my peers, I developed a penchant for violent films in my early teens. This was amplified by *Street Fighter II* on the Super Nintendo, which to me was the greatest invention since fire. Better, even. I now have a full-size *Street Fighter II* arcade machine set up in our kitchen: a sore for my wife's eyes and the apple of mine. Having not yet refined my taste for story arcs and character development, I found not only Jean-Claude Van Damme's acting acceptable, but his 720° spinning kicks amazing. Given that my parents were much stricter than my friends' in terms of my curfew, the company I kept, my extracurricular activities and my financial independence, rather inexplicably they had absolutely no qualms in allowing me to hire 18-certificate videos every Friday night from Blockbusters (RIP) from my early teens. It was the violence that drew me in. *Robocop*, *Terminator 2* and *Boyz n the Hood* left a dent in my impressionable mind. As they once again pulled me out of my dull textbook-heavy life as a young teenager into a fantasy domain, I was oblivious to the fact that I would be regularly rubbing shoulders with violent offenders two decades later.

Keen to get as far away as possible from soporific Cheshire, I attended Edinburgh medical school in 1997 from the age of eighteen to twenty-four. I had the same level of street cred as a choirboy, but the determination to reinvent myself. I drifted aimlessly through my degree. The attitude of my friends and me was, shall we say, atypical: instead of an opportunity to learn our craft and occasionally social-ise, we treated university as one big party, occasionally inconvenienced by pesky lectures and clinical attachments. Attendance was the bare minimum to avoid getting kicked off the course. Nowadays, attendance is far more fervently overseen, but back in my day, on the rare occasion when we had to sign in (like when examining cadavers for our anatomy module), we would select the equivalent of a designated driver to peel themselves out of bed, suppress their hangover and sign all our names. On the odd day when I did attend anatomy classes, seeing dead bodies was underwhelming to me. They looked and smelt so unreal, discoloured and pickled in formaldehyde, that I found it hard to accept that they had once been living, breathing people. There were repercussions for my actions (or lack thereof). I failed almost all of my exams in the first year and had to re-sit them in the summer holidays, a hair's breadth (ninety-nine micro-metres, thanks anatomy) from having to resit the entire year. I resolved to take the course seriously and hit those books much harder. When my mates returned at the start of the second year, frankly my resolve was weak-ened. Still, I managed to at least tread water throughout the rest of my degree. Looking back, my attitude was sheer immaturity. Now, in my early forties, I am driven and pas-sionate about my work. But back in my medical school days, my mindset was still that of a teenager. The only difference was that I no longer had a curfew from my parents and no longer needed a fake ID to buy booze.

I took a year out halfway through medical school to do an intercalated MSc in pharmacology. I would love to say that I had an interest in this topic, but in reality I just wanted to delay the inevitable slog of becoming a junior doctor. After this year, I was twenty-two as I entered my fourth year, and I first encountered psychiatry. I was assigned a placement within a liaison psychiatry team based in a hospital in Edinburgh, and I had an immediate affinity for the specialism. The doctors and nurses were very welcoming and friendly to all the medical students. This contrasted with some of my other experiences of placements where we had been treated like a persistent flatulence that followed the senior doctors around, mostly too scared to make eye contact, let alone ask any medical questions.

Like all of my clinical attachments, I initially blagged my way through my psychiatry placement, intending to cram all the information for the exams within the last couple of weeks. However, to my surprise, what I lacked in clinical knowledge I made up for with empathy and communication skills. When patients would come in post-paracetamol overdose, after the basic risk assessment and necessary medical treatment, they needed the catharsis of sitting with somebody who would listen to their problems and not judge them. I could do that!

To be honest, my empathy had not really been tested before. I had never known much tragedy among my friends and family; nobody close to me had died and I'd grown up in a typically stoic Asian family. For the first time I was encountering real people with real problems. Abuse, poverty, alcoholism, homelessness, relationship breakdowns and, of course, mental illness. I had been vaguely aware of this world, but until then it had been as far removed from me as Snoop Doggy Dogg's drive-bys and gang turf wars. But here I could actually make a difference.

During the latter part of my placement, I was stationed across a few different psychiatric wards. I spoke to dozens of psychotic patients and was immediately fascinated by their stories and experiences, some of which existed outside of reality. Conversing with them about their delusional beliefs was sometimes surreal, scary even, but always fascinating. I quickly saw that there was a fine line between empathising with their bizarre experiences and encouraging them. There was the pub landlord who believed he was shrinking and would eventually disappear. A former university professor who believed she was a reincarnation of Cleopatra. A skeletal anorexic teenage boy who lived in shame of being overweight. The patient who touched me the most was a middle-aged teacher named Freda Millican, who had been in a horrific car accident seven months earlier that had taken her teenage son's life. She was brought to the accident and emergency department by her husband because she had not slept for the previous three nights. I had never seen anybody so consumed by sadness. As I had shown keenness and competency on the ward in the previous weeks, the psychiatrist in charge of the team, Dr Porter, let me assess her fully independently, without observation. Although I had sympathised and felt some connection with the pub landlord I had assessed the previous day, his psychosis was so bizarre, so alien, it felt as unreal to me as those cadavers. Freda's situation was different. This could happen to anybody. This could happen to me.

Several times a day, Freda described experiencing 'a balloon blowing up in my stomach', identical to when the car left the ground, as well as intrusive images of her son's blood dribbling across the cracked windshield moments afterwards. She told me she was 'stuck on that day on repeat' and had to 'live it over and over again'. Other symptoms and behaviours she reported included feeling constantly miserable, feeling too tired to look after herself or to do housework and being unable to follow conversations or even TV programmes. Her husband forced her to go to bingo which she did avidly and weekly before the accident.

'It was miserable,' she told me. 'No joy whatsoever. It felt like everybody was staring at me because of what happened. I couldn't wait to get home.'

Freda was terrified of leaving her house. She dreaded seeing teenage boys, especially tall skinny ones with shaggy hair who reminded her of her son. The mere sight of them would upset her and send her spiralling into hours of intrusive visual images.

As she relayed this, she burst into tears. I held Freda's hand and offered her tissues. I kept telling her how sorry I was. An unfamiliar icy cold feeling crept into my chest. I had never felt this intensity of pity. I pushed away the recently memorised template of a psychiatric interview. Instinctively, I changed tack and started asking questions about her son. A barrage of questions about psychiatric symptoms was too clinical, too callous for that moment.

What was his personality like? What music was he into? What was his favourite food? His name was Angus but his mates called him Mongoose. He was seventeen and obsessed with hip hop and video games: a kid after my own heart. His most prized possession was his recently acquired 'decks' (vinyl turntables). He worked part-time at the local Scotmid (the Scottish version of Budgens) after school and spent most of his time and money on rare records. The more she described her fond memories, the greater the gaps were between her sobs. I gently introduced the necessary enquiries later. Around a decade later, as a junior doctor training in psychiatry, I was taught how to slip questions into conversation subtly, rather than listing them. I didn't realise it when I was speaking to Freda about Mongoose, but I was doing this intuitively.

Later, as I presented my case to Dr Porter, I was able to match Freda's descriptions with actual symptoms. As I spoke, snippets of information from textbooks tumbled into my head and a diagnostic light bulb twinkled. Her visions were flashbacks!

'These issues have lasted too long to be explained by typical grief,' I said to Dr Porter over coffee. 'This woman is suffering from post-traumatic stress disorder.'

Not only was Dr Porter the first doctor I had met who allowed coffee in his ward rounds, but he actually bought it for the whole team. Were all psychiatrists this nice? I wondered.

'Good. Anything else?'

'I think she suffers from clinical depression. Well, an adjustment disorder that has progressed to clinical depression.'

'On what basis?'

'She had a lack of energy and motivation, problems concentrating and maybe anhedonia?' This last symptom is a lack of pleasure in previous activities, a core sign of depression.

'What treatment options might be appropriate?'

I started reeling off answers, surprising myself. 'Cognitive behavioural therapy, eye movement desensitisation and reprocessing, anti-depressants.'

'Which anti-depressant is licensed for post-traumatic stress disorder?'

'Er, paroxetine?'

'Good,' Dr Porter said with a nod.

'And I think she's got agoraphobia too. She's afraid to leave the house.'

'Steady on. I think Freda's avoidance behaviour is related to her PTSD. Reminders of her son trigger flashbacks so she avoids them.'

That did make more sense.

'Remember, psychiatry shouldn't be over-complicated. Unnecessarily diagnosing always labels but rarely helps the individual. Simplicity is key.'

Simplicity. That's me! I thought.

I walked out of the ward with mixed emotions. A taste of Freda's pain and a glimpse of real-world hardships penetrated my paltry cocooned student life of partying. But I also experienced something completely novel. I felt like a doctor.

I came to realise that psychiatry is one of the only medical specialties (I would also include general practitioners in this category) where personality and bedside manner were not just a bonus, they were essential. You would want your cardiothoracic surgeon to be polite and pleasant to talk to, but as long as they carried out heart surgery effectively, it doesn't really matter. Psychiatry was different. I could see that it was more of an art than a science. The difference between a patient letting you into their very private and sometimes even paranoid inner world and them rejecting you was all in the communication skills and empathy.

A pettier inspiration for me was the fact that I was as good as, and often better at, forming connections with patients and teasing out their symptoms than my geekier medical student peers. I discovered a skill for putting whoever was in front of me at ease, no matter their background or demographics: from the young gang member with schizophrenia, to the teenage girl who had taken an overdose as revenge towards her cheating boyfriend, to the elderly woman with dementia. I could charm and disarm, and stealthily coax out their emotions. Those medical students who would study relentlessly and dominate me and my friends in our exams often had stilted communication skills. Maybe all those disinhibited chats with random strangers in drum and bass clubs (sometimes sweaty, sometimes topless), throughout my previous four years at university had rubbed off on me.

As my confidence grew, I developed a thirst for learning. I was fascinated by all these strange symptoms, from cata-tonia to thought block and flight of ideas. I was captivated by the bizarre. For the first time in my life, I was studying for me and not to appease my parents or under the fearful shadow of looming exams. Every psychiatric sign, symptom and syndrome I learnt would be another potential piece of the puzzle that would eventually reveal the diagnosis. I also wanted to learn about the myriad of medications and their effects on receptors, neurones and neurotransmitters, to add to an arsenal of options for treatment.

I was a newly qualified doctor at the age of twenty-four. Instead of committing to a career as a psychiatrist straight away, I felt I still had some fun to get out of my system. As well as an unsuccessful stint as a trainee surgeon, this included gallivanting around Australia for eighteen months. Here, in between shifts in an emergency department and on a psychiatric unit, I would soak up the Antipodean lifestyle. By which I mean string vests, miniature pints of beer, barbecues and beaches (though clearly I didn't need to work on my tan). Of course, at job interviews I said that I had stalled my training to broaden my horizons, experience different cultures and because I wanted to immerse myself in a disparate mental health system to truly objectively appreciate the uniqueness of our own. However, in truth, I can't deny that I was also dodging the inevitable series of exams that were necessary to climb up the professional psychiatry hierarchy, including becoming a member of the Royal College of Psychiatrists, the professional body responsible for education and training, and setting and raising standards in the UK. I managed to shirk this inevitable progression by taking on a number of standalone non-training posts for a few years. In the time period leading up to treating offenders, I had made some huge personal commitments and hit some landmarks. Maybe this dissuaded me from dedicating myself to my career too soon. I had turned thirty, bought a flat in Islington (with a lot of help from my parents and sister), fallen in love and got married. I'd even got a gold tooth and my first tattoo.

When I first entered the world of forensic psychiatry in 2010, I had already wriggled my way through the exams that I had previously been dodging. I was in core training as a senior house officer, a junior position for graduate doctors who have completed their obligatory sentence as the whipping boys on the medical and surgical wards. This training involved cycling through six-month placements within numerous mental health sub-specialties on different wards and clinics. This was before I had taken the plunge into my higher training and specialised in treating mentally disordered offenders as a specialist registrar (where I would receive advanced training to become a consultant). In breakfast cereal analogy, senior house officer training is like a variety pack, whereas the specialist registrar position is one big, crunchy, delicious but fairly samey box.

As I started my first six-month placement in forensic psychiatry, friends and family would often ask questions about my imminent duties. I must admit that even when I started I hadn't fully grasped what this area entailed. I had even fallen for some of the fantasies I had seen on TV.

Chapter 2

What I do (and What I do Not)

Psychiatrists assess, diagnose and treat mental illnesses. Just like surgeons specialising in different parts of the body, there are numerous types of sub-specialist psychiatrists. More than you can stroke a beard at, each with expertise in treating particular categories of mental illness. General adult psychiatrists are the most common breed. There are also old-age psychiatrists and addiction specialists. Forensic psychiatrists are a different species from other psychiatrists; we assess, treat and rehabilitate offenders, usually perpetrators of violent and sexual crimes. This is where somebody who is morbidly fascinated with gangsta rap and violent films might gravitate. We also sometimes act as expert witnesses to advise judges and juries in criminal trials about individual defendants who have, or are suspected of having, psychiatric issues.

Contrary to popular belief, including my own, I quickly learnt that forensic psychiatrists have no business whatsoever at crime scenes. Jaded TV homicide detectives might take a swig of their coffee and ask a minion for 'forensics' on bullets, and the very charming Dick Van Dyke might visit the local morgue and ask for 'forensics' on a dead body, but they are asking for ballistics and pathological examinations, respectively. The term 'forensics' is often associated with *solving* crimes. The word comes from the Latin word 'forēnsis', meaning 'before the forum'; in Roman times, criminal charges would be discussed before a public group of individuals, in a kind of precursor to the modern-day criminal trial. The term encompasses offending, the legal system and courts in general. In psychiatry, it's about the juxtaposition of mental illness and criminality. The context is often one of ascertaining the mental state of an offender during a crime, by examining the evidence afterwards. It's about deciphering an individual's risk factors for future violence, and reducing them through intense long-term rehabilitation and treatment. So, pretty much everything *except* for solving crimes.

We cannot figure out if Colonel Mustard killed Professor Plum in the kitchen with the candlestick or not. But after he is charged, we can figure out which personality traits and psychotic symptoms drove Colonel Mustard to act so violently and impulsively, ascertain whether he was criminally culpable, and rehabilitate him so he is safe to rejoin society.

Criminal profiling is also not on the agenda for a forensic psychiatrist. This is the practice of identifying likely suspects to assist the police or of linking cases that may have been committed by the same perpetrator. It also involves predicting the future actions of a criminal at large (occasionally, according to the programmes I've seen, through telepathy).

'Judging by the way he's taunting the detectives, this man is a narcissist and probably works in advertising.'

'His crimes are escalating and he's becoming more emboldened. I think his next attack will be in broad daylight, superintendent.'

. . . are a couple of sentences I have never uttered.

In my opinion, criminal profiling is at best a pseudoscience and at worst a scam, even though people (not qualified forensic psychiatrists) have made careers out of it. There is a lack of scientific research or evidence to support its usefulness, reliability and validity. It works on the assumption that criminals operate in a predictable manner. And also that there is consistency within their modus operandi and their motivation, both within one particular perpetrator and between them. Having read hundreds of case papers outlining details of offences, including some by the same individual, and having discussed culprits' thought processes with them, I can confidently say that these patterns do sometimes occur. But equally, they don't. There is chaos, randomness and opportunism in many serious crimes. There is not enough consistency or even enough data to predict the profile of an offender, in my humble opinion.

One of the most high-profile cases where this dark art has hindered a police investigation was the murder of Rachel Nickell. One morning in July 1992, Ms Nickell, a twenty-three-year-old former model, was sexually assaulted and stabbed forty-nine times while walking her dog with her two-year-old son on Wimbledon Common. The prime suspect was a man named Colin Stagg, but the authorities had little evidence linking him to the murder scene. The police therefore asked a renowned criminal psychologist to create an offender profile of the killer, which fitted Stagg. They then set up an entrapment-style sting, with the psychologist's assistance, where an attractive under-cover policewoman befriended and flirted with Stagg to coax out and secretly record violent fantasies and, they hoped, a confession from him. Although he played along to a degree, Stagg did not admit to Ms Nickell's murder, but was prosecuted anyway. The mind doth boggle. At trial, the case was thrown out by the judge at the Old Bailey, who declared that the police had tried to incriminate the suspect by 'deceptive conduct of the grossest kind'. The police and criminal psychologist were criticised (the latter was charged with professional misconduct by the British Psychological Society, though the case was later dropped). In July 2006, after re-examining some evidence, the police interviewed a convicted murderer named Robert Napper, who had paranoid schizophrenia and Asperger's syndrome, at Broadmoor Hospital, where he had been a patient for a decade. He had already been convicted of a very simi-lar murder of another young woman named Samantha Bisset and her four-year-old daughter in November 1993. At trial, he pleaded guilty to the manslaughter of Ms Nickell on the grounds of diminished responsibility. The judge ordered that Napper would be held at Broadmoor Hospital, indefinitely.

What is particularly upsetting for me about this whole debacle is that Samantha Bisset and her four-year-old daughter's deaths might have been prevented had this rogue criminal profiler-led sting operation not distracted the authorities.

Interviewing suspects is another area I had wrongly assumed we might be involved in when I first paddled into the ocean of forensic psychiatry. The idea of sitting across the table from a suspected murderer, with police officers observing incredulously behind a one-way mirror as I play intellectual chess to coax the slippery mastermind into incriminating himself does sound enticing. I'm sure experienced detectives have sharpened their skills and perfected their mind games to do this very thing. Any questionable abilities I may claim to have in this area are strictly from watching Netflix crime dramas. If you put a biro in front of the accused and they don't play with it, they are too calm, calculated and unemotional. They are definitely, 100 per cent guilty. Or was that not guilty? These techniques are categorically never utilised in my profession.

Having said that, I do look at the consistency and reliability of the interviewee during my own assessments. Defendants fabricating mental illness is certainly not unusual. But this is all in the context of eliciting symptoms in order to refute or validate a diagnosis, not for confessions of murder.

To this day, I am frequently asked about delving into the minds of serial killers or terrorists and explaining their behaviour. This included being a guest on a podcast about Ted Bundy, the American serial killer and rapist who is believed to have murdered at least twenty-eight women in the 1970s. I suggested that he had the superficial charm, callous disregard for the rights of others and the glib, manipulative nature of a psychopath. The host, clearly unsatisfied, pushed me repeatedly to explain *why* Bundy carried out his dozens of rapes and homicides, almost as if I was in the dock. As I told her, I'm not sure there's an answer that makes sense to anybody other than Ted Bundy. In my career, I have assessed a handful of perpetrators of multiple murders and acts of terror. The vast majority have been initial assessments to rule out acute severe mental illness, allowing the defendant to be dealt with by the usual criminal justice route. If they have no discernible mental illness, there is no room for curing, and therefore no role for my services or expertise. These horrific acts are thankfully uncommon. But for them to be directly driven by psychiatric symptoms, as opposed to simple hatred, is as rare as chicken's fangs. I have been asked on several occasions, including once on live radio, about what drives serial killers and terrorists. The truth is that the answers lie outside of psychiatry, and more in the field of criminology.

Some might proffer that the very acts of serial killers and terrorists prove that they must be mentally ill. This boils down to how you define mental illness. If you consider having murderous thoughts or ideas of extreme fundamentalist hatred, as well as having the conviction to carry these out, as automatically being mentally ill, then yes, clearly these people are ill. However, for psychiatrists, hatred, anger, fascism and even religious fanaticism are not in themselves psychiatric symptoms. It is only in exceptional cases that they are the product of, or the outward expression of, underlying mental illness. Only those in this minuscule category could potentially be treated by us.

One of the first cases I was sent to assess by my team during my first placement was an example of that very rarity.

Chapter 3

Do Terrorists Need a Psychiatrist?

Mr Stevie McGrew was a gruff, brooding Scottish man in his mid-fifties who led a solitary, somewhat reclusive life. His index offences (as in, the ones that brought him in to psychiatric services) were those of putting persons in fear of violence by harassment, perpetrating a bomb hoax and sending electronic communications with intent to cause distress or anxiety. He had already been charged and remanded to a psychiatric unit when I saw him, early on in my first forensic psychiatry placement in north London in 2010.

Of the handful of potential terrorists I have assessed, Stevie was the only one who was genuinely psychotic. In my naivety back then, I used to carry around numerous textbooks, assuming wrongly that I would have nuggets of time to study between assessments. That day, travelling to the general adult psychiatric ward he was residing in, I had a brutal accident involving a loose Tupperware lid and a lot of salad. Not only did I ruin a couple of hundred pounds' worth of books, but tragically I also lost my lunch.

Stevie's only previous contact with mental health services was about three years prior, when he was convinced that cars on the street with registration plates that contained letters from his surname were mocking him. This is a 'delusional perception', a perfectly normal perception, to which the individual attributes a false meaning. He took a baseball bat to one of the cars (a Porsche, no less!) and was arrested. He was then sectioned straight from court to the same general psychiatric ward where I would see him a few years later. He was diagnosed with schizophrenia, prescribed antipsychotic medications, improved within a few weeks, and was discharged. Job done. For the time being.

At home, Stevie was supposed to keep taking his tablets every day, for the foreseeable future. He told me that the medication 'gave me ants in my pants' – i.e. an overwhelming urge to constantly fidget, which could only be resolved by walking around or 'jiggling my hips, like Elvis'. This is a well-recognised side effect of some anti-psychotic drugs, though our psychiatric parlance is a little less colourful than Stevie's. *Akathesia*. It is related to blocking dopamine, a chemical in the brain that controls movement and is also associated with schizophrenia. Stevie became non-compliant with his tablets. This is a very common act in patients and the bane of many of their psychiatrists. But it is also understandable. I wouldn't take tablets with side effects for a disease I didn't recognise, composed of symptoms I didn't believe, by a doctor I didn't trust. Stevie appreciated that vehicular mockery was all in his mind, so he figured that as long as he ignored any contemptuous number plates, there would be no need to take such an unpalatable medication.

A couple of years after stopping his anti-psychotics, Stevie received a phone call out of the blue from a marketing company asking him for feedback about a recent renewable energy seminar he'd supposedly attended. Stevie had never been to such an event and was perturbed when the caller was then able to relay his personal details, including his address and National Insurance number. This might have freaked out you or me, but we would possibly swear, probably hang up, chalk it down as an attempt at a scam and move on with our lives. But Stevie was convinced that the government had intentionally leaked his personal information and so he phoned up the Citizens Advice Bureau (an organisation specialising in giving information about legal, debt, consumer, housing and other problems in the UK) to complain. He spent hours every day, for days on end, trying to get a satisfactory answer, but according to him, there was either no reply or he was kept on hold or he wasn't called back as promised. Stevie became increasingly incensed and was certain that the bureau was goading him and therefore must be part of this conspiracy. This paranoia was amplified when he finally received an email from them with his surname misspelt. He complained to the police, who predictably dismissed him, and so Stevie started sending increasingly aggressive emails to the bureau. This escalated to direct threats to kill the staff. The case papers sent to me included printouts of around three hundred of his emails, though I think I got the gist in the first. The titles of his messages included: 'You are not safe. I will detonate bomb in your office today!' and 'I guarantee a horrific death to your entire department'. Now the police paid attention. When they searched his bedsit, they found household ingredients known for making explosives. I cringe at the prospect of where this was leading.

Visiting Stevie on a normal ward felt strange to me. Even though I had only spent a couple of weeks within the confines of a secure forensic unit for offenders in my new role, I had grown accustomed to hyper-cautious security. This ward had only one thin blue door with a flimsy lock, which did not look kick-proof, to prevent patients escaping into the wider world. Visitors were not searched and there was even mixing of genders on the ward. It felt paradoxically riskier than my usual work habitat. To my amazement, Stevie, a man with a slight frame ('wee', to adopt his terminology), a hooked nose and thinning hair was even allowed to carry his very hot drink into the interview room. He clearly hadn't been informed of my visit. He came across as a prickly man, particularly annoyed that I had interrupted his cappuccino. He was paranoid, checking my ID for well over three minutes, which was two minutes and fifty-nine seconds longer than the staff at reception had spent on it.

He seemed perturbed that I had been sent the case papers for his alleged offences in advance and repeatedly asked questions about how they'd been sent and if they were password-protected. He was abrasive, constantly interrupting me and deliberately misinterpreting my words. These would be deliberate tactics used by barristers cross-examining me years later after I had become an expert witness.

Stevie tossed my ID onto my lap. 'I've already got a psychiatrist. And I don't even need that buffoon. Why do I need you?'

'Fair question, Mr McGrew.' To avoid being presumptuous, I generally use surnames for clients I see for one-off assessments, though use their first names if I treat them in the long term on my own ward. 'Your team referred you to our services, as they wanted a forensic opinion. They really should have informed—'

'So, my psychiatrist is not clever enough to assess me herself? That's what you're saying?'

'No. It's just that we are the experts in mental illness related to offending.'

'Oh, so I'm mentally ill, am I? And an offender as well? Looks like you've already done your assessment, doctor.' He put his coffee down on a table to give me a slow sarcastic clap. 'Outstanding job, I must say. Have you got a card? I might refer you to those Citizens Advice Bureau pricks.'

During my assessment of Stevie, two thoughts sprang to mind. The first was that his beliefs appeared to be delusional and were therefore potentially treatable. A delusion is a firm, unshakeable belief that originates from an ununderstandable source, which is not amenable to rational argument or opposing evidence. It is also not compatible with regional, cultural or educational background: a clause to exclude odd beliefs that are 'taught' in certain communities, and not related to mental illness, such as the somewhat ironic belief in Scientology that all of psychiatry is bogus, or in some religious sects that non-believers merit execution or in some socio-economic strata that bright-orange fake tans are attractive. Delusions are characteristic of a particular type of illness (known as 'pathognomic' in psych jargon), namely psychotic disorders. My second thought was of all those times I had been put on hold by various services and not called back when I was promised (and fantasies I may have had about how to get their attention).

I concluded that despite being near the cusp, Stevie was unfit to plead. He was so utterly preoccupied with his own beliefs of being targeted and victimised, he was unable to absorb or analyse other information, including that which would be pertinent to his court case. Although I was not directly involved in Stevie's treatment beyond my initial assessment, I was intrigued by him and stayed in touch with his hospital psychiatrist via email to keep tabs on his journey towards recovery. His doctor was sensible enough to trial another anti-psychotic medication with more tolerable side effects; this would, of course, decrease the risk of Stevie's future non-compliance (ants-in-pants-related or otherwise). After months of treatment, he still felt like he was the victim. He still felt mistreated and that his phone calls should have been returned. However, of significance, he was no longer preoccupied with a conspiracy against him. He now believed that the Citizens Advice Bureau's behaviour was down to incompetence. The delusions about intentional malice and treachery had been eradicated. This meant he could carry on his previous life without being constantly distressed by thoughts of persecution. And, vitally, without ravenous intentions for revenge.

As a side note, one aspect of Stevie that I found fascinating was his ability to justify his actions. 'I only wrote such extreme emails so that these arseholes can no longer ignore me.' He stressed that the chemicals he had gathered were not for explosives, were not illegal, and were for general household use. His barrister successfully argued this in court and the charges related to bomb-making were dropped. (Really, though? Pool sanitiser, even though he has no pool?) This is known as an 'external locus of control'. It boils down to refusing to accept responsibility. It is very common in offenders as an internal justification for their misdeeds, whether they have a mental illness or not. Defendants' statements from my career which illustrate this curious psychological anomaly include:

'If the government hadn't stopped my benefits, I wouldn't need to go out and burgle houses.'

'My mate shouldn't have asked me to carry that knife for him in the first place.'

'It was the alcohol, doctor. It makes me nippy and it makes her answer back to me. It was inevitable really.'

Stevie's case and his motivations differ from those of the vast majority of terrorists. Dylann Roof, the American white supremacist who committed the mass shooting in a church in Charleston, South Carolina on 17 June 2015, would be a good example. He had a history of drug and alcohol use and petty offending, but he did not have a mental illness that made him lose touch with reality (or, crucially, that excused him of criminal culpability). He purportedly often claimed that 'Blacks were taking over the world' and his actions were clearly influenced by deep-rooted racism and hate. But to be clear, his beliefs, however revolting, were not delusional. They were not born of insanity and so no amount of medication or psychological therapy could change them.

Many offenders, from petty criminals to serial killers, have severe character flaws, from minimal empathy to narcissism. Returning to the case of the charming Ted Bundy, he would be a prime example of this. His superficial charisma, insincerity, lack of nervousness, pathological ego-centricity and lack of remorse exemplified his ability to live a double life. He had a long-term relationship, attended college and built a political career, all while carrying out brutal murders. His handsomeness and personality allowed him to win the trust of his victims and even charm law enforcement and legal professionals, to a degree: the textbook traits of a psychopath. Some criminals may cross the threshold for a personality disorder: deeply ingrained, pervasive faults in the subject's natural temperament and nature. Personality disorders, like psychopathy, are not altered states and are technically mental *disorders*, as opposed to mental *illnesses*. They can sometimes be treated, but it takes years of intense therapy, and cannot be cured with medication.

Notwithstanding the nebulous sphere of disturbed personality, the vast majority of people who commit atrocities, including serial murders or acts of terrorism, do so outside of the context of a diagnosable, biologically understandable, chemically reversible, treatable mental illness. In the same way that the majority of angry, hateful people – religious fanatics, right-wing racists or that old man down the road who refused to return my wayward football when I was a kid – don't have psychiatric disorders. Being extreme, just like being odd or being provocative, isn't enough.

Forensic psychiatrists cannot help people like Dylann Roof and cannot decrease his future risks any more effectively than the criminal justice system or probation services. We may have a small role in the initial assessments of these characters to rule out psychiatric issues, but after that we are of as much value as a pool sanitiser when you don't have a pool.

Chapter 4

Punched on Duty

One dreary muggy Monday morning in August, I was approaching the end of my core training. I had just started my placement as a senior house officer on a medium secure ward in a forensic unit. My dreaded exams were behind me. My next hurdle was to decide which sub-specialty I would sign my life away to as a specialist registrar the following year. After a week of induction, this was my first day on the front line. Keen to make an impression on my colleagues, I went to my allocated ward to interview some of the patients before the ward round later that day. I was speaking to a patient in a private interview room in the corner of the ward. He was an overweight young man, Dennis, whose offence of stabbing his brother frantically while hearing voices was at odds with his phlegmatic presentation. Luckily, his brother, a bodybuilder, managed to overpower Dennis before he sustained any real damage and only required a dozen or so stitches to his forearms (though I imagine future Christmases were doomed to be awkward). For safety, all the interview rooms on the ward had huge wire-reinforced windows so that staff were visible. I noticed another tall young man looking in through the window, seemingly fascinated by me. He kept tapping on the window, waving and smiling. He even brazenly interrupted the interview a couple of times by bursting through the door and commenting on random topics, mostly related to religion.

'Everybody can be a god, but there has to be a king of gods.'

I politely bustled him out of the room.

He put his head round the door a minute later. 'I didn't mean everybody. Only the righteous.'

He seemed convinced that we were childhood friends and kept asking me about a cricket match we supposedly played together. I treated him like I do those 'charity muggers' in fluorescent jackets on the high street. I looked away, put my head down and ignored him.

My interview with Dennis had only scratched the surface. I had many more queries, particularly about how he had arrived at his beliefs that his brother had been telepathically planting suggestions in Dennis to get a tattoo of a penis on his cheek (a psychiatric phenomenon known as 'thought insertion'). But that would all have to wait for another assessment when I would have more time. This meeting was merely to introduce myself and to get a skeletal overview of his psychiatric issues (and if I'm being honest, to impress my new consultant). I walked out of the interview room, smug smile on my face, notebook in hand, totally unaware of what was about to follow. The young man who had been interrupting ran up behind me, punched me hard on the side of the head and scuttled off. It happened so fast that I didn't even realise I had been hit. I just found myself on the floor, confused, with a throbbing temple. As the nurses helped me up to my feet, the perpetrator had already retreated to his room.

I wasn't too shaken up. Perhaps because the assault was so sudden, I didn't have time to process any threat. But I know of several colleagues who have been seriously injured at work. In fact, barely a month later, one of the other senior house officers was trapped inside an interview room by a psychotic man who had delusional beliefs that the doctor was working undercover for social services. He wouldn't let her leave, insisting that she knew the whereabouts of his young son who had been removed from him and given up for adoption. Although the perpetrator didn't physically harm her, it took well over half an hour of negotiations with the ward staff through the window before he would allow my colleague to leave. She was unscathed, though clearly traumatised. Her time off for stress kept extending every week and eventually lasted longer than two months. It was interesting to see the sympathy of her peers, including me, slowly peter out. Every day, between the other five senior house officers, we had to cover her clinics as well as her evening, night-time and weekend on-call shifts.

Being assaulted can, and does, have a profound impact on people's lives, confidence and careers. For me personally, it was more embarrassing than anything. For both patients and staff, I went from being *one of the new doctors* to *that new doctor who got punched*. I found out later that the man who had punched me had schizoaffective disorder and was suffering from a specific type of delusional misidentification syndrome, known as a 'Fregoli syndrome': the delusional belief that a stranger is actually a familiar person. This had driven his original offence; he had walked into a random café, picked up a chair and thrown it at an unsuspecting group of strangers, whom he believed to be undercover policemen who had arrested him years previously. That morning, he was convinced that I was really an old school bully in disguise. I have no hard feelings. In his mind, his actions were justified. As he was relatively settled within moments of assaulting me, he didn't need to be transferred to the seclusion room, but his medications were increased. Even though I didn't directly treat him, I would frequently bump into him on the ward. To be fair to him, he did try to apologise once, but he suffered from a formal thought disorder, which is a symptom of psychosis where the flow of one's thoughts is jumbled and disconnected.

'Yeah, doctor. You was a cricket guy, not the other guy. Shouldn't have happened, but who knows who playing cricket and who really a god or not. You can't really blame me if we're all gods.'

I guess it's the thought that counts.

Of course, now I know that what I should have done was alert staff to my presence as soon as I entered the ward and ask if there was anybody who was agitated or unpredictable. After the young man's first couple of interruptions, I should have stopped my interview with Dennis and informed the nurses who worked with the patient group daily. They would have known far better than me if my assailant's fixation on me was concerning.

At least the experience solidified these lessons that have since developed into natural instinct every time I step into a secure unit. To be honest, I should have known better. I had just completed a whole week of induction for all new staff on medium secure units, including safety strategies. It was a blur of talks and PowerPoint slides. I was distracted by the free doughnuts and coffee at the back of the classroom. My concentration should have been guided by an innate sense of self-preservation, rather than by the levels of carbohydrates, sugar and caffeine in my system.

Had I been paying attention, I would have learnt that security within these specialist units is categorised into three areas: environmental/physical security, relational security and procedural security.

Environmental security includes a fence around the hospital grounds, which must be a minimum of 5.2 metres in height and have very small gaps in the wiring, making them climb-resistant, as well as restricting the passing of objects such as weapons or drugs through the mesh. Doors on every ward are locked and there are airlocks in the main exits: two locked doors that are electronically controlled so that only one can be opened at a time, manned by reception or security staff on the other side of a Perspex or reinforced window. They check personnel in the space between the doors to prevent any slippery patients who might try to bolt through. Staff also carry keychains which have to be attached to belts. It is not unheard of for even familiar, regular staff to be turned away from their shifts because they came into work without a belt. This is so patients can't run off with the keys (at least without a human attached, which tends to impede mobility, thereby making the whole escape process somewhat awkward).

Relational security is the process of forming trusting relationships with patients. As well as empathy, politeness and good communication, ward-based recreational activities are key in building a sense of camaraderie; these might be anything from playing pool, to communal meals to newspaper discussion groups. Nurses oversee these sessions and are therefore invaluable in establishing the ward atmosphere.

Procedural security is all about the protocols to minimise risk. This includes searching patients on admission and when they come back from leave, regularly undertaking urine drugs screens and having occasional unannounced visits from police sniffer dogs.

Of course, these psychiatric units for offenders are not relentlessly dangerous environments, but the potential is always there. The frequency of violence and other untoward incidents (such as death threats, hostage-taking, severe self-harm or fires) is low but hugely variable. It also depends on the patient mix. Sometimes, there is relative harmony and camaraderie between the patients. At other times, not unlike prisons, there may be beefs. These can be anything from deep, long-standing tensions between two or more residents who crossed paths years ago (there is a frustratingly mammoth proportion of regular attenders within the system) to patients falling out over the state that the communal bathroom has been left in. I've even seen a fist fight over who took more than their fair share of the ward's communal takeaway the night before. There were no serious injuries, though it led to both men having their leave suspended for two weeks. Even the most succulent, flavoursome chicken tikka masala surely couldn't have been worth that.

In my career, I've seen cliques formed on forensic psychiatric units, with competition for that coveted alpha-male spot. I've seen this crown won and lost by rivals spreading rumours about each other, threatening each other, physical fights or simple popularity contests. As well as aggression towards staff, bullying between patients and drug smuggling, I have also seen great compassion and friendship between residents. Patients buying snacks for those without money. Those in recovery donating their time to explain concepts to their less knowledgeable and often unwell peers, like their rights under the Mental Health Act or side effects of medication. I've seen lifelong bonds forged by those who have previously been marginalised, shunned and ignored by their own families, let alone society. Dennis, the man I had assessed on my very first morning on the forensic ward, had his leave stopped after he tested positive for cannabis. This resulted in the return of his unsavoury voices, telling him to attack others. He had so far resisted them but was clearly now a danger to the public. One of his peers, a quiet older man with a peppery grey beard, Seamus, went on an errand for him, using his own money to buy Dennis toiletries, a huge bar of Toblerone and a bodybuilding magazine. Ignoring the irony of the simultaneous purchase of industrial-size chocolate and that particular magazine, I asked Seamus why he'd gone out of his way for a man he barely spoke to and who had threatened him a couple of weeks earlier.

'Dennis didn't know what he was saying. His voices told him I had used all the loo roll on purpose.'

'Well, it's nice of you to look out for him.'

'Mental illness is a wretched thing. I've not heard voices for years, but I still remember. They are relentless. Really test your sanity, doc.'

'I can only imagine.'

'Also, you can't hold a grudge. Just like when you got punched,' he said with a wink.

'Yeah, thanks for bringing that up, Seamus.'

'Hey, you're not going to tell the nurses, are you?'

Patients buying or lending items to or from each other is strongly discouraged. It allows the vulnerable to be exploited or bullied. It requires specialist documented permission and must be overseen by nurses, which involves queueing and paperwork. Clearly, this wasn't a dodgy scenario, though.

'I won't tell if you don't.' I winked back.

My twelve-year-old, *Karate Kid*-inspired, martial arts-obsessed self may have been excited to know that almost two decades later I would be given combat training. Every year, like all members of staff in these units, forensic psychiatrists have to undergo 'control and restraint training'. This varies between hospitals but in one unit I worked in, we had to do this for an entire week annually. We would rock up in tracksuits and trainers, and instructors talked us through everything from de-escalation techniques to how to defend ourselves. We learnt how to forcibly restrain and move patients whilst causing minimal damage with a series of holds and grips. I have mixed feelings about this training. Ever the cynic, I can't help but recognise that this covers the hospital, so if staff try to sue them for injuries suffered during an assault at work, the organisation can say, 'Hey, we did our bit'. Plus, even the best-taught techniques are often forgotten in that split-second fight-or-flight moment when a seething patient with a history of assaults is hearing voices and leaning over you with clenched fists.

I often get asked if I feel safe in my line of work. The majority of the time, yes. Defendants whom I see in prison or court are generally on their best behaviour; they know I'm writing a court report about them as evidence for their trials, so it is in their interests to make a good impression. The exceptions to this are defendants who are so enraged at the criminal justice system that they show disdain towards any of its representatives. Or people so psychiatrically unwell that they are not in control of their actions.

Patients detained in psychiatric units are a different cauldron of tadpoles. Whereas in prisons or in courts, defendants merely have to keep it together for an hour or two during an assessment, once stuck in hospital, the residents' behaviour is under the microscope for years. They still may acquiesce to the forensic psychiatrist as this is the person who decides on their leave and ultimately their discharge. Those who lash out often do so in the context of boundaries being set (e.g. having leave stopped or access to groups denied due to recent violence), failing drug tests or following arguments with other patients. Again, uncontainable florid symptoms of mental illness also trigger violence.

The danger of the job really boils down to a numbers

game. Even if 95 per cent of assessees are settled, I might see two or three people in court in one session, up to ten in a prison clinic and have eighteen inpatients on a psychiatric ward. If I'm working with a patient group specifically deemed to be high risk, with histories of violence, tempers will flare sooner or later. Verbal outbursts and threats are far more common than actual violence. Some of my patients grew up in environments where this was standard practice for conflict resolution. I try not to take it personally. At the end of the day, I get to leave whichever establishment that the confrontation occurred in, and go home to my family (and my precious *Street Fighter II* arcade). They don't.

As well as being punched, other hairy moments have included being kept hostage during a ward round. I don't mean demands for a ransom, and a helicopter and a police negotiator with a megaphone type of hostage. This happened in 2012, a good two years after I was punched, around halfway into being a specialist registrar. On a forensic unit in east London, one of my patients, Johnny Benson, was a six-foot-three, naturally muscular young man with a psychotic disorder, who used to be a semi-professional mixed martial arts fighter: never a good sign. He was admitted after allegedly raping a woman in a crack den, though the charges were eventually dropped. His medication had only recently been increased and he was extremely paranoid and disorientated during a ward-round meeting. He had been given some bad news – his brother had died from cancer – and in his fragile mental state, he deteriorated instantly. In his confusion, Johnny concocted delusional beliefs that the hospital staff must have poisoned his sibling with carcinogens. He stood in front of the door, barring our exit in a fighting stance and interrogated, threatened and insulted each of the staff members in turn. We momentarily managed to placate him a few times. He would become apologetic and bemused. But I could see the tension and rage build up within his disorientated psyche within seconds and filter through to his facial expressions, before he would start ranting again. As I had only joined the team for a new placement, this was the very first time I had met Johnny. I remember feeling very unsure if I should attempt to calm him down. Would a new person talking to him agitate him further? Would it add to his disorientated paranoia? In the end, I didn't address him directly, but stood up, casually walked across the room, poured myself some squash in a plastic cup and offered him some. He took it and thanked me, temporarily distracted from the fury inside. The whole ordeal lasted an hour. Sensing no way out, the social worker on our team pulled his alarm, which alerted the Emergency Response Team, who came in, restrained Johnny and coaxed him into the seclusion room. Although perplexed and incensed, he cooperated. Fortunately, our annual weekly control and restraint techniques were not pitted against Johnny's decades of daily mixed martial arts training that day. I know who I would have put my money on.

I was beginning to appreciate that the field I had chosen would invoke the most extreme of emotions. Arguably more than any other area of medicine. I had been moved by the sympathy I felt towards Freda Millican losing her son, the admiration I had for Seamus' generosity towards Dennis, and more than a little flustered by the hair-raising antics of Johnny. But I was about to experience the heartache of one of the most tragic cases of my career.

Chapter 5

Demons Lurking Inside

I still think about my first day at the Old Bailey. Everything about it – the wind, the nervous pacing, the chain-smoking, the pomposity, the marble pillars, the Latin Scriptures – made me giddy. Trial for murder from Ms Yasmin Khan's perspective, trial by fire from mine.

I was in my early thirties and was a lowly specialist registrar, a middle-grade psychiatrist, eight years out of medical school, but still in the earlier part of my three years of higher training, before I would emerge out of the chrysalis as a fully formed consultant forensic psychiatrist.

I was also newly married to Rizma, a very pretty, funny and quirky A-level psychology teacher with a profound knowledge of movie trivia (which I have piggybacked on several times to win various quizzes over the years). She told me months later that when we had first met at a party in Central London, she didn't believe I was a doctor, dissuaded by my smoking, gold tooth and scruffy, baggy black and white chequered hoody. When she finally was convinced (not by my own reassurances, I should add, but by asking some mutual acquaintances) the only reason she agreed to see me again was to persuade me to give a talk to her students about my career as a psychiatrist, which I did that year and have done every year since. Our romance bloomed relatively quickly, and we were married within two years, jumping the queue of many of my tight-knit set of university friends, some of whom had been in relationships for over a decade (inadvertently pressurising some of them to propose, I'm sure). Our wedding was one of many in 2011, one of my favourite years, punctuated with multiple holy matrimonies and more importantly, stag dos. Our wedding stood out with a surprise musical act, an Indian Elvis impersonator, who closely represented the eccentricity of both me and Rizma. I may have had to tell him a little porky pie about the depth of our Elvis fandom to book him.

Even though I was not familiar with the Old Bailey, I had observed my previous consultants giving evidence on a handful of occasions in other less grandiose criminal courts with a notable lack of Latin. I had also practised with the other junior doctors on my rotation a few times during our scheduled teaching sessions. But Yasmin's trial was only around the fourth time I'd taken the witness stand myself.

Yasmin was a well-educated eighteen-year-old school-girl with an unblemished past. There was no history of offending, anti-social behaviour or even being disruptive as a child. From what I had read in various reports, she was seemingly far less trouble as an adolescent than I'd been. She was shy and timid, with only a couple of close friends. Accepted, but very much in the cheap seats at the theatre of high school. Studious and quiet, she was, according to her teachers, a pleasure to teach. Yasmin had never been known to use alcohol or drugs. She was one of four siblings and had immigrant parents who toiled in a family-owned newsagent's and pushed all of their children towards professional careers. They were a close but insular family unit. Yasmin did voluntary shifts in the local hospital, to enhance her recent application to medical school. All of the above distinguished her from my typical clientele. Many of my patients' backgrounds are a cocktail of poverty, neglect, prominent criminal records and drug use. Very much blemished pasts.

According to witness statements from neighbours and interviews with the family, in the weeks leading up to the killing in spring 2012, Yasmin had been displaying some uncharacteristic behaviours. This included reprimanding her family for watching 'smut' on TV (though they assured me that it was the same sitcom they had watched together for years), listening to bizarre instrumental flute music (instead of her usual Miley Cyrus), chanting and making weird comments (including that she could see her own soul and how the sky had been painted on a very high ceiling). This was clearly unusual but hardly a harbinger of killing. In retrospect, I believe that this behaviour was a prodrome of psychosis – a period, usually lasting a few weeks, during which some individuals experience changes in feelings, thoughts, perceptions and behaviour, before they develop full-blown psychotic symptoms such as hallucinations or delusions. I've always thought of a prodrome as the starter to the main course of insanity.

Yasmin's eldest brother, a software designer, lived at the family home, along with his wife and son, Sonny. Yasmin had babysat two-year-old Sonny many times before that fateful day. That morning, witnesses saw her clapping, singing and chanting loudly at her fifth-floor bedroom window, which faced the apartment complex's communal courtyard. She muttered something about seeing angels in the clouds to her younger sister, who responded with a dismissive eye-roll. Her other family members left for school and work, and Yasmin, who had a couple of free periods, was left with little Sonny for the morning.

Her mother came home from the newsagent's after a few hours and initially assumed that Sonny was asleep. It was only half an hour later that she discovered that he was unresponsive. When the police arrived, Yasmin seemed incredulous that everyone was making such a fuss and demanded that they 'march to the Houses of Parliament to arrest the corrupt and flood the streets with adoration instead of drugs'. She reassured the police that she had smothered Sonny only to remove the demons from him and she claimed that he would 'wake up stronger than ever when the next full moon comes out'. When challenged, she nonchalantly replied, 'You shall all see, and you shall feel foolish'. Chaos prevailed, as Sonny's parents arrived. Yells echoed across the courtyard, causing the throbbing throng of people to swell further. Yasmin seemed calm on the surface. 'Spookily placid', is how her brother described her to me many months later. She kept reassuring the increasingly distraught crowd that everything would be fine, as long as they 'all dared to believe in angels'.

In police custody, Yasmin acted bizarrely, eating tissue paper and making herself sick. She urinated through her clothes. The officers were concerned and the possibility of calling a psychiatrist was raised, though there was some resistance. Some of the policemen didn't want to give her a 'get-out-of-jail-free card'. So, she was remanded to Holloway Prison instead.

Yasmin festered behind bars for a while, barely engaging with prison officers and ignoring the other inmates. She refused visits from her family and spent entire days making origami shapes and ripping out pictures of young children from magazines. Odd behaviour perhaps, but at least on the surface, not indicative of florid psychosis or the intense paranoia she later disclosed. Yasmin slipped under the radar of prison staff who appeared to have read her general lack of cooperation and prickliness as a young woman resigning herself to her terrible crime and insulating herself in guilt.

Prison is a chaotic, hectic place, where severe agitation is not uncommon, often as a result of fights, beefs, gangs, bullying and illicit drugs, let alone psychiatric disorders. As well as a long waiting list of mentally ill inmates who need to be sectioned to secure forensic psychiatric units, there are also those trying their luck by fabricating or exaggerating mental illness in the hope of hospital transfer or of being prescribed medication that gives them a buzz. Throw in budget cuts and recruitment issues and most Mental Health In-Reach Teams (usually consisting of forensic psychiatrists, nurses and psychologists) are perennially crippled under the weight of their caseloads. The isolated, unobtrusively psychotic, like Yasmin, are the faulty wheel, not squeaking loudly enough to get the proverbial grease. This, in part, explains the delay in her referral burrowing its way to the female medium secure unit ward where I was working at the time.

Walking through the prison gates to meet her for the first time, my confidence wavered. I wanted to prove to my consultant that I could handle the pressure, but anxieties niggled under the magnitude of the case. There is no room for sloppiness in a murder trial. What if I missed something? After queueing, airport-style security searches and sniffer dogs, I found myself sitting in the visiting hall, twiddling my thumbs. I have never been very good at waiting, especially without any form of stimulation. Anything considered non-essential, such as books or even a cup of coffee, let alone phones, is not allowed through the prison gates, to decrease the chances of smuggling. My only distraction was the row of patronising posters for prisoners that I have since become accustomed to ('Spice – it's not legal, it's not healthy, it's not worth it!'). The hall was unexpectedly spacious, with garish turquoise vinyl seats and grey plastic tables. All the furniture was bolted down, in case interactions during the inmates' visits turned a bit colourful. There was an ironic gloom in the luminous coloured plastic building blocks and desolate bright-green playmat in the corner. The huge room filled up with prisoners, family and lawyers, each identifiable by their attire, posture and degree of scowling. Time passed. Where was she? Half an hour into the scheduled appointment, a prison officer took pity on me. She made enquiries through her radio, then escorted me through the long snaking corridors of the main prison, through a plethora of heavy gates and doors and many stares from the inmates: some curious, some suspicious, some marking their territory through the medium of eye contact. The officer showed me to Yasmin's cell, opened the door and waited outside. I had assessed a few violent assailants before, but meeting Yasmin would be the first time I'd be coming face-to-face with an actual killer. Unfairly and somewhat judgementally, my imagination had been stoked. I had been expecting to see something akin to a horror movie scene. I thought she would be dishevelled and possibly cowering in a corner with her head in her hands. But Yasmin had long, dark, neatly plaited hair, framing an unassuming face. Her eyebrows had been plucked to within an inch of their lives. She sat forward on the edge of her bed. Poised. As if she was the one about to interrogate me. Her smile was the strangest thing about her. It seemed painted on. A veneer.

Yasmin said she had forgotten about the appointment, though I was sceptical, presuming her schedule to be rather empty. Throughout my assessment, she kept up the façade of normality. She completely denied any of her reported odd behaviour in the weeks leading up to the death of her nephew (my suspected prodrome) and claimed a complete memory lapse of the incident. Her answers seemed as fake as her smile. She even dismissed her strange activities in prison, despite the mountain of origami visibly stashed under her sink. Yasmin was guarded and evasive, yet ostensibly pleasant. I tried to form a rapport by making anodyne, non-threatening enquiries about her background and school life, before digging around about any mental health issues. Her responses were passive aggressive, such as: 'I've already told you, I can't remember,' and 'I don't really see how that is relevant, doctor.' I failed to extract any psychopathology to consolidate into a psychiatric diagnosis. Blood. Stone. 'Spookily placid' was spot-on.

I left the prison through more locked doors, queues and suspicious stares. During my commute home that day, I felt a little uneasy, and it wasn't just the constant swaying and waves of body odour on the London Underground. It just didn't add up. The statement to the police about her nephew waking up at the next full moon. Demons and angels. Her other aberrant behaviour at home, in the police station and in prison. The horrific and random nature of the killing. Her prickly indifference during my assessment. Doubts bubbled. Could I have squeezed more information out of her? Was there something about my approach that caused her to reject me? Should I have been more confrontational? Or more casual? Alarm bells were ringing. A young life had already been lost and another one was on the chopping block. A murder conviction carries an automatic life sentence. Despite Yasmin's resistance, if there was any chance that her actions, however unpalatable, were caused by mental illness and she was not culpable, then she deserved a thorough psychiatric assessment. Most importantly, if there was a chance that she could be cured and the risk of her committing violence in the future could be ameliorated, then she deserved that opportunity.

I applied to the Ministry of Justice for a warrant and managed to get Yasmin transferred to our ward, under the provisions of a special criminal section of the Mental Health Act. Her court case was adjourned to give our services time to intervene. Six weeks. Then I would have to give evidence at the Old Bailey. A blink of an eye in the world of trenchant mental illness.

Yasmin was observed closely by me and the rest of the mental health team in the hospital. After a couple of weeks, we were convinced that behind Yasmin's mask of sanity, something prowled. She was mostly stone-faced and robotic, yet when asked, she would describe her mood as being 'happy, very happy. I am at utter peace'. It was all *incongruous*: a phrase within psychiatric vernacular that has since become very familiar. She also let some odd comments slip, which she would later deny or dismiss, such as asking nurses how to purify evil spirits and asking me to send her all the available scientific literature about reincarnation.

Yasmin initially refused to take oral anti-psychotic medication. Not unreasonable from her perspective; she didn't believe she was mentally unwell. This lack of insight is very common in psychosis, and explains why many patients, such as Stevie McGrew, the Scottish man who threatened the Citizens Advice Bureau, become non-compliant further down the line. As her next court hearing loomed, Yasmin's medication defiance posed a predicament. By slowly building a therapeutic relationship, could we gradually convince her to try tablets? Or should we bite the bullet and use our powers under the Mental Health Act to inject her against her will? Despite my efforts, she failed to develop insight into her illness. But on the bright side, I developed an insight into my flaccid powers of persuasion.

In the end, we restrained Yasmin and gave her an anti-psychotic injection known as a 'depot'. I mean the royal we; although psychiatrists prescribe medication, nurses are burdened with the dirty work. Yasmin needed the needle every two weeks. The first time involved some kicking and screaming. To this day, having to watch my patients being pinned down and stuck with needles is one of the most uncomfortable aspects of my job. But it is very much a necessary evil. Yasmin's compliance improved after the second dose. To the great relief of everyone involved, she then agreed to take tablets, daily. Like most patients when a new medication regime is started, she had to be observed to swallow the pills with water, followed by a quick tongue-out mouth inspection.

After a few weeks of medication, Yasmin opened up a little. The rare glimpses into her psyche revealed her thought processes and psychiatric symptoms during her heinous act. Some of her odd beliefs were substantiated by interviews with members of her family. I spoke to her brother on several occasions, who in his devastation and incredulity was nonetheless very supportive and sympathetic. I remember struggling during my conversations with him, worried that I would come across as patronising. I couldn't help over-analysing my words, my tone and even my facial expressions. Trying to convey hope about the future of his sister, and the deepest condolences for the death of his son, but also trying to be, pretending to be, the unflummoxed professional who is supposed to know what's going to happen. More than anything, I just felt sorry for the guy.

Ahead of Yasmin's trial, I submitted a very detailed court report to be used as formal evidence. It weighed in at a whopping sixty A4-pages, the longest I had written at that point. I made the case for a diagnosis of schizoaffective disorder. This mental illness is a combination of schizophrenia symptoms, such as hallucinations or delusions, and mood disorder symptoms, such as depression or mania. The worst of both worlds.

My recommendation to the court was the defence of 'not guilty by reason of insanity', aka the 'insanity plea' or the 'special verdict'. This is defined by the M'Naghten rules, courtesy of a man who suffered from paranoid delusions, Daniel M'Naghten, who, on 20 January 1843, attempted to assassinate the Prime Minister, Robert Peel, but instead shot his private secretary in the back. These rules state that this defence is open if, at the material time, there is evidence to suggest that the defendant was suffering from:

(a) A defect of reason which was caused by a disease of the mind.

(b) The mental disorder was such that the accused ought not to be held responsible for the act alleged by reason of the fact:

   i) The Defendant did not know the nature and quality of the act, or

   ii) Did not know the act was wrong.

Despite Yasmin's secrecy, using all the objective evidence I was able to establish that at the time of the incident, on the balance of probabilities (more likely than not), Yasmin was suffering from a defect of reason which was caused by a disease of the mind; due to her schizoaffective disorder, she was acting under the delusional belief that her nephew had demons lurking inside him, which she had to remove to save him. She also believed that she could later resurrect him, harnessing the power of a full moon. Additionally, her disorder led her to experience an elevated mood, which disinhibited her thinking and behaviour, and in turn, her ability to weigh up the consequences of her actions. I opined that although she may have known the nature and quality of the act (i.e. suffocating her nephew), on the balance of probabilities, she did not know the act was legally (or indeed morally) wrong.

In case the court rejected this defence, I had a Plan B. Diminished responsibility is a *partial* psychiatric defence, which does not fully exonerate but does downgrade murder to manslaughter; the former carries a mandatory life sentence, whereas sentencing for the latter is completely at the judge's discretion. The medico-legal criteria for this defence are not the same as the M'Naghten rules, but there is a big overlap in the evidence required and the arguments that can be made.

Tuts of disapproval might be forthcoming from some. They would not be unfounded. Yasmin did kill an innocent two-year-old boy. Those tuts would also certainly not be unprecedented. I have discussed this and other similar cases (completely anonymising those involved, in case the General Medical Council asks), with others. I have been told by close friends, a member of my family and even another doctor that the perpetrator had 'got away with murder' (and by inference, that I was an accomplice). As a side note, not too long ago, I was told by a horrified barber who had asked me what I did for a living, that no criminals, *especially* those with mental illnesses, deserved rehabilitation. He literally used the phrase: 'they should lock them up and throw away the key'. I could pretend that I argued that sometimes mental illness can reduce culpability. That I insisted that everybody deserves a chance at rehabilitation and redemption. But the man was halfway through my haircut, so I just shrugged.

To reassure any doubters, 'not guilty by reason of insanity' means that technically the defendant is innocent in the eyes of the law, but that doesn't mean that there are no consequences. Occasionally, if the offence is minor, the court may fully acquit. Particularly if the offence is unlikely to recur and if the defendant will be returning to a stable, supported environment, such as a care home. More often, particularly if the index offence is serious or if there is ongoing potential risk, the insanity plea leads to the defendant being admitted to a psychiatric unit for the foreseeable future. In the case of Yasmin, this would mean returning to the same female medium secure unit to continue her treatment and rehabilitation. A third option if the severity of offence, utilising the Goldilocks model, is not too hot and not too cold, is for the culprit to be released into the community under a supervision order, where they are closely observed by a professional such as a probation officer.

I constructed my report meticulously, in the knowledge that my words would heavily influence the court's judgement on disposal: whether Yasmin would spend all of her life at her Majesty's pleasure or years of her life in hospital. I recommended a 'hospital order' to the court, which is another criminal section of the Mental Health Act (section 37) as well as an additional 'restriction order' (section 41). This is for the upper echelons of high-risk detainees. For these cases, the Ministry of Justice shares decision-making responsibility with the consultant forensic psychiatrist in charge of the care of the patient in hospital. Usually, it is the psychiatrist's autonomous decision when each individual can have leave in the community, and when the patient has undergone enough rehabilitation and treatment to be finally discharged. However, with a restriction order in place, the Ministry of Justice has to give their own nod for all of the above milestones. The ministry also keeps tabs on these individuals after they have left hospital.

Contrary to popular belief, being sectioned to a secure forensic hospital is not an easy ride. In the majority of cases the length of a prison sentence is finite and pre-determined. Admission to one of our units lasts as long as the consultant forensic psychiatrist (and in aforementioned special cases, the Ministry of Justice) deems necessary to reduce the patient's risk. This could take years or even decades if the patient has a treatment-resistant illness, refuses medication, breaks boundaries, displays aggression on the ward, doesn't engage in therapy, or doesn't wash behind their ears (just kidding); potentially stretching their admission beyond the equivalent prison sentence for their original offence (formerly known as the 'tariff').

There are certainly some similarities between a secure forensic hospital and a prison: stigma, rationed food, restricted freedom, locked doors, a strict regime, an influx of illegal drugs and, at times, violence. But a hospital is an environment for healing and rehabilitation. The patients' eventual discharge depends on their compliance, which is a pretty powerful motivator, although the *threat* of never being discharged, I'm sure, probably feels more stick-ish than carrot-ish. They also need to undergo educational or vocational training to set them up for life after discharge. These interventions exist, to varying degrees, in prison. But they are not forced onto prisoners and do not directly affect an individual's stretch in custody (with the exception of very long sentences, when the inmate has to apply for parole).

As I sweated and stuttered through my evidence that blustery day at the Old Bailey, despite the barrister for the prosecution's underhand tactics and efforts to reduce my credibility, the judge accepted my recommendation of a 'not guilty by reason of insanity' verdict and the continued hospitalisation of Yasmin under the provisions of a hospital order and a restriction order. I knew that a lengthy sentence in prison would never have allowed Yasmin to return to her normal self. Maybe my performance on the witness stand was persuasive, but I'm fairly sure the circumstances were more so: a previously untarnished, polite, deferential young woman; a supportive, forgiving family; a precipitous tsunami of psychosis; and an inexplicable offence.

Yasmin's eventual recovery in hospital did happen, but sadly, it was a transformation I would not fully witness. To my great frustration, a couple of months after her trial, I had to move on from my placement on the medium secure female ward back onto the conveyor belt of my training. However, I did stay in touch with Yasmin's treating team and learnt that after almost a year of medication and therapy, her psychotic mask fell even further. She disclosed a barrage of paranoid and grandiose delusions that she had been hiding in the (not entirely incorrect) fear that people would think her crazy. She described seeing hidden messages from God within patterns in the curtains at home, then within stains on her prison cell wall, then within shapes in a carpet on the ward. She was absolutely convinced that she was an angel who had the ability to purify and reincarnate souls. However, with medication these beliefs loosened. She started questioning them, then doubting them, and finally denouncing them.

Yasmin's symptoms dissolving was only the beginning of her rehabilitation. An inevitable, deep, dark, insidious depression bubbled once the horror of her heinous actions gradually seeped into her consciousness. This needed treatment with medication and also cognitive behavioural therapy from the ward psychologist. Family therapy – gradually reconnecting with her relatives in a controlled, supervised space – was also a priority. Yasmin's brother, Sonny's father, not only forgave her, but was very supportive and present in her recovery.

My experience at the Old Bailey taught me so much about medico-legal intricacies, and exposed me to barristers' brutal strategies to undermine. Yasmin's case was an invaluable educational opportunity at that stage in my career. I was given the autonomy to form my own independent opinion about psychiatric defences as well as a restriction order and to give evidence at the Old Bailey.

But more importantly, I learnt about the human cost of violence caused by mental illness. Something that I had read plenty about in textbooks and journals and had heard about in lectures and conferences, but had not *felt* until I spoke to a guarded, paranoid eighteen-year-old who refused to accept what she had done. Until I sat with her brother, as we both tried to make sense of this senseless act. As a forensic psychiatrist, I have encountered abundant tragedy since then. But there was something so *visceral* about Yasmin's act. What is more devastating than the death of a defenceless child? And by a relative who was supposed to be caring for them. This case also made me reflect on the magnitude of forgiveness from Yasmin's brother and other family. Would I have been capable of such magnanimity? I didn't know back then. I've since had two children and I still don't know.

Psychosis very rarely comes out of the blue like that. And it's even rarer for it to lead to such grave consequences. But it can and does. I already had knowledge of the system that finds these needles of mental illness in the chaotic tangled haystacks of killers and other offenders. But Yasmin's case also taught me *why* this system is vital. It brought to the front of my mind a needling awareness of the fine balance between justice and treatment, and the complex intertwined ethical issues. The need to protect and rehabilitate the mentally disordered offender has to be weighed up against the need for justice for the victim.

Chapter 6

Mad or Bad?

Mr Reggie Wallace was detained on a male ward in the same medium secure unit in north London as Yasmin, at around the same time, from late 2012 to around 2014. He had a litany of previous offences. So many that the court clerk had to email over the police case papers to me in three separate attachments. That wasn't a good sign. Over a hundred offences for seventy-two convictions. Not the highest tally I've ever seen, but an honourable mention.

His crimes were a smorgasbord of delinquency: driving offences, numerous assaults and more than a dozen charges of drug possession (cannabis, crack cocaine and heroin). Reggie's more colourful transgressions included kidnapping and torturing a man for over four days: burning him with cigarettes, stabbing him and even urinating into his wounds. I suspect the victim was a rival drug dealer, but obviously he didn't volunteer this during the police investigation.

With the exception of my barber, most people would

generally sympathise with Yasmin Khan. We accept that her acute symptoms of mental illness directly caused her to kill her nephew. She didn't have any history of violence or offending. She wasn't criminalistic or aggressive at any time outside of this context. Mad, not bad. Simple.

Reggie was the antithesis of this. He was a drug dealer, originally from Ghana, latterly from south London, in his mid-forties. Six-foot-four, with a facial tattoo (of a rose, somewhat ironically) and built like a brick poo-home, Reggie was not someone you'd want to meet in a dark alley. He had a history of antisocial behaviour, from shoplifting arrests at the age of eleven to reportedly breaking a teacher's nose with a chalkboard eraser in the second year of high school. Incidentally, my friend's son, then aged seven, once overheard me talking about this case at a barbecue and asked me what chalk was. 'Before touchscreen boards, teachers used to write on black sheets of slate with sticks of compressed coloured dust, invented by cavemen,' was my answer.

Reggie's first contact with mental health services was during a stint at Pentonville Prison for sexual assault of his stepsister. According to the probation reports, he would allegedly lure women addicts to his drug den, encourage them to run up debts for crack and heroin and then get them to work them off by becoming sex slaves for him and his gang. His stepsister said no. There were suspicions that many more vulnerable women accepted this arrangement, though they too were not forthcoming to the police.

In prison, Reggie was deemed to be paranoid. He was convinced that other prisoners from rival south London gangs were plotting to stab him. So far, so feasible. But the clinical picture changed when he became convinced that prisoners, officers and even the prison governor were chanting at night to entice voodoo spirits to shrink his genitals. He was prescribed anti-psychotics by the prison mental health team and improved after a fortnight.

After serving four years, he was back 'on road' (see, I'm down with the lingo). In between dropping off packages, laundering money and torturing his 'opps' (I'm still down), Reggie failed to attend any of his psychiatric outpatient appointments. He wasn't registered with a GP, and therefore couldn't collect the prescribed medication that he was advised to continue taking.

The crime that brought Reggie to the attention of our specialist services (his index offence), was the assault of a random stranger on a bus who he claimed was a rival gang leader in disguise, following him. It was chalked down to mistaken identity, but I couldn't help wondering if it was an overlooked resurgence of his psychotic illness. This was never investigated. No forensic psychiatrist was instructed and an expert opinion about his mental state at the time of his misdemeanour was never sought.

Back in prison, Reggie's paranoia resurfaced, followed by the previous delusions about black magic. This time, he refused medication, believing that the governor had been putting hormone-replacement chemicals inside the tablets to change him into a Mrs Reggie Wallace. He deteriorated quickly. He started lashing out at other prisoners. He smashed a kettle over his cellmate's head, culminating in a trip to the segregation unit (custodial terminology for solitary confinement). Reggie was placed on a 'two-man unlock', meaning that he was deemed to be so high risk that his cell door could not be opened unless two prison officers were present. They had to escort him everywhere to protect others, akin to reverse bodyguards.

When psychosis was diagnosed, Reggie was eventually transferred to the medium secure unit in north London. Here, his challenging behaviour seemingly worsened. Maybe it was the natural fluctuation of his illness, or maybe he felt more emboldened away from a locked cell and constant shadowing by burly prison officers. He would threaten and lash out at patients and staff. He established himself as the alpha on the ward: no walk in the park, considering the patient mix at that time. His actions were often in the context of paranoid beliefs, born from mental illness; he thought that other patients were affiliating with rival drug gangs and had been planted to spy on him, and that the forensic psychiatrist in charge of his case was implicit in this. However, his persecutory perspective also seemed to be related to his natural personality and outlook. Reggie clearly did not like being told what to do and would often act out when boundaries were enforced on the ward. Even basic rules such as turning down his music and handing over his money after visits to the on-site shop (this is standard policy to prevent some patients' cash going missing) were met with impressively loud teeth-sucking, grumbling, swearing and sometimes shouting, often peppered with slang which, to my embarrassment, I was not familiar with. I think I even Googled 'wasteman' (I guess I wasn't quite as down with the lingo as I had hoped). Ever the entrepreneur, Reggie also smuggled in his products to sell to other patients. He didn't have any leave or visitors for the first couple of months, making this feat even more remarkable.

Once medicated effectively, Reggie's psychotic delusions subsided. An underlying milder paranoia remained in the background. As well as his aforementioned natural personality structure, this seemed to be associated with his experiences and upbringing. His trade must have also contributed; I imagine being under surveillance by rivals and by police is fairly standard in his line of work. Plus, his facial tattoo would attract a few extra stares from strangers. Not an ideal accessory for someone with a naturally ultra-suspicious mind, but I certainly wasn't going to point that out to him.

Even with his delusions medicated, much of Reggie's acerbic anti-authoritarian behaviour did not assuage and neither did his bullying and intimidation of other patients, both overt and covert. Frankly, this made him a nightmare to treat and even to be around at times. Although the treating team set boundaries, emphasised the rules and wagged our fingers, this had minimal effect. We are nurses and doctors. We don't have the physiques to control or intimidate like prison officers. Our team, myself included, carried haggard exasperation in our eyes, from going through the rigmarole of chastising him and repeating ward rules several times a week, only to be verbally abused and teeth-sucked at.

I would assess Yasmin's mental state in the female ward across the courtyard, often on the same days. My interactions with her, although challenging in their own way, were far more pleasant and less belligerent. Like a schoolboy resisting sinful thoughts, I couldn't help sacrilegious questions forming in my mind. Does Yasmin deserve our treatment more than Reggie? Should we only treat mad and only punish bad? There are a range of opinions on this, according to my interactions with psychiatrists, other mental healthcare professionals, friends, neighbours and barbers.

Around this time, I was finding my feet as a specialist registrar. I had been exposed to dozens of cases, in hospital as well as prison assessments, and had provided evidence in criminal court on a few more occasions. Spotting patterns within clusters of symptoms and extracting relevant risk factors had started to become instinctual. When I sent drafts of court reports I had written to be checked by my consultant, they were being returned with less red ink. Time and time again I faced a conundrum. Determining whether a defendant or patient was 'mad' or 'bad'. This is a crude distillation of an inescapable core concept within forensic psychiatry. But is this distinction fair? And does it matter? Kind of and yes.

When the public hear about a heinous crime, they bay for blood. The mother who killed her own children. The teenager who stabbed a stranger. Reggie assaulting a random man on a bus and sexually assaulting his own stepsister. If the perpetrator has a mental illness, the 'mad versus bad' distinction is essential to apportion blame. Is our disdain justified? What fraction of liability should we attribute to the shady-looking perpetrator in the newspaper, and what to mental illness?

When the judge hears a case in court, this demarcation

is crystallised by the evidence of a forensic psychiatrist. It guides His or Her Honour as to whether the defendant is culpable. Whether they should be sent to hospital instead of prison. Even if the perpetrator doesn't meet this threshold (i.e. the criteria for detention under the criminal sections of the Mental Health Act) any evidence that they were mentally ill while they carried out their offence might act in mitigation and lessen their custodial sentence.

For the forensic psychiatrist on the witness stand, we make this distinction to guide the court. For the forensic psychiatrist in hospital, it is also vital to guide our risk assessments and our rehabilitation of the individual, who is technically now a patient, and no longer a defendant, once they pass through the industrial-strength, escape-resistant, bolted and locked doors of our secure unit. Simply put, people who are more 'bad' than 'mad' are more dangerous and are harder to treat. It takes more resources, scrutiny and support to contain their future risks. For us, 'mad versus bad' shouldn't be a moral but a clinical judgement, though in some cases the boundaries are blurred. It takes a hardened heart to ignore the egregious nature of some offences. We must also be prepared to deal with the antisocial personalities on the ward. Some of our patients can be particularly … *abrasive*, to put it politely. 'Mad' generally indicates psychosis. 'Bad' generally indicates personality disorder. Antisocial personality disorder is the most common and significant amongst lawbreakers, though other brands are available.

Personality describes the characteristic patterns of thinking, feeling and behaviour that make up who we are and how we feel about ourselves and the world around us. It's what makes us, us. Your grumpy aunt. Your excessively friendly, overly chatty neighbour with the inexplicably punchable face. The six-year-old son who always promises to eat, though spits out the first mouthful after you've toiled for almost two hours making a chicken and mushroom pie intentionally so bland and unseasoned that he could tolerate it, to name some random examples. When an individual's personality is disordered, they may experience difficulties in how they think and feel about themselves and others. These difficulties are ongoing and problematic, negatively affecting their well-being, mental health and relationships with others. The main distinction between errant personality traits and an actual diagnosable disorder is all about functioning. If you struggle to relate to people to the extent that it affects your daily life and hinders most relationships (friendship, familial and romantic), you have crossed this threshold.

A large proportion of my patients have personality disorders. This is not surprising, given the harsh, horrible and chaotic childhoods they have been dealt. Antisocial personality disorder, sometimes called dissocial personality disorder, the younger brother of psychopathy, is a mental condition in which a person consistently shows no regard for right and wrong and ignores the rights and feelings of others. People with this disorder tend to antagonise, manipulate or treat others harshly or with callous indifference. They show no guilt or remorse for their behaviour. These individuals often violate the law. They may lie, behave violently or impulsively, and have problems with drug and alcohol use. Because of these characteristics, people with this disorder typically can't fulfil responsibilities related to family, work or school. Unsurprisingly, this diagnosis is over-represented in males. This was the label given to Reggie Wallace after thorough evaluation on our unit.

Very broadly speaking, from my experience, people with antisocial personality disorder are career criminals. They enjoy the lavish life and gangster image. Many are forced into it from an early age. They keep rebellious and unruly company. Many continue to offend even after coming out of the psychotherapy and medication tumble drier that is our rehabilitation process. The notorious Kray twins would certainly fit this picture. They were celebrity gangsters from London who operated in the swinging sixties until they were both convicted for various crimes in 1969, including murder. The Krays were versatile criminals, with their fingers in numerous illicit pies, from extortion to arson to assault to witness intimidation to killing. Incidentally, one of them, Ronnie, was diagnosed with paranoid schizophrenia and spent almost two decades in Broadmoor Hospital, suggesting he was both mad *and* bad.

We also commonly see borderline (also known as emotionally unstable) personality disorder, which occurs more frequently in females. This is a serious mental abnormality that causes unstable moods, behaviour and relationships. It is characterised by unstable or changing relationships, impulsive or self-damaging behaviours (e.g. excessive spending, unsafe sex, substance abuse, reckless driving, binge eating, self-harm) and problems with anger, including frequent loss of temper or physical fights. Although

I've obviously never had the pleasure of assessing him in person, I've always suspected that one of the most talented and original lyricists of all time, Eminem, has this diagnosis. His relationships are the very textbook definition of explosive and turbulent; he's been sued by his own mother, has married the same woman, Kim, twice and has written very graphic songs about raping the former and killing the latter. He has 'dissed' a multitude of other rappers and celebrities and has struggled with depression and addiction. These personality traits clearly haven't stifled Eminem's musical prowess and creativity, and have arguably even fuelled his unique and fascinating lyrical content.

Again, with some liberal generalisation, my experience is that people with borderline personality disorder do not intend to offend, but they cannot contain their emotions, especially during a crisis or confrontation. They will lash out impulsively, aggressively and excessively. Unlike their antisocial personality disorder peers, they often regret their actions afterwards but they cannot help themselves at the time. After being analysed on our unit, Reggie was deemed to have 'traits' of this disorder, but he didn't cross the threshold for a full diagnosis.

Less common, but certainly an inductee to the forensic-psychiatry Hall of Fame, is paranoid personality disorder. As the name suggests, sufferers of this disorder are very suspicious. They mistrust the motives of others and believe that people want to harm them. Additional hallmarks of this condition include being reluctant to confide in anybody, bearing grudges and finding demeaning or threatening subtext in even the most innocent of comments or events.

Sufferers can be quick to feel anger and hostility towards others. Cases from my career have given me the impression that people with paranoid personality disorder will not offend if left alone, though they will not tolerate perceived injustice or insults, often with violent retaliation. Again, Reggie exhibited traits of this.

My perspective on Reggie and the mad-versus-bad issue blurred once I happened to look more closely into his background. One aspect of working with offenders in secure units that attracted me in the first place is how deeply and intimately we get to know our patients. They are on the wards for years, during which time we carry out exhaustive explorations of their familial relationships, their previous lives, childhood experiences and historical traumas to identify emotional and behavioural triggers and the resultant character flaws. Psychologists are invaluable; not only are they tasked with eliciting this material, but also with trying to change deeply ingrained negative cognitions, emotions and attitudes. They are the tattoo removalists of the psyche.

Our team's psychologist gradually managed to tease out the details of Reggie's tragic upbringing. It was as hard-knock a life as you could imagine. He had oscillated between his indifferent mother and care homes. On the rare occasion that his father showed up, he was abusive towards Reggie, his other three siblings and his mother. He even fractured one-year-old Reggie's arm because he wouldn't stop crying. No matter how disagreeable I might find the intimidating forty-six-year-old tattooed version in front of me, and no matter how unpalatable his previous crimes of kidnapping, torture and sexual assaults were, I could not feel anything but deep sympathy and terror for that baby. Completely oblivious and in tremendous pain. It's my job to understand why people occasionally harm babies in the context of florid psychosis, like Yasmin. But even after all the violence I have seen and treated over the years, I cannot comprehend how anybody could intentionally hurt such an innocent being.

After some education sessions from the occupational therapist, it became apparent that Reggie had severe dyslexia and could barely read and write. This was seemingly never explored by his teachers. To be fair, this would have been a taxing task while dodging flying objects. Was Reggie's bad behaviour perhaps frustration at his educational needs never being considered? Was his foray into drug dealing at least reinforced by his lack of alternative career options?

Reggie also revealed to the psychologist that his older brother Bobby was murdered in his late teens, stabbed in a pub over a game of pool. 'The only member of my family who gave even the tiniest shit about me, growing up' was how he described Bobby. Reggie wanted to join a gang for a sense of belonging, though he also felt compelled to for protection. He reportedly felt guilty about his shenanigans at first. This included taking the bus to the posher west London boroughs to relieve the schoolkids of their pocket money and their Game Boys (other brands were also stolen). He recalled an incident when his friends had shoved a younger kid onto the floor in McDonald's and stamped on his glasses. Reggie relayed how they had all guffawed and sauntered off. He had laughed along, but looking back over his shoulder, he'd felt awful watching the boy pick up his broken frames with a bloody nose. The image stayed with him for weeks. But over the years, Reggie became inured to the daily brutality he witnessed and perpetuated. He stopped feeling guilty. Repeated exposure to violence eventually softens its impact. As I well know.

Reggie's origin story is very familiar to me. Similar tragedies are revealed when I explore the background of the majority of the patients within the forensic psychiatric system. These vicissitudes commonly predispose to both offending and also mental illness (known as confounding factors), so are almost ubiquitous at their crossroads. This includes exposure to physical aggression, especially at an early age, as well as other forms of neglect, emotional and sexual abuse. Behind every 'bad' there is inevitably 'sad'. An uncomfortable but inescapable truth is that the majority of perpetrators of physical violence were once victims themselves. Employment droughts, poverty and homelessness are also often experienced by those with psychiatric and criminal histories. Perhaps the most significant confounding factor is substance abuse. Some vices, particularly alcohol and cocaine, are renowned for increasing aggression in those who are susceptible; others, such as amphetamine and 'skunk' cannabis, are notorious for triggering psychosis.

Reading the psychology report, I wondered what resources had been denied to Reggie and how steep his playing field must have been. Not only a lack of basic care from his parents but also basic support from his teachers. The very system that I represent could also have been implicit. If he was potentially mentally ill during his most recent offence, why was this not picked up by the police who arrested him, the solicitors who discussed the case with him, or the barristers and the judge who tried him? Or by the prison staff (including a forensic psychiatrist, I hasten to add) when he was on remand? He could have been pulled out of the quicksand of paranoid delusions earlier. Missed opportunities were rife.

It was also disappointing to see how easily Reggie fell between the cracks of the mental health system after he was released from his previous prison stay. Not taking his prescribed medication and not registering with a GP didn't help. But this is hardly unique behaviour and I have seen many other patients with compliance issues being more assertively supported in the community. Other more middle class, more congenial and less Black patients. Would Yasmin, for example, a small, placid, polite, unblemished, vulnerable female with a loving, supportive family, be fobbed off in such a passive manner if she didn't cooperate with treatment?

The 'mad versus bad' distinction is necessary in my opinion, but only from a clinical, not judgemental, perspective. As forensic psychiatrists, we risk-assess our patients to decide when to discharge them into the community and how to contain their dangerousness afterwards. To do this, we need to analyse the factors that are likely to lead to relapse of violence and of mental illness. We must also allocate our limited resources wisely. To be blunt, if my patient is purely mad, like Yasmin, then all I have to do is remove the mad from the equation. The main focus is to ensure her compliance with medication after discharge. This is relatively simple. Even though her original crime was incredibly tragic, the likelihood of it recurring is very low and if it were to happen, this is very likely to be in similar circumstances. She had also (eventually) been compliant and cooperative in hospital. All of this indicated a good prognosis.

With Reggie on the other hand, it was far more difficult to contain his risks. After we removed the mad, the bad (his antisocial personality disorder, his anti-authoritarian stance and his general unwillingness to cooperate) was a much more persistent stain. Can bad be cured? This is a complex, multifaceted issue that polarises forensic psychiatrists as much as the rest of society. We could travel down an at times philosophical wormhole together. Instead, I'll save us both a headache by giving the short answer: sometimes. But only with internal motivation from the patient. As the old adage goes, forensic psychiatrists can lead a horse to water, but we cannot alter its personality. On the depressingly rare occasions that this redemption does happen, from my experience, it usually follows the repeated cycle of prison/hospital/handcuffs/police station/weeping relatives/standing in the dock. Only then does the patient finally gain insight. When their antisocial peers have all moved on with careers and family and they are the last one left at the party, realising it's time to go to bed.

It took the younger, naive junior doctor version of myself a few years of seeing promising patients – seemingly on the straight and narrow – eventually deteriorate, re-offend and get churned back into the system before I came to a rather gloomy realisation: our enforced moralistic boundaries and values rarely, if ever, change a patient's attitude without their own personal internal epiphany.

Reggie didn't change his ways and didn't even pretend to. This meant that even if he did keep his mental illness at bay after discharge, there were many other risk factors for him re-offending: his personality, his core beliefs, his lifestyle, his occupation, his associates, his recreational drug use and his limited alternative career options, to name a few. Reggie's chance of recidivism was much higher than Yasmin's and he required far more attention and resources, even if his actual recent offence (assaulting a stranger on a bus) was far less heinous. There were many forms of offending and violence he might foreseeably commit. In his case, we knew we couldn't manage all of his risk factors, but we at least knew our limits. Close supervision from MAPPA (multi-agency public protection arrangements, a communication network formed of the police, probation and prison services and other agencies to manage violent and sexual offenders) was the most effective safety net.

Incidentally, another anomaly in my line of work compared to other doctors' is very limited customer gratitude: comparable to that given to football referees, the tax man and traffic wardens. We work with people with a history of violence; we intervene (they might say interfere) when they are at their lowest ebb, lock them up for significant lengths of time and enforce medications that they don't like taking, for symptoms they don't recognise. We also chastise fully-grown adults like Reggie, who already have a problem with authority, for misbehaving according to our rules on the ward. I can count on one hand (without using two fingers) the number of Christmas cards I have received from patients over the years. I will have to be satisfied that I am, in my own little way, saving the public (from harm), some patients (from prison) and some trees (from being pulped into card).

Reggie understandably had no love for our services. The only thing that remotely indicated any fondness (or at least, a dip in animosity) towards me from him was one conversation we had on the ward about an underground old-school British hip-hop tune that he had blasting from his room that I knew and loved ('Riddim Killa' by Rodney P). However, on the day he left the ward, Reggie's sister attended his final discharge meeting. Afterwards, she made a point to thank all the staff involved in his care. She told us that this was the first time that anybody had tried to help him. Those words moved me more than I expected. Not just because of the seldom-received thanks for our services so much as the heart-breaking thought that Reggie had lived such a marginalised and ignored existence. On the drive home that day, I clocked a traffic warden and felt a kind of thankless-job-kinship. A recognition of the fact that he was helping decrease congestion on our roads. Although since then, I've had around a dozen parking tickets. To hell with them all!

Yasmin and Reggie are at extreme ends of the spectrum. Most of my patients are somewhere in between. Those ethical waters were muddied further and those philosophical fires stoked by another case where mad and bad were less well demarcated.

Chapter 7

Muddied Waters

Mr Charlie Wedger was a thirty-year-old man who had a diagnosis of autism. Autistic spectrum disorder covers a range of disorders, from severe autism to milder disability. Symptoms occur in three main areas, namely social interactions, verbal and nonverbal communication and repetitive or ritualistic behaviours. Common symptoms of autism in adults include difficulty interpreting what others are thinking or feeling, and trouble interpreting facial expressions, body language or social cues. Although the vast majority of people with autism are categorically not violent, there have been a couple of recent, tragic high-profile cases that have highlighted this very rare correlation.

One extreme example is Alek Minassian, a twenty-five-year-old with no prior criminal history, who on 23 April 2018 rented a van with the explicit intention of running over dozens of strangers in Toronto because he wanted to be famous. His legal team tried to use his autism as a defence, even erroneously comparing it to a psychosis. He was found guilty of ten counts of first-degree murder and sixteen of attempted murder.

During his trial, it emerged that Minassian had studied spree killers and openly admitted fantasising about school shootings. He'd also researched Elliot Rodger who, in 2014, had stabbed, shot and run over six people before killing himself and had a manifesto which was linked to the incel population. This term, an abbreviation of 'involuntary celibate', describes a recent internet-driven movement of young men who have not had carnal knowledge; as a result, they have disturbing misogynistic views about their entitlement to sex and direct their vitriol towards all women, particularly the attractive ones who they believe ignore them. Personally, having experienced being a spotty virgin with very little 'game' in my teenage years, I can't fathom why they don't find other . . . ahem, solitary activities to release their sexual frustrations and bide their time until they eventually find meaningful relationships. Whereas the vast majority of incel members egg each other on with childish sexist comments and theories, a very small proportion justify extreme violence through their shared agenda. Closer to home than Minassian was the case of Jake Davison, a twenty-two-year-old who shot and killed five people (including his own mother and a three-year-old girl) and injured two others before turning the gun on himself, in Plymouth in the UK in August 2021; this was the first mass shooting on British soil in a decade. He also openly declared an allegiance to the incel philosophy.

Looking at Minassian's background, there were certainly some factors that may have contributed to his anger and sense of isolation. He was bullied at school and was a social outcast. He had a hatred of being rejected, especially by women, as is the incel way. In fact, during his court hearings, a particular incident was raised when he had tried to flirt with a woman in a college library and was rejected, which he particularly took to heart. It is likely that some of the features of his autism may have contributed to him being marginalised and made him more likely to be the target of bullying and to be spurned by females. He probably struggled with interactional reciprocity and figuring out social cues, which would have hindered his ability to flirt. One could postulate that as he had restricted interests, his penchant for spree killers could have led him to become more obsessed than the average person. Another factor in sufferers of this disorder is their inability to express emotions like anger and frustration in a healthy and acceptable manner.

Despite Minassian's attempt to get a finding of 'not criminally responsible', the Canadian equivalent to the aforementioned 'not guilty by reason of insanity' defence, this was (correctly in my view) not recognised by the court.

It emerged that Minassian's actions were deliberate and pre-planned. He had hired the van on that day with the distinct purpose of killing random people and he even stated to a psychiatrist that he wished he had run over more attractive young females and that he was happy with the attention he was getting. It could be argued that due to his autism and inability to appreciate other people's perspectives, he would not have fully understood the magnitude of pain and suffering he had caused. But this would not have any direct bearing on his criminal culpability.

Not long afterwards a horrendous case sent shockwaves through the UK and beyond. Jonty Bravery, aged seventeen, picked up a six-year-old French boy, and dropped him over the railings of the Tate Modern gallery in London on 4 August 2019. He initially travelled by Underground to London Bridge and made his way to the Shard. He asked a member of staff about the entry price but it was too steep so he ended up going to the Tate instead. He took a lift up to the tenth-floor viewing platform, walked casually towards the edge and peered over. Witnesses described him as looking relaxed and smiling at children, but the children felt something was off, so they moved away. The victim and his family arrived in the lift, and when the door opened, the young boy skipped out to the balcony. Bravery scooped him up and threw him over the edge where he plunged thirty metres to what was very nearly his death. Bravery was smiling as he was detained by members of the public and was said to be calm and lacking emotion. He stated: 'It's not my fault; it's social services' fault' and then asked if it was going to be on the news. That poor boy suffered a bleed to the brain, spinal fractures and broken legs and arms. He was incapacitated and wheelchair-bound for several months, though is now making a very gradual recovery.

Almost a year later, Bravery appeared at his court hearing via video link from Broadmoor Hospital to be sentenced after pleading guilty to attempted murder. Bravery was clearly criminally culpable.

With spooky echoes of the Minassian case, his attack was pre-planned. Not only had he tried to go to the Shard first, and then had to adjust his plans, but he'd used the internet in some incriminating searches on that very morning of the incident ('are you guaranteed to escape prison if you have autism?'). Evidently, stating that he wanted to be on the news indicated he knew what he was doing was legally wrong. At his trial, the judge ruled that Bravery's autism spectrum disorder did not explain the attack, and that he presented 'a grave and immediate risk to the public'. He was sentenced to prison for a minimum of fifteen years for attempted murder.

I was entering my third and final year of higher training in 2013, when my consultant asked me to assess Charlie Wedger. This was a one-off evaluation in order to write a court report, assessing his fitness to plead. I visited him on a specialist psychiatric ward for offenders with learning disabilities like autism, situated on the other side of the east London hospital where I was working. Charlie had spent most of his thirty-odd years in institutions, from special needs boarding schools to various care homes. He wore sunglasses and a bright Hawaiian shirt, even though the ward and the weather were gloomy. As there was already a ward round in full swing in the main meeting room that morning, and the only other office was being used for some kind of paperwork audit, I was asked to conduct the evaluation in the patients' recreation room. Writing notes on top of a pool table added to the already surreal flavour of our interaction.

Charlie's original crime was the sexual assault of a random woman who was waiting at a bus stop with her baby in a pram. He approached her, asked her a few questions about the timetable and then suddenly fondled her breasts and tried to kiss her. She pushed him away and screamed. Charlie scarpered, though remarkably returned minutes later to ask for her phone number. She shrieked at him and then he ran away again. His care home was only around the corner and the victim saw which door he went through. She called the police and Charlie was promptly arrested.

Police enquiries revealed that there had been previous similar incidents; Charlie had approached numerous lone females and made sexual advances. Although he wasn't overtly threatening or violent during his approaches, they would clearly have been very distressing for his victims. He'd even been arrested three times before, though each time the case had been dropped by the police with the unofficial 'he's just a bit cuckoo' defence that some officers seem to adopt (a kind of warped positive discrimination). Each time, stern words had been had with and fingers had been wagged at Charlie. Each time, the staff who worked at his care home promised to be more vigilant and only allow him out on his own when he seemed stable. However, the doors were not locked and Charlie was not detained under the Mental Health Act, so legally they could not stop him from leaving. There was also a four-to-one ratio of staff to clients, all of whom had significant needs. Like a modern-day Murdock from *The A-Team*, Charlie kept giving them the slip. To me, this has echoes of Jonty Bravery's case; he was also regularly allowed out of his care home by himself before that fateful day when he threw the innocent boy off the balcony of Tate Modern, despite the fact that there were concerns about his level of risk and his violence towards staff. Nobody seems to have considered legally detaining Bravery.

I appreciated that Charlie's actions during his offence did seem jumbled and confused and not quite the characteristics of a dangerous sexual predator. But I had to consider, why did he flee? Was this genuine remorse? Or fear of retribution? Or embarrassment at being rejected? Then he returned to ask for her number, indicating a lack of understanding of the inappropriateness of his act or any sense of harm he may have caused.

During my assessment, after establishing the routine background information (such as his childhood and his attitudes towards any previous offending), I tried to explore my queries. Charlie was very open about this incident and the others. Too open, almost childlike, seemingly oblivious to the impression he might be giving me: in itself another suggestion of an inability to fully appreciate the consequences of his actions. Did he know what he was doing was wrong? Upon detailed questioning, he explained that he had sexual urges and wanted relief. I tried to gauge his concept of consent.

'You try to snog them and if they do it, that is consent,' he said.

'And if they say no?' I asked.

Charlie shrugged. 'Then it's not.'

'What would you do in that situation?'

'You keep trying and they might say yes.'

This reminded me of a certain ex-president's philosophy on consent. I asked Charlie why he had absconded after the woman had pushed him away.

'Because she was angry. I was in trouble,' he answered.

We were getting to the crux of the matter. 'Why was she angry?'

'Because I was too ugly for her.'

I asked Charlie how he felt about his victims being upset. He pondered this for a while and fiddled with his shades. 'I still should be allowed to try to get a girlfriend. It's my human rights.' This seemed like a simplified, fatuous version of the core belief of the incel movement.

Charlie was befuddled by the complexities of consent, despite having a superficial understanding. His lack of reciprocity and conceptualisation of social norms due to his autism contributed to this. Yet simultaneously, he also felt sexually entitled and this trumped the emotions of his victims. Clearly this is also the thought process of a rapist.

Charlie's rehabilitation would require schooling him about consent, respect and possibly even the concept of sex as a whole. He would need an intense psychotherapy regime, tailored to his intelligence level and cognitive idiosyncrasies. This was not a quick fix. And certainly not something I was able to even begin to unpick during a one-off interview. Despite my temptations to correct him and educate him, I knew I had no authority in his eventual future treatment. This would've been discourteous to his treating team, who would want to approach his issues in a measured and structured way.

In this particular case, I found Charlie to be unfit to plead.

Despite having a very basic understanding of the court process, he could not comprehend anything complex (once again evoking comparisons to a certain ex-president). This was reflected by Charlie's repeated pleas to tell the judge he was sorry, promising he would never speak to a woman again, and begging just to be released. His swearing at me when I tried to explain that I didn't have the authority to do this further cemented my suspicions of him not grasping the legalities of his situation. He received a hospital order from the judge and returned to the learning disability unit for long-term rehabilitation. Therefore, there was no trial and his culpability was not scrutinised in court. Even though I was never asked during the course of my evidence, I found myself wondering where Charlie's attitudes lay on the 'mad versus bad' scale. As the court was satisfied with my opinions on his fitness to plead and as his treatment was not my jurisdiction, I had no further contact with Charlie. Given the timescale, he may well have since been discharged. Autism is not an illness that can be 'cured', but Charlie's cognitive outlooks and behavioural patterns can be adapted. Hopefully, he has learnt to change his attitude and the way he interacts with women.

Around a year later, I assessed another similar case of a nineteen-year-old with Asperger's syndrome (a form of autism with less severe symptoms and the absence of language delays), named Talal, who had allegedly raped his younger cousin and tried to convince her to keep it a secret. The focus of my assessment was similar to Charlie's: a court report regarding fitness to plead. Talal was quiet and unassuming, and a bit of a loner – all fairly typical for this disorder. He was seventeen and the victim was thirteen at the time. He claimed to have absolutely no memory of the three alleged incidents, which had only occurred a year and a half earlier during a summer holiday, when the whole family had gone camping for a month. As I relayed in my court report, this didn't seem consistent with the rest of his reporting. He was able to outline articulately and in detail most other aspects of his life, with no lapses in his recall. In actuality, a defendant claiming that they have no memory of an alleged crime has no bearing whatsoever on their overall fitness to plead, as it would not have on their guilt or innocence. Anybody can say they cannot remember, and it is hard to disprove.

I assessed Talal at his solicitors' office, in the main meeting room, crammed against the wall by a gargantuan oak table, evoking memories of the inconvenient and un-ergonomic pool table (clearly not enough space to swing a cue for a decent shot) shunting me to the side of the room during Charlie's assessment. Not only was Talal dressed in a suit, but his entire countenance was formal. He had limited reactivity in his facial expression, again, not uncommon for Asperger's syndrome. Talal answered questions like he was in a job interview. The assessment felt even more uncomfortable due to his mother's presence. She had clearly coached him in what to say, and he constantly looked over to her for answers. She was also disruptive at points in the interview, talking over me and her son, making very leading statements.

'Obviously, doctor, he's suffered from this horrid illness

for so long, it leaves him confused. He doesn't always know what he's doing.'

'Surely an expert like yourself can't expect my boy to remember such insignificant incidents from so long ago, especially if nothing untoward actually happened.'

'He is intelligent, but it's all too stressful. Too complicated for him to understand what's going on in court. He finds the judge intimidating, with his silly wig. You know what they're like, with the jargon.'

There was a palpable desire from Talal and his mother for this case to miraculously disappear, and reluctance for him to be involved. Despite this, after some dodging and weaving, I still found him fit to plead. Months later, I heard that he received a custodial sentence of three years.

Back in the office, out of curiosity I pulled up my report on Charlie. Reading through it, I could sense that within the space of a year I had become much more familiar with legal terms and concepts which had initially flummoxed me. Areas that I remember feeling indecisive about now seemed obvious to me. I found myself wondering if Talal was actually guilty of the allegations, whether he could be classified as fully *bad*. Probably. He must have understood that his actions were immoral if he wanted his victim to hide them. His case had many similarities to Alek Minassian's. In both cases, Asperger's must have limited the perpetrators' ability to feel empathy and fully understand the impact of their horrific crimes. I wondered if, like Minassian, Talal would have carried out his actions if his disorder didn't hinder him from forming healthy romantic and sexual relationships? Probably not. But is that an excuse? Definitely not.

These questions are complex and the very concepts are nebulous. There are many grey areas. I sometimes still struggle with them. But the law does not care for uncertainty. It doesn't tolerate maybes. A defendant is either eligible for a psychiatric defence or not. Guilty or innocent. Prison or hospital. I was coming to realise that being an expert witness was far more Byzantine than I had expected. But instead of these philosophical, ethical, medical and legal minefields being a deterrent, they drew me in like a moth to a flame.

Chapter 8

The Most Surreal Interaction

As I approached my final year as a specialist registrar, I was tasked with evaluating a man named Mr Josef Jefferson in a low secure unit one afternoon. This hospital was affiliated with our medium secure unit in east London, and only a half-hour bus ride away. While he was suffering from an acute phase of mania, Josef had walked into a clothes shop in his underwear and stolen a mannequin. His reasons were unknown. I had imagined a couple of potential scenarios, both unsavoury and neither of them great for the mannequin. He had been chased by the store security guard and run across a busy main road causing a not particularly serious, but what I can only picture to be a fairly comical, slap-stick accident. He was sectioned and had been stable, though the day before I met him, Josef's consultant psychiatrist had been told by nursing staff on the ward that he had deteriorated in the last week.

Training in forensic psychiatry, as in all fields of medicine, involves annual appraisal and innumerable workplace-based assessments, which are about as much fun as they sound. These include carrying out specific clinical tasks while being observed by a senior colleague who marks your performance on a pro forma. My assignment was to carry out a full mental state examination. This is the psychiatrist's equivalent of a doctor examining somebody with a physical health issue. But instead of listening to your chest, making you gag with a massive lollipop stick, or sharing the smell of our last meal on our breath while blinding you with a torch, we enquire about or covertly assess manifestations of your mental state, including your mood, your speech (e.g. rate, tone and volume), whether your thought content is delusional, and your intentions with any kidnapped mannequins.

With the consultant observing me, I entered the clinical room to find Josef lounging prostrate across a chair. He was a plump fellow in his late forties, with a mischievous, cherub-like face, and a Salvador Dali-esque moustache. He was wearing a bow-tie, a luminous yellow waistcoat and glasses without any lenses. He also sported what I can only describe as a 'reverse mohawk': a puff of hair with an inch-wide strip shaved off in the middle. He was sipping tea from a small china cup, lifting his pinkie up with every gulp. Mania makes sufferers disinhibited, excitable and outlandish. Sometimes this is reflected in their dress sense. A common malady within my patient cohort, it is an acute phase of bipolar affective disorder. Sufferers oscillate between periods of depression, normal mood (known as euthymia) and mania. Symptoms of the latter include feeling very happy, talking quickly, feeling self-important (grandi-ose), bursting with great new ideas and having important plans, being extremely distractable, being easily irritated or agitated, generally feeling full of energy and not requiring much sleep. There is also disinhibition leading to impulsive acts and very poor decisions without the ability to consider the consequences. I'm sure many of us have said or done something we shouldn't have (possibly with a colleague) after one too many gin and tonics at the office Christmas party. And I'm sure we can remember the stinging shame and embarrassment the next day in the cold light of sobriety. Now, imagine several weeks of poor judgement caused by mental illness. Uncharacteristic and impulsive risk-taking in the form of drugs, promiscuity, excessive spending and giving away possessions are common behaviours during a manic episode. Within a proportion of my patient group, sexually disinhibited behaviour, from flashing to public masturbation to actual rape, occurs too.

As soon as he saw us, Josef jumped up and curtsied. 'This is a Monet original,' he said, pointing to a bland painting of a barn in a booming posh voice. 'And this is one of Van Gogh's finest works.' He nodded at a photo of a beach. He grinned, patted his belly, took a swig from the china cup and then ducked his head towards me. 'I'm out of famous artists, dude. Help me out,' he whispered.

I was conscious that I had not even introduced myself and I might get marked down by the consultant. I asked Josef to sit, which he did, though he was squirming with excite-ment. Halfway through my explanation of why I had come to see him, he bolted up.

'Dammit, man! I can't remember all those painters by name, but you get the gist. They're worth millions.' He rubbed his hands together. 'This building is worth at least a billion. For two noble gents such as yourself, an esteemed pair of psychologists, I will sell it for £300 million.' He spat on his palm and held out his hand. He was disorientated and disinhibited, with a flight of ideas. Classic mania.

'Josef, we're psychiatrists, not psychologists.'

Josef cocked his head back and guffawed, making his belly jingle. I found myself smiling. Elevated mood: another textbook symptom of mania. Even the countertransference (when a therapist feels emotions towards a client) in this situation, namely his infectious laughter, was typical of this disorder.

I took in a deep breath and suppressed my urge to giggle. 'Could we please talk about your symptoms?' I asked.

'That's my final offer. And we both know it's a veritable bargain,' he boomed.

At this point, the consultant intervened by asking Josef to listen to my questions. Josef shushed my colleague (who was at least twenty years my senior) and said: 'Silence! The grown-ups are talking.'

Josef eventually let me speak and we had a surreal exchange about his symptoms, which felt like a sketch show.

'Do you feel like your thoughts are speeded up?'

'Well yes, compared to mere mortals. But it's not my fault I'm a genius.'

'Okay, when you say you're a genius, what makes you think that? Can you give me some examples?' I was trying to elicit the specifics of his grandiosity. At this point, there was no doubt about the diagnosis. However, it would be helpful to document all symptoms as a benchmark of severity. This way, after adjusting Josef's medication doses, he could be assessed a couple of weeks down the line and his future mental state examination could be compared to the one I was undertaking.

Josef cackled and sipped from his cup of tea. He pulled out a crumpled piece of paper from his sock and handed it to me. There were a few drawings of various cylinders inside what looked like a spider's web with random arrows and a nonsensical equation: '$x = x+1 = y = z+2$'. At the top, in childlike writing, were the words 'Dezine for newclear oprated power plant'.

Josef snatched the paper out of my hand and eyed me suspiciously. 'You can see it properly once the patents are through.' He took a sip of his tea. 'John Naps, the great mathematician, won a Nobel Peace Prize. He had schizophrenia, you know.'

'Nash.'

'Nats?'

'No, Nash. His name was John Nash. And I think it was the Nobel Prize in Economics.'

Josef smirked. 'Sure, my young boy, if you believe everything you read in the papers.'

'Is that what you're hoping for, a Nobel Prize?'

'Nope, already got one.' He'd really nailed that grandiosity.

'Oh yeah? For what?'

'For awesomeness. Do you know that I can do ten thousand press-ups?' Josef lay on the floor and did around five.

He stood up to wipe his brow with his waistcoat and said, 'I'll finish them later'.

He was easily distractible with pressured speech and formal thought disorder (jumping between topics), other typical signs of his diagnosis. We proceeded to go through the list of symptoms of mania and Josef claimed that he had them all, though was not unwell. The consultant jotted away in the background. I had no idea if I was impressing my assessor. The interview was so random and disjointed but at the same time I *was* eliciting numerous symptoms.

Over the next ten minutes, I finally managed to get through my list of enquiries, with Josef stopping to do some star jumps and answering some of my questions in song. Just as I was about to say goodbye, he told me I had not enquired about his one major symptom.

'The salient of ailments,' he called it.

'Please, do tell, Josef.'

'Piles, young doctor. Piles.'

I looked over at the consultant who remained stone-faced. I politely explained that I would be happy to alert his ward doctor, but this was not associated with mania, which was the focus of my assessment.

'Oh yeah? Then how do you explain this?' He undid his belt and grabbed the top of his trousers. I froze. The consultant jumped up. 'We're done!' he barked.

'But I haven't asked him about thoughts of self-harm,' I said, but the consultant had already grabbed his notes and was scurrying out the door. 'It's fine. I'll give you the marks. Let's just go.'

Josef winked at me again. 'Don't worry, doc. I was

kidding, I'm not that mad,' he said, grinning and fastening his belt back up. 'I just wanted to freak out that stuffy older doctor fellow.'

'Well, I think you succeeded,' I said, winking back.

Josef's roaring maniacal laughter echoed behind me as I walked away.

Another day at the office. I didn't come across Josef again, as I was based on another unit. I do hope that he recovered from his mania (and his piles), but retained his sense of humour.

I passed the assessment. The consultant had ticked the 'good' boxes for all categories and wrote nothing in the 'recommended areas for development' section. Which suggested to me that either he found my assessing prowess flawless, or perhaps he viewed the whole task as yet another inconvenient, administrative burden and he wanted to forget about the whole afternoon – and Josef's piles.

I completed numerous other types of assessment for my training in forensic psychiatry, though that must have been the most surreal interaction. I also had to send out questionnaires to multiple colleagues and patients for feedback on my skill and competencies. For me, like the traffic-laden commutes or the protracted security checks at secure units and prisons, these bureaucratic tasks were forgettable and inconvenient necessities, part and parcel of the role. The most enlightening aspect of my training, by far, was observing consultants work their trade. They were a mixed bag. Most were helpful, supportive and knowledgeable. The two that I learnt the most from happen to be the best and the worst. The best, Dr Linford, was my boss around halfway through my three years as a specialist registrar. He was very focused and driven, despite his reserved exterior. He had the demeanour and slow, calculated speech of a wise kung fu sensei. He knew his patients intimately and had their care plans meticulously mapped out in his head. He led the team effectively and always knew who was supposed to be doing what and when. Most admirably, he *always* had time for his patients, no matter how busy he was, often working well past his scheduled hours. Even for the minority who were hostile towards him, usually because he'd had to stop their leave (e.g. if they had tested positive for drugs). He would endure the occasional tirade of abuse, even though he could easily have avoided these individuals and delayed any confrontation until the next ward round, when multiple staff members would be present. I respected that Dr Linford treated me fairly and he pushed me. He critiqued every mistake I made in a pernickety but constructive manner. His natural personality was civil but not over-friendly. This led me to constantly seek his approval. His anankastic ways forced me to fully focus all the time, which eventually became habit. Once, after a ward round, Dr Linford pulled me aside and told me that he'd noticed me making a few mistakes (I'd forgotten to prescribe the medication from a previous conversation, and also accidentally mixed up the background information of two patients with similar presentations). He was polite but firm, and this made me hyper aware of his level of scrutiny, preventing me from making future errors.

Immediately after working with Dr Linford, I began a six-month placement with Dr Peck, the worst consultant I encountered. She was sloppy and disorganised, and had a ghostly countenance despite wearing so much make-up that she was bordering on clown territory. She was pathologically late to almost every meeting, often leaving a room full of professionals (sometimes including external visitors who had made a long journey specifically to discuss a patient with her) waiting with no apologies or explanation. Her ward rounds were chaotic and shambolic, and at times, I wasn't even sure which patient we were discussing. Worse, they were excruciatingly long and boring and I had fallen asleep more than once (which, to be fair, was inexcusable). She loved the sound of her own voice and would recycle the same hypotheses about a patient's psychodynamics that were neither interesting, nor relevant. One such conversation went like this:

'Of course, Fred always played second fiddle to his brother. He could barely hold down a job at the supermarket, but his brother went on to be a pilot. Fred has deep-rooted insecurities, and victimises those whom he feels intellectually inferior to,' she said.

'Sure, Dr Peck. But the nurses need to know if you think he is stable enough to have leave?' I asked, probably not masking my passive aggressive attitude enough.

She would shy away from decisions and offered no guidance to the treating team. As her lieutenant, she dumped the dullest tasks onto me, as opposed to the ones that I could learn from, and would either turn up very late or not at all to the weekly supervision meetings we were supposed to have. To be fair, I was not completely without fault. I was not as diplomatic as I should have been and perhaps ignorant to the chain of command. I was brash and outspoken. I would interrupt Dr Peck to repeat questions that she had dodged with rambling psychological formulations. We clashed. I admittedly went above my station and occasionally gave instructions to my team. This is a solid faux pas for a doctor of my seniority. She saw this as extreme arrogance, but honestly, I felt that somebody should be leading the team, and hey, I actually bothered turning up to the meetings and at times was the only doctor in the room. Dr Peck had never challenged me on this, so I had assumed there was no huge issue.

During my annual progress meeting with the training programme director, who oversaw all registrar training placements, I entered her office expecting a fairly relaxed chat about my future goals and training needs, but was instead ambushed with a barrage of negative criticism, courtesy of Dr Peck. Although I felt that some of this disparagement was justified, much of it wasn't. And *all* of it should have been discussed with me before being escalated. One of Dr Peck's litany of vexations against me was that I had apparently booked Christmas leave on the same days she had told me she was away (as the only two doctors on the team, one of us had to always be on duty). If we had had this conversation, I had genuinely forgotten. Surely she could have just reminded me instead of dobbing me in to the person in charge of the rest of my training? Suddenly, I could sympathise with my patient group's prison-influenced attitude towards snitches.

'And you apparently make repeated sarcastic comments in ward rounds,' she said.

'Really? Like what?'

She lifted up a file with my name printed out on the front and leafed through it.

'Dr Peck said you have a patient named Martin on Floral ward. Once, you said in front of the whole team that you didn't think there was a decent treating plan in place.' She flipped over a page and examined it, peering over her lenses. 'Dr Peck thought this was very disrespectful to the treating team who had been working so hard.'

My heart thundered. I felt like I was melting into the low-set chair.

That's bullshit! I thought. The nurses and psychologists were fed up with Dr Peck not doing anything for Martin. They literally told me that one morning while we were all waiting for her to turn up for the ward round! But I couldn't badmouth my boss. Shit always flows downwards, not upwards. I knew that.

'But I really *did* think we needed a better plan,' I said feebly.

'But can you see how that might come across as . . . ' she cleared her throat, 'jarring?'

Had I had any idea this diatribe was coming, I could at least have prepared some defences, but I was blindsided. I felt faint and I just wanted to get out of the office.

The training programme director was seriously considering halting my training or extending it with extra remedial supervision with Dr Peck. I begged her to let me change consultants as I knew I could prove myself, working for a better boss. She relented and I eventually managed to redeem myself. The whole experience was a devastating blow to my ego and my sense of worth. Up until that point, I had received positive feedback from previous bosses and had assumed that I was a decent doctor. Now, I was questioning if I was really up to the task. The aftermath was a few months of second guessing my decisions, a crisis of confidence in my clinical skills. I also suffered paranoia and awkwardness at work, feeling like a cashier on his final warning after being caught with his hands in the till.

I had to sign off my appraisal and was given a copy of Dr Peck's feedback, which my training programme director had been peering at over her lenses. Dr Peck had written almost four pages in what was supposed to be one small box at the bottom of the page for 'areas for development'. Dr Peck, who never turned up to meetings on time and submitted half-written reports, had spent probably the most effort on any one piece of work I had seen in my tenure with her. Nowadays, I keep that appraisal document in the top drawer of my office desk and occasionally peruse it when I need inspiration to remind myself of the struggles that I have had to overcome to become a consultant.

Fortunately, the rest of my higher training went relatively smoothly. And I am grateful to Dr Peck for teaching me two things: how not to be a consultant and how to keep my mouth shut (at least while I was still a trainee).

Patience has never been one of my virtues. As the last stretch of my three-year tenure of higher training approached, I was confident that I had it sorted and was chomping at the bit to be a consultant. I was naive. I didn't realise that the true essence of this status wasn't in diagnosing and treating patients. That was a given. It was actually in the art of *management*. Management of the mental health team; overseeing junior doctors, nurses, psychologists, occupational therapists and social workers. Ensuring that every member feels valued, is content and is pulling their weight. Managing expectations; accepting that whereas most patients' journeys to recovery are reasonably predictable and roughly linear, the best-laid plans o' mice an' consultants gang aft agley. It is also about managing time and paperwork. One was scarce, the other abundant. And managing risk: finding an equanimity in the knowledge that, despite all our efforts in hospital, we cannot control external influential forces on the patient after discharge. An acceptance that a proportion of patients will relapse, will deteriorate and will re-offend once they have escaped the shadows of our bulwark. I had some ideas of these concepts of course, but it took a rude awakening to really hammer these points home. This involved me stepping up for three months to take on a temporary consultant role, and it could not have come at a worse time.

Chapter 9

Christening of Lava

Shortly after starting my final year of higher training, I was offered a fixed three-month post to 'act up' as a consultant. One of the mental health teams in the medium secure unit in east London didn't have one and, for reasons I was not privy too, senior management did not want to find a replacement. Instead, they recruited a series of final-year trainees for three months at a time (the maximum allowed, so as not to detract from formal training). I knew that the job was a poisoned chalice. The team were disillusioned. Who could blame them? Their supposed leader was replaced every three months but they were still burdened with having to rehabilitate dangerous patients. But how could I say no? This was an opportunity to take on full responsibility and have a taste of what could potentially be the rest of my career. Although I had experienced the other incarnations of a forensic psychiatrist (running clinics in prison, diverting the mentally ill from criminal court and working as an expert witness), I had assumed that I would work, at least initially, as an inpatient consultant within a secure psychiatric hospital, simply because I was most familiar with that setting.

I started my three-month post shortly after my wife, Rizma, had given birth to our first child, Kamran. A wrinkly baby boy with huge hands, a shock of jet-black hair and a comically suspicious furrowed brow graced us. My very first fortnight on the job was the only time I could take paternity leave. Hardly a great introduction and not the best way to make an already neglected, rudderless disgruntled team feel less neglected, more ruddered and ... gruntled. During my paternity leave, I stupidly took on a couple of independent psychiatric reports paid for by the criminal courts. A tidy cash injection for a car seat, nappies and the inexplicable plethora of muslins, was my thinking. I even planned to go to a friend's wedding in Poland, but my wife refused, insisting a newborn would be way too much to cope with abroad. I thought she was being a bit precious, but she had a tiny human suckling at her teat (eventually giving her mastitis) and I did not. Being the youngest of my siblings and my cousins, I had never really been around babies before. But they don't do much. If they cry, you just feed them and/ or rock them, right? I had never been more wrong in my life. Even though Rizma took far more of an emotional and physical battering for the entire first six months of the little dude's life, and even though my nipples were left largely unscathed, every day felt like sprinting up a mountain and then tumbling back down it, hitting every single sharp rock on the descent. Ah well, at least I had the most important and high-pressured phase of my career at that point to help distract me.

To be honest, this whole period was a blur of various bodily fluids, crying and sleepless nights (and not all from the baby!) I'm not sure if my foggy recollection is a defence mechanism from the trauma or simply because I didn't sleep enough to be able to encode memories. I do remember having to bed down on a fold-out mattress in the living room in our cramped flat in Muswell Hill just to get a crumb of something that resembled slumber, before getting up and putting on a suit every morning. I felt like a smartly dressed refugee.

Arguably, the most intense part of any consultant job is the beginning. I had to learn the background information and risk factors of all eighteen patients on the ward and get to know them and their foibles, including their personalities and behaviours. Then I had to get up to speed with the foibles, personalities and behaviours of my own team. I had to study the previous action plans, as sanctioned by my predecessor, and adapt some of them, after my own evaluation. Understandably, this particular team already felt under-appreciated. Personality clashes with some of the previous consultants didn't help. My reception was not exactly cold, but, let's say, tepid. I think they were sizing me up to see if I cared enough to actually engage with the work, confront the clinical dilemmas and make the tricky decisions, as opposed to just keeping the throne warm for three months for the next sucker, while plumping up my CV.

I had bought a brand-new navy pinstripe suit, hoping

that if I looked like an authoritative senior doctor, I might feel like one. Within my first two-minute walk from my office to the ward, I was already being approached by nurses and bombarded with dilemmas. This included how to keep two alpha males apart (one who was a member of a notorious gang, the other who had almost stabbed his son's social worker to death) after their fight the previous week, whether to allow another patient visits from his wife (who was the victim of the assault that got him imprisoned in the first place) and how to support and protect another resident (who had been charged with downloading child pornography) from being relentlessly bullied.

We work with a complex, difficult and potentially very dangerous patient cohort. So, naturally, opinions can be strong, emotional and often contradictory between different staff members. Within this christening of lava, I quickly learnt that there was an art to managing everyone's opinions and input. This involved coaxing contributions from our timid, oversized spectacle-wearing occupational therapist, Emelia. After a few weeks I realised that she had very good ideas, though would not volunteer them unless asked directly. The two warring alpha males were both wannabe hip-hop producers. Emelia could wrangle some free studio time in a local youth centre. She could perhaps broker peace between the men by inviting them to supervised sessions, on the premise that continuation of any musical projects would be dependent on their behaviour. I also noticed that a couple of members of the team didn't always follow through on tasks that had been agreed. Not wanting to single them out or embarrass them, I emailed a detailed list of jobs to everybody after each ward round, making it harder for everybody, myself included, to dodge duties.

My next hurdle was the very pessimistic social worker, Margo, who looked, spoke and waddled like a bulldog, and basically said no to everything.

'I don't think Henry should have leave. He's too unpredictable,' she grumbled during one ward round.

The trick, I discovered after a few exasperating weeks, was to acknowledge her opinion, politely agree with her and then politely disagree. 'You're right. Henry is unpredictable and he's probably still hearing voices, even if he denies this,' was my overly jovial counter argument. 'But he's not lashed out in over four months and I'm not sure we can realistically reduce his symptoms any further. Let's bite the bullet and trial one short, escorted trip. Otherwise, we might never discharge him.'

'There's no point referring Marcus to that particular community drug and alcohol team,' she said later. 'I've dealt with them before and they never respond. It's a waste of time.'

'You're right. Their track record isn't great, and it's frustrating to be ignored. But even if the service doesn't reply, at least we have the documentation to say we tried. That way the Community Mental Health Team who will supervise him after he leaves hospital can re-refer him in the future. They can even copy our paperwork.'

She sighed. 'I don't see why we should do all the work.'

'Because until the point of discharge, he's still our patient. Tell you what, I'll draft the referral letter. All you have to do is email it,' I said, beaming a smile while clenching my fists under the table.

By the end of the first month, I had managed to get to know the patients and gained some level of trust from most of them (although one elderly man with a delusional disorder was convinced that I was trying to marry his ex-wife and was keeping him detained in hospital to get him out of the picture). I had squeezed out ideas from Emelia and got some of the slackers to follow through on their chores. A few weeks later, I began to shake off the feeling of being a little kid trying on his daddy's jacket and shoes, pretending to be a grown-up. As I had once, as a medical student, emulated being approachable and then become so, here I faked being a leader and then became one. I grafted through my three-month tenure. With numerous nocturnal baby-related awakenings at home, and occasional nightmares of turning up to my ward round naked, I was utterly exhausted. However, my team and I managed to discharge four patients, including two long-term very high-risk individuals who had eluded my predecessors. This included a prolific fire-setter with schizophrenia in his fifties. For over two decades he had gone through the same cycle of functioning relatively well outside of hospital, but inevitably relapsing after stopping his medication. This resulted in delusional beliefs about being able to control flames. The trick wasn't to cure him, it was to keep his schizophrenia at bay in the long term. We stabilised him on a depot anti-psychotic injection, which would be administered by a nurse and therefore couldn't be avoided like tablets could. We sent him to supported accommodation, with staff members on site for twelve hours of the day. He was discharged on a contract (known as a community treatment order) meaning he had to take his anti-psychotic medication every month or face being recalled to hospital immediately. We also released an alcoholic man with crippling anxiety in his late thirties, who had robbed two post offices with an imitation hand-gun. After intense psychotherapy centred around building confidence, tinkering with his medication and alcohol reha-bilitation, his mental state vastly improved. His botched robberies were in the context of having limited financial options and being too anxious to work. During the one he was arrested for, he used a gun-shaped piece of wood which he had coloured black with a marker pen; he was caught out when the staff member saw ink on his palms, smelt a rat and wrestled him to the floor. Working with Emelia, this patient not only trained to become a barista, but secured a part-time job in a local café. He was too anxious even to speak to me when we first met, but by the time he left, he was even making jokes – something about having studied so much law during his trial, he could've trained as a barrister instead of a barista (good effort, three stars). He managed to reconnect with his estranged mother while he was in hospi-tal, and she even offered him accommodation after he left.

Equally importantly, I eventually earned the respect of the team. Some of the more memorable moments during my stint at the helm included a minor car crash and a staff member bursting into tears in the middle of a ward round (related to a cheating fiancé, not my chairing abilities). On my last week, I walked around unknowingly with a red pen leaking in my shirt pocket which made me look as if I had just been stabbed in the chest. Arguably, not a good look in any hospital, but especially a forensic psychiatric ward, where several of the detainees had previously stabbed people, and at least one had attacked a psychiatrist in the past. This caused a nurse to pull her alarm and start screaming, which led to me running towards the nursing office where she was. Other staff members saw me running, covered in blood, and put out the call for the Emergency Response Team. I burst through the door, and the nurse ran up to me and started unbuttoning my shirt, which was flattering, but mostly confusing. The Emergency Response Team arrived and rushed over to add to the mayhem. A lot of apologising later, they left. My face matched my shirt from utter embarrassment (which is quite remarkable when you consider my skin tone).

As well as learning to lead the mental health team, I also came to realise that there was far more paperwork, emails and general administration involved behind the scenes than I had imagined, some of which felt pointless to me. This planted a seed of doubt that would later blossom.

But I also learnt that I was ready. I could be a consultant with little sleep, chaos at home and a malcontent team. I was capable of making important decisions without any support, supervision or backup. Surely this meant I could thrive under normal conditions? I felt like a long-distance runner who had been training at high altitude. Once I got back down to sea level, the marathon could only get easier, right?

Chapter 10

The Microcosmic Secure Psychiatric Ward

It was May 2014 when I first met Jordan Dorian, one of my most challenging patients. Weeks earlier, I had been awarded my 'Certificate of Completion of Training' in forensic psychiatry, which confirms a doctor has completed an approved UK training programme and is a fully fledged consultant. No more supervision. No more seeking approval for my decisions. It made me feel like a made man in the Mafia. Some doctors would frame this certificate in their office. Those are the type you would not want to sit next to at a dinner party. I'm not even fully sure where mine is right now.

I had some anxieties about finding a permanent consultant role that was in or near London. A couple of my predecessors had had to relocate their whole families to another area after they had finished training, due to an anaemic job market. Despite my fears, I was fortunate enough to be selected for a role in a small secluded secure unit in Essex, around an hour's drive from our home. I had opted for a part-time post, working three days a week, so I could spend my spare days building up my own freelance medico-legal practice. This was a sizeable risk, because this type of work was not contracted, and therefore not guaranteed, but my experience of giving evidence at the Old Bailey had given me an itch I just couldn't scratch.

At home, our son was approaching his first birthday, was getting chubby, still had a comically furrowed brow, and wrestled me with such ferocity during every nappy change that it felt like he was trying to protect his faeces from being stolen. My wife had returned to work as an A-level psychology teacher after maternity leave, and adult company had helped restore her sanity. Our nights remained traumatic, but the degree of tears and wailing was gradually improving. I graduated back to our double bed, which felt luxurious compared to the fold-out mattress.

I was now a proper grown-up consultant and Jordan was the first patient I was fully responsible for throughout the entirety of his rehabilitation voyage through hospital. From the initial assessment, sectioning him under the Mental Health Act, overseeing his treatment and his convalescence to rehabilitation and finally his discharge. No boss to oversee my clinical work. Full autonomy.

When I first crossed paths with him, Jordan was nineteen, incarcerated and in a bad way. Before we met, I had read from the court documents that he had been imprisoned for a charge of arson with intent to endanger life. He had locked all the doors of his house while his mother was asleep upstairs. He used lighter fluid to start a fire in the kitchen. Even as an atheist, I thank God that his mother woke up from the smell of smoke. She tried to escape, and – from what I can gather – made no attempt to move Jordan who was sitting at the breakfast table of the cramped kitchen, transfixed on the blooming yellow flames. The front door was locked and the key was missing. Jordan was unresponsive to his mother's screams, scratches and slaps. She alerted neighbours who called the police and put a brick through the lounge window, allowing her to escape. Firemen literally had to drag Jordan out.

My assessment of him in Thameside Prison lasted a paltry ten minutes after negotiating two hours of London traffic, half an hour of queueing at the prison gates and then forty-five minutes of prison security (body search, fingerprint scan, magnetic wand, sniffer dogs). Having opened in March 2012, HMP Thameside was new and more modern than the institutions it shared its grounds with, including Belmarsh Prison. The décor had an airport-chic vibe to me. I had held a slight grudge against Thameside Prison ever since my first scheduled assessment of an inmate there, around one year earlier, when I was kept waiting in a random corridor for more than two hours and eventually told my visit was cancelled without any explanation in a very abrupt and unapologetic manner (one star).

As a gaggle of lawyers and I were being led through yet another set of gargantuan locked gates by a prison officer, I got a tap on my shoulder from one of the guards. My heart sank as I assumed that Jordan had refused to see me, or perhaps there had been another admin error and my visit was cancelled again. Either way it meant a wasted morning I could have used to burn through (unfortunately not literally) my perennial mountain of paperwork. However, the prison officer told me that he would have to take me directly to Jordan as he had been refusing to leave his cell for the entire week. Many staff would not do this as it involves taking a colleague off the wing; prisons are chronically understaffed, with officers as short in supply as nurses within psychiatric units. This proposal suggested that they must have been especially worried about Jordan. As usual, during my walk through the bowels of the penitentiary, I had to politely but firmly bat away several prisoners who approached me. Some asked me who I was. Some had guessed I was a doctor (my ethnicity and my suit, no doubt) and tried to refer themselves for various ailments. One man even hopped alongside me, lifting up his bandaged foot to ask about a slow-healing wound. I imagine he was used to being fobbed off by prison staff, and so he did not accept my explanation that I had very little expertise in his ailment, though eventually I managed to thwart him with a flight of steps. The prison officer explained that Jordan had not spoken to anybody since being remanded, hadn't showered and hadn't eaten recently (though unhelpfully did not know exactly how long this starvation had been going on for). Jordan had also been muttering to himself. Jesus and heaven were common themes in his mostly indecipherable speech. After the resounding clank and shrill screech of the door being unlocked and opened, I entered his cell. He was huddled in a corner, clutching his knees, looking equally perplexed and petrified. He was young-looking, very pale, with straggly hair and a wispy beard. His fingers were twitching, nails covered in dirt, as if playing an invisible keyboard. His cell was completely bare. No provocative naked women pasted up on the walls as I have seen in almost every other male prison cell I have visited. Jordan barely acknowledged me. The stench in the room was overbearing, but ever the professional (and with a one-year-old at home, somewhat inured to a range of nasty pongs) I crouched down next to him and introduced myself.

'Mr Dorian, right?'

Nothing.

'Can I call you Jordan?'

Still nothing.

I asked him a few more questions, about where he was, the last thing he remembered, whether he was hearing voices and whether he felt safe, but again, to no avail. I stared into his eyes for a full minute. I wasn't sure what I was hoping to see, but there was only emptiness. I told Jordan that I felt he needed to be transferred to my psychiatric unit. 'Don't worry. Whatever is going on, we can help you,' I said.

I could see a flicker of a grimace as he struggled to process this information.

I *hope*, I thought to myself.

Jordan exhibited pronounced thought block and poverty of speech. Thought block is like a brain fog, when you suddenly forget a word or somebody's name, but it is far more powerful and interferes with every thought. Even witnessing it is unnerving. Poverty of speech is the fancy psychiatric term for 'not saying much' and is the outward expression of thought block. This all suggested psychosis.

I left the prison without a single word from Jordan and wrote up the application paperwork, requesting a transfer warrant from the Ministry of Justice. Jordan was relocated to the microcosm of our unit a few days later. I was now fully responsible for his treatment and rehabilitation and, more imminently, given his refusal to eat, his life.

Once he was on our ward, Jordan's paranoia dwindled within days. He went from looking petrified to plain old scared. His eyes were less fixed on the empty space in front of him and he started to venture around the room. At this point he had not yet been medicated so I could only assume that this improvement was attributable to moving to the safer environment of a hospital. Metal bars, burly officers and locked gates had been replaced by plastic plants, kind nurses and locked doors. Although I remained tentative, this was a good sign. On some level, through the thick psychotic fog, Jordan must have been aware of his surroundings.

The soft ethereal voices of the ward staff had managed to convince Jordan to drink a couple of bottles of Fortisip per day. Like a milkshake for the malnourished, this is a drink packed with calories, protein, vitamins and minerals for patients who struggle to eat, such as those with anorexia or recovering from bowel surgery. His ongoing refusal of solid food wasn't ideal, but at least the Fortisips bought us some time and avoided the nuclear option of force-feeding via a nasogastric tube.

It took some medication, a fair amount of time and a lot of coaxing to eventually persuade Jordan to eat solid food.

Successfully medicating him was the next war of attrition: him with no insight, not understanding he was unwell, and me with his best interests at heart, trying to persuade him, charm him and everything short of bully him. He was just about talking in sentences, though they were short and mumbling.

I would be the first to admit that anti-psychotics (like most psychiatric drugs) are not perfect. The sedative effects kick in after around half an hour, though the reversal of psychosis takes four to six weeks, and sometimes more. Which is a long time to be imprisoned in insanity, outside of the realm of reality. I think even the most hardened hippie would baulk at an acid trip that lasted a couple of months. These medications have nasty side effects, including sedation, agitation, involuntary movement disorders, impotence, weight gain and diabetes. Often, the initial choice of medication is not effective, meaning that we have to trial a few different types. I've had dozens of patients accuse me of experimenting on them with drugs. They are not completely wrong. Though, I think the fundamental issue is that they sometimes feel that we psychiatrists are doing so for our own personal gain, perhaps to promote a particular brand for money under the table. Whereas from the psychiatrist's perspective, sometimes we have to test a few tablets, because although we know that they generally do work, we have no way of predicting the efficacy of any one tablet for any particular individual. We do work with blunt tools but we're not barbarians. For these reasons, I appreciate why many patients like Jordan, Stevie McGrew and Yasmin Khan would refuse psychiatric drugs. I would not like to ingest chemicals on a daily basis that made me foggy, fat, sleepy and diabetic. But as the alternative is being plagued by terrifying psychotic symptoms, surely medication is the lesser of the two evils. I had a duty to treat Jordan and, dare I say it, I had the power under the Mental Health Act to enforce this against his will, if necessary. I could summon a team of nurses to physically restrain Jordan and give him injectable depot medication, though I knew this might damage an already fragile relationship and crush any gradually nurtured trust. This dilemma echoed Yasmin's case, though there was less of the urgency that is brought about by a pending murder trial.

For the first couple of months there was minimal resistance. Jordan took the tablets, I suspect because he was told to and his thoughts were too unclear to consider his options. Gradual improvement was marked with little ventures outside his room, sitting in the lounge area with other patients and eventually initiating conversation. He still had odd religious preoccupations, asking staff and patients bizarre questions such as whether there were any Jewish terrorists, or if a Muslim eats pork by accident they'd still go to hell.

For me, the clearest sign of Jordan improving was in his eyes. His previously furrowed brow and wild, darting stare, which I had seen on our first meeting, started to assuage. His whole facial expression equilibrated: from bunny in headlights to concerned curiosity to eventual normality. This is the most rewarding part of my job. I don't get to run to an emergency with my quiff wobbling and my white coat flapping behind me like a cape. I don't get to shout 'Ten milligrams of adrenaline, stat,' grab the defibrillator paddles and yell 'He's in ventricular fibrillation. Not on my watch! Everybody stand back. Clear!' (Actually, I do get to do some of those things once a year on a dummy during mandatory life support training that all mental health staff undertake.) But I do get to very gradually break the chains of mental illness, release the sufferers' minds and rescue them from horrid inner turmoil and confusion. I get to witness their salvation in sanity.

Once Jordan had gained insight, his defiance surfaced. He was caught secreting his tablets: hiding them in his mouth, spitting them out in his room and stashing them. Stockpiling medications is a potential suicide risk and could not be tolerated on the ward. I prescribed Velotabs, dissolvable (and as the pharmacist would regularly remind me, very expensive) medications placed under the tongue that melt in the mouth. Jordan was then found intentionally making himself sick in his room after taking Velotabs. Had he had the physiology lectures I had from medical school, he would have known that the chemicals directly diffuse into the bloodstream, bypassing the digestive system. His vomiting would merely relieve himself of his last meal.

Jordan extended his admission by several months with his medication shenanigans and by refusing to engage with the team's psychologist and occupational therapist. This was incredibly frustrating to witness. He was young and at the prime of his life. Thus started a familiar dance. I visited Jordan on the ward every couple of days to cajole him into compliance, feeling like a used-car salesman trying to pitch his own rehabilitation plan to him. Jordan would nod along passively, not unlike a surly teenager getting yet another lecture from his nagging parents. Meanwhile, Jordan was having supervised visits from his mother. She lived in Milton Keynes and, due to the distance and her own work commitments, her visits were infrequent. She was rotund with an excess of gold rings and bangles and a powerful stench of cigarettes (I was in between relapses of smoking at that time, so I was allowed to judge). Clearly their relationship was complex. Jordan had, to be fair, tried to burn her alive. She seemed far more concerned about her son's finances than his treatment and I suspected that she was siphoning money off him. When invited to the ward round, she didn't have any questions about his medication or how long he would be in hospital, but plenty about his bank account and his benefits. I bit my tongue. Doctors are not supposed to be judgmental. She also frequently cancelled visits with Jordan at the last minute. He seemed indifferent to this but I couldn't help feeling offended on his behalf.

Jordan's overall appearance also began to change. He had a stylish haircut from the visiting barber (an ex-patient who had been trained up while in hospital). He wore trendy clothes ('peng garms', I believe, in his vernacular), most of which he bought online. He had a bank account that was topped up regularly. He claimed this was by his mother, but I doubted this. 'Ask me no questions, and I'll tell you no lies,' he told our social worker once, with a glint in his eye. The pallor from weeks inside his prison cell was replaced by a warm glow. Even his facial hair seemed less wispy, though that might have been an optical illusion. He was younger and slicker than most of the other patients, some of whom had been suffering from severe mental illness for decades.

This had ravaged their looks, their health and, in some cases, their fashion sense.

Jordan slotted in well into the patient group. He was funny and charming when he wanted to be. The medication seemed to have not only eliminated his thought block and poverty of speech but somehow caused the opposite effects. He had banter with the nurses and managed to straddle the fine line between being cheeky and flirtatious. But he also had a sinister side which occasionally reared its head. If he felt he was being disrespected, if a patient denied him a cigarette or a nurse made him wait too long to take him to the hospital tuck shop, he could explode in a tirade of threats and expletives in an unnervingly instantaneous transformation to Mr Hyde. It felt calculated and very much within his control. He knew exactly when to rein it in (such as when faced with the threat of seclusion or a sedative injection). This contrasted with other patients on the ward at the time, whose occasional angry outbursts were caused by mental illnesses, such as bipolar affective disorder.

Around nine months into his hospital stay, Jordan started to cooperate more. I suspect he saw other less capable patients getting leave out of the hospital or being discharged. He wanted to move on, on *his* terms, not mine. On the days when Jordan was congenial, insightful about his rehabilitation needs and seemed keen to work with us, I'd walk away with something resembling a sense of achievement. I genuinely enjoyed some of our interactions. He would frequently do impersonations of staff, which were freakishly accurate, leaving me equally amused and uncomfortable as I was passively permitting him to do them.

Although I had no qualms enforcing official hospital rules, I have always felt some discomfort in chastising patients when it comes to the grey areas. I remember sitting down at his table in the communal hospital café and having a cup of coffee with him one morning. This was unusual practice. There was an unofficial side for patients and another for staff: an unwritten voluntary apartheid. This generated a lot of stares and whispers from both factions. People looked at us as if we were rival gang members who had sat together in a maximum-security penitentiary chow hall. But it was just a cup of coffee. On other days, Jordan would be dismissive or sarcastic, speaking to me as if I was a cop who'd brought him in for interrogation. We both know you've got nothin' on me; I'm gonna beat the case, his scowl seemed to say.

The story of Jordan, however, wouldn't be complete without talking about his compassion and humanity. He showed a fondness towards a couple of the older, chronically unwell, vulnerable patients whose functioning and capabilities had been all but decimated by chronic mental illness. He would give them cigarettes, buy them cans of Coke, and let them beat him at pool. He seemed to go out of his way to take care of Stanley, an elderly man with the countenance and huge bushy beard of a sailor. Stanley, a weathered soul with chronic treatment-resistant schizophrenia, spent almost the entire day sitting in his favourite armchair in the patient lounge. He was perennially confused despite all our treatment and would mutter unintelligibly. His original offence wasn't particularly serious: a botched robbery of a warehouse while carrying a machete. Yet due to the intractable nature of his psychosis, he had been in hospital for well over fifteen years. The occasional few words I could decipher from Stanley were either delusions about ghosts or him asking where he was. When I told him, he would snort at me and call me a liar. Jordan would occasionally tidy Stanley's room and would shoo other patients off his armchair. I often wondered why Jordan took a shine to Stanley. Perhaps he recalled glimpses of his own comparatively brief trip into the world of psychosis that Stanley represented and was grateful to have escaped. Jordan was a multi-dimensional and complex character and one aspect, as much as he tried to hide it, was his benevolence.

I found this consultant post in Essex quite stressful. But more than Jordan or any of my other patients, it was the demands on my time. I was working part-time and my own medico-legal practice was blossoming, which was great news for my bank account. But my court work began to leak outside of my two spare days a week. As being with my family was immutable, the only way I could manage was to wake up sacrilegiously early (anywhere from 4.30 to 5.30 am) just to cram in a couple of hours of report writing. This drifted insidiously from the rare occasion to the norm, and then into my weekends. I'd even shoved in a couple of hours every morning on a two-week family holiday to Portugal. Rizma was, and always has been, understanding about the pressures of my work. She has always given me space: no questions asked and no added guilt-tax.

In the second half of 2014, our second bambino sprouted inside my wife, which prompted us to move from our small flat in Muswell Hill to a house in a leafier, slightly more northern area in north London, Enfield. Around this time, my social life was decimated. Techno festivals with my university friends were replaced with endless brunches. Brunches, I came to learn, where instead of chastising our toddlers at home for throwing half-full yoghurt pots, plastic spoons and scrambled eggs on the floor, we would pay for the privilege of doing this in public, with other parents, while we seemed to talk only about the many difficulties of child rearing, taking some sadomasochistic pleasure in comparing how disruptive our nights were. In retrospect, I became a bit too preoccupied with my medico-legal work. I would constantly check emails and snatch moments in between kids' naps, bath time and walking from one brunch to another, to read over draft reports or scrawl through case papers and witness statements on my iPad. In all honesty, this wasn't necessary. Deadlines constantly loomed, but there was always time. I was becoming obsessed. I couldn't stop thinking about cases. And even stranger, on the rare occasion when I was ahead of my work and had no pending reports, I felt restless. I was unsure if this was a strong work ethic or anxiety. Perhaps both? Oddly, it was not the crimes, violence or risky behaviour of the clients I was assessing for criminal trials or my patient group in hospital that drove this anxiety. It was the thought of my professionalism being tainted. I had never missed a deadline for a court report, and was determined to keep my record untarnished (which I have done to this day). I would fret excessively over forgetting to reply to an email, even though several of mine were ignored daily. Some of my consultant peers were not so conscientious, and a few occasionally asked for adjournments of court hearings because they had underestimated how long it would take to submit their reports. Why was I so bothered about my professional image? Perhaps a deep-rooted, insentient fear from the barrage of criticism from Dr Peck had infected my very soul.

When I was at the psychiatric unit in Essex, I was pulled between innumerable meetings (of varying value), supervising my junior doctor, writing a constant stream of medical notes, liaising with a range of other professionals and speaking with patients' family members. On some busy weeks, I really struggled to spend time with my patients on the ward. Not only to carry out specific assessments, but simply to be present. A chat. The odd game of chess. The occasional game of Twister (not really). I was ultimately responsible for the detainees. I felt that my absence would be disrespectful towards them (many of whom already had authority issues and abandonment complexes). During my training years, I had witnessed a wide range of consultants' attitudes and efforts to touch base with their patients. From those, like Dr Linford, who would be a regular feature on the ward to others, like Dr Peck, whose presence would be like spotting the yeti. I vowed never to be *that* guy.

Jordan was progressing. Not as fast as I would have liked, but at least he was moving in the right direction. His numerous acts of rebellion gifted me a few grey hairs and a relapse in nicotine-based solace. Finally, almost eighteen months after Jordan arrived through the gates of the hospital, I felt that he was stable enough to be tested on leave. That's when the problems really started.

Chapter 11

Why Won't You Just Let Me Discharge You?

Leave from psychiatric units is granted once patients have settled and are engaging in therapy. This is at the discretion of the consultant psychiatrist in charge for the majority of detainees (though for those under a restriction order, like Yasmin, the doctor has to also obtain permission from the Ministry of Justice). Although it was ultimately my call, I wanted to get the whole team on board. They carried a lot of the burden of Jordan's rehabilitation, so it seemed only courteous to take this step with their endorsement. But Jordan didn't make it easy. Within this particular team, I was blessed with a very good psychologist, Pamela, who managed to pierce the defensive shields of many patients. Although she made laudable progress with Jordan, she often found him prickly. Jordan would open up to her about his feelings of inadequacy as a child and tell her about how his mother, a party animal, would jump around pubs and friends and men, and made him feel like an inconvenient accessory, that she no longer wanted but had lost the receipt for. Yet just when Pamela was making headway, he would snap shut like a Venus flytrap, pushing her away with sarcasm, insincere clichés or overt hostility. A defence mechanism, to protect his fragile psyche.

Psychiatrists and psychologists have been confused with each other since the dawn of time. *Psychiatrists* are primarily medical doctors who have been to medical school: white coats, cadavers, hospital placements, waddling behind real doctors like chicks following the mother hen around. Therefore, we have specialist knowledge of physical illness and how this is linked to mental health disorders. We deal only with actual mental illness. We can also prescribe medication and have the power to section people. *Psychologists* focus on assessing emotions and personality, usually, but not always, in the context of mental illness; sports psychologists would be an example of an exception. They provide psychotherapy (talking therapy) to patients, some of whom prefer to be called clients, as they are not mentally ill, often delving into previous traumas and relationships. They train exclusively in mental health issues and not general physical health. If they have a doctorate degree, they can be called 'Dr X', but are not medical doctors. Neither of us make you lie on a couch. My experience of people mixing up my job title and calling me a psychologist is surpassed only by them mixing up my first name. I'm not exaggerating when I say this happens to me on an almost daily basis in my emails. For clarity, *Sohom* (inconveniently, pronounced Sh-hom) is the moniker that my parents bestowed upon me for people to struggle with for my entire life. *Soham*, on the other hand, is a little village in Cambridgeshire, infamous for the murders of two ten-year-old girls by Ian Huntley in August 2002.

Our occupational therapist, Elaine, also had a turbulent relationship with Jordan. In the UK, all forensic psychiatric units have occupational therapists, who help facilitate a range of activities for the patients, from dog-walking to baking, football matches to gym sessions. Most of the hospital residents are long-term unemployed (years in prisons and mental institutes tend to blemish one's CV) and often have low levels of educational attainment. Some are embedded or even born into the criminal underworld. Discharging patients into the wild with limited options to earn a legitimate living is setting them up to fail. Occupational therapists also help with obtaining education and qualifications through online or local college courses. Alternatively, they train patients in basic skills such as T-shirt printing, working a till, being a barista (like the alcoholic man with crippling anxiety who had robbed the post offices) or hairdressing (like the barber who gave Jordan a trendy haircut).

Elaine informed our team that Jordan had achieved below average grades at school, despite clearly being bright. We soon ran out of learning materials and books that were challenging enough for him, yet he was resistant to the idea of honing a future vocation in hospital. He only had ambitions to be a DJ and since the hospital could provide him neither gigs nor decks, he wasn't interested. We strongly suspected that he had alternative, potentially unsavoury, classified means of making money after discharge.

Proving once again that his rehabilitation was on his

terms, Jordan was fully cooperative, disarmingly charming and keen to engage with our social worker, Mary. She would help with his finances and organise his visits. Another typical task for the social worker in a psychiatric hospital is liaising with family and friends on behalf of the patient. However, in Jordan's case, Mary explained that he kept his cards close to his chest, seemingly wanting minimal inter-action with his nearest and dearest.

The aforementioned staff members are known collec-tively as the 'multi-disciplinary team', which for some reason always evokes images of Shaolin monks from the 18-certificate ultra-violent films I used to watch as a kid, who are trained in numerous disciplines of martial arts. Most members of the team have offices based off the wards, which can be oases of tranquillity. Nurses on the other hand are very much in the eye of the storm. They are based on the ward for their entire shifts. They are expected to supervise patients 24/7. They carry out a whole range of day-to-day activities, some of which are more stimulating than others. This is a fairly mothering role, involving getting patients out of bed, encouraging them to get dressed, supervising their meals, dispensing their medications and giving them access to their money and valuables which are kept locked up in the nursing station for safekeeping. They also escort some patients during leave in the community. In addition, nurses closely observe high-risk patients (where there is a possibility of either aggression towards others or deliberate self-harm). Good nurses (of whom there are plenty) make a concerted effort to bond with their patients. They have one-to-one sessions and act like a confidant, parent and friend.

Bad nurses (of whom there are fewer) only focus on the authoritarian and restrictive aspects of their roles. Too much stick, not enough carrot.

The nurses are very much the backbone of the system. They are also the eyes. Although forensic psychiatrists carry out regular mental state examinations, we only get snapshots of our patients. Nurses spend all day with them and so they can pick up on subtler symptoms. Who's hearing voices but hiding it? Who's over-sedated with medication? Who claims to suffer from side effects but only shakes when the doctor is with them? I do not envy nurses. The environment on secure psychiatric wards varies depending on the patient mix and how unwell the individuals are. But they can be chaotic and tense places. It felt claustrophobic at times for me, though I got to leave. With some manic, angry, agitated and distressed patients, nurses have to bear the brunt of abuse and swearing. They do not get a fair wage, in my opinion. Which just goes to show that the majority must be doing it because they are compassionate. Jordan's interactions with our nurses were once again a mixed bag. He would be pleasant and charming on a good day, but woe betide any nurse who chastised him. His scathing, argumentative and sarcastic side would reveal itself. He was adroit at finding a personal angle for his abuse, whether it be his target's weight, age, race or sexuality.

Once he was relatively settled, despite the tightening of a couple of lips and the odd frown, the majority view of the team was that it was time to take the plunge and test Jordan out on leave.

This is initially escorted (i.e. accompanied by a nurse) for fifteen minutes, then thirty, then an hour. As long as there are no issues, this advances to unescorted leave, still within the confines of the hospital. Most psychiatric units have a shop, café, gym and communal areas, such as a garden. Before the smoking ban a few years ago (which went down even worse than one might expect), patients would often congregate on benches and chain-smoke while gossiping with their peers from other wards. The vast majority of detainees manage their leave within the unit's grounds with no problem. My naive younger self used to think it would be nigh on impossible for patients to get up to mischief within the confines of the hospital boundary. The most noteworthy shenanigan I know of was a male and a transgender female being caught naked in the hospital café toilets. Awkward, not to mention unhygienic. If patients use hospital leave appropriately, they graduate to escorted community leave. Again, this starts off as brief periods, extended by small increments.

As we expected, Jordan was fine during his escorted leave, though once again pushed the limit when he advanced to unescorted. He frequently returned just a few minutes late: enough time to make my heart flutter but not enough to justify curbing his freedom.

When patients are granted unescorted community leave, they need to have a purpose and some structure; whether it be going to the cinema, to college, to an internet café, shopping or to visit family. Inevitably, unescorted leave is potential exposure to a number of temptations (or 'destabilisers' in psych jargon). As well as intoxicants, there might be certain people they shouldn't visit, such as ex-partners, ex-victims (often the same person) or criminal associates who might entice them towards illicit activities. Obviously, a detainee absconding is a major concern every time a doctor grants leave. Some detainees even do this when they're being escorted. This has happened once or twice per year within the secure units I have worked in. The residents are not criminal masterminds, and with little money and addresses of family members known by police, it doesn't usually take long to retrieve these prodigal patients.

It's the residents who escape directly from hospitals rather than when on leave that raise staff and hospital managers' blood pressure, as they have been deemed too dangerous to be out in public in the first place. Escape from inside secure psychiatric hospitals is very rare. As it should be. Those climb-proof, 5.2m-tall, Home Office-spec mesh perimeter fences don't come cheap. I've only known this to happen twice in my career on units I have worked on.

Both times were during my specialist registrar higher training in the early 2010s. The first time, it was a busy summer afternoon with numerous visitors going in and out of the airlock and the patient simply snuck in among the crowd on the way out, giving his escort the slip. The security guards checking IDs must have been lax that day. The other time, the escapee managed to sneak through a staff-only admin-corridor door which was left unlocked, force entry into an empty office and unscrew the entire window frame. Fortunately, disaster was averted both times. Both detainees went on drugs binges and were found by authorities, without having committed any vio-lence. After I left, there was a serious incident in one of the medium secure units where I trained in east London. During a siege in July 2015, six staff members were trapped inside an office as five patients reportedly armed themselves with broken glass. Thankfully, nobody was seriously injured and taser-equipped police officers helped to contain the perpetrators. They were charged with violent disorder, false imprisonment and public order offences. Two were sent to Broadmoor Hospital (where security levels were massively elevated), and three were shipped off to prison.

A far more scandalous and macabre case was when serial killer John Straffen murdered a little girl just a few hours after scaling a ten-foot-high wall and escaping Broadmoor Hospital in 1952. The victim was Linda Bowyer and she was just five years old. She was out riding her bike in Arborfield village, Berkshire, near the high secure hospital. Straffen kidnapped the girl before strangling her, within just four hours of him escaping. The child's body was found in a field the following day.

In 1951, Straffen had been sent to Hortham Colony in Bristol, an institution for the 'mentally handicapped' where medical officers labelled him 'mentally retarded' and said he had the cognitive age of a ten-year-old. Straffen purportedly had a 'smouldering hatred' and an 'intense resentment' of the police as a child, and causing them the maximum amount of grief appears to be one of his motivations for repeatedly killing. On the same day he was sent to Hortham Colony, he murdered a young girl named Christine Butcher. Shortly afterwards, Straffen killed five-year-old Brenda Goddard by leading her into a copse, strangling her and using a stone to bash her head. After leaving her body there, he went to the cinema to watch a film about a murderer. He then killed a girl named Cicely Batstone three weeks later in Bath; he strangled her and left her in a field. He confessed openly to the murders. He was declared unfit for trial and sent to Broadmoor, where he worked as a cleaner. He escaped by climbing onto a shed after being told to clean an outbuilding. He had civilian clothes on at the time and managed to travel seven miles during his escape, which lasted a few hours.

Police eventually picked him up in Aborfield, and he told them 'I'm done with crime.' The next day, Linda's body was found and Straffen was arrested and charged with her murder. Following a ruling that the previous murders could be included in a trial, a jury found him guilty. He was sentenced to death, but just over a month after the original sentence, the Home Secretary changed the sentence to life in prison on the grounds that he was a 'feeble-minded person'. Straffen became Britain's longest serving prisoner at that time, with the infamous 'Moors Murderer' Ian Brady being the only man to beat his record since. Straffen spent fifty-five years in jail and died in Frankland Prison in 2007.

Of course, phrases like 'feeble-minded person', 'mentally handicapped,' and 'mentally retarded' have since been replaced by the far more palatable 'learning disabilities'.

There were never any fears that Jordan would escape and go on a murderous rampage like Straffen, but he did give me headaches as his leave advanced. Around two months after unescorted leave was granted, Jordan was seen by a staff member sat outside a coffee shop, canoodling with an unknown brunette. He hadn't told us about her and he denied her existence in a hostile, defensive manner when questioned. Our team must be informed about romantic relationships and even friendships outside of the hospital. This part of the job, the Orwellian Big Brother role, always made me feel uncomfortable. I didn't sit gruelling exams and memorise textbooks to become a glorified babysitter to surly rebellious young men. On some level, it felt inherently wrong to tell a grown man what he can and cannot do in his love life. But what if this unknown receiver of his affection was vulnerable? Or, God forbid, underage? What if he suddenly relapsed and hurt her? What if he set another fire, but this time the emergency services couldn't intervene in time? As unlikely as a scenario this seemed to me, it wasn't beyond the realms of possibility. And I had ultimate responsibility for Jordan.

This mystery female became a bone of contention and a thorn in our relationship. Jordan vehemently and indignantly denied the existence of any such person. We didn't have any proof. The staff member could have been mistaken. I was unsure about whether it would be fair to stop Jordan's leave. I suspected he was lying, but this was hardly beyond reasonable doubt. There didn't seem to be a viable solution that was both fair to him and ensured the safety of this potentially non-existent young woman. When I reluctantly challenged him about her, Jordan swore and threw a stapler at the window in the back of the ward office. The window didn't smash as it was reinforced with wire, but the stapler, tragically, would never bind documents together again. He then launched a tirade of racist insults at me. I should have been scared, but I felt little at the time. I don't know if it was my naturally unfluster-able personality, or maybe I had become inured. Two nurses popped their heads around the door when they heard raised voices. Jordan calmed down and his words were replaced by a death stare. I shooed the nurses away with a shake of my head, though in all honesty most other patients would have been dealt a needle and/or a trip to the seclusion room. I always seemed to give Jordan a pass, sometimes subconsciously. But his verbal abuse was enough to stop his leave for two weeks. Dilemma solved, albeit a Pyrrhic victory.

Jordan barely spoke to me for around six weeks. I was relieved to a degree, after taking such a vocal battering. Despite my stoicism at the time of the incident, over the next few days I felt resentment towards Jordan. I'm not sure why, but I felt betrayed. There was also an escalating disappointment that this capable, intelligent young man, now twenty-one, had lengthened his ever-extending hospital stay. Even recognising my emotional overinvestment couldn't stop this sentiment.

After several months, our icy relationship started to thaw, and Jordan utilised his leave appropriately. But then, one afternoon, he came back from his supposed leave to the high-street gym smelling of alcohol. When the nurses commented on this, he was overly defensive, with Oscar-worthy pleas of indignation. But what he didn't know was that we had a breathalyser. I was once again called to the ward to have a word. Jordan explained that he had had just one pint as it was such a sunny afternoon. The breathalyser suggested three pints, and it was overcast. He begged me not to stop his leave. It seemed a pity to do this for the umpteenth time and delay his progress yet again. I personally didn't care whether Jordan had had two, three or four pints. Alcohol was not one of his risk factors, and played no part in his original arson. In contrast, though, I drank only theoretically at that point, as brunches and fatherhood had bulldozed into my life.

Aside from his flagrant dishonesty, the problem was that allowing this sort of behaviour would set a precedent. Unlike Jordan, some of my patients were on high doses of medications which interact with alcohol, and some became disinhibited and violent when drinking. Some were recovering alcoholics. Relaxing the rules with Jordan might send ripples amongst the other detainees. They might sense favouritism or sniff out an exploitable weakness.

The final straw came one rainy afternoon. I was in my office, hours from finishing an urgent court report that I had to submit the next morning, when I got a call from the nursing staff.

'He's done it again,' the nurse said. I knew who she meant and exactly what had happened before she uttered another word. Possibly sensing a chink in my armour for giving him a pass on the boozy leave, this time Jordan had returned completely drunk. He denied this, of course, and refused a breathalyser test. I slammed down the phone, shut the door and screamed. I walked down to the ward taking deep breaths. I had to see Jordan in his bedroom as he refused to come out. The waft of beer hit me as soon as I opened his door. After first denying that he had been drinking, then claiming that I had told him he was allowed to drink on leave, he suddenly snapped. He ran up to me, shoved a finger in my face and pushed me against his wardrobe, cracking a mirror. His eyes were wild, his cheeks were an incandescent shade of red and spittle oozed from the side of his mouth. His tirade was targeted. In between bursts of very racist language, he ironically accused *me* of being racist towards him. He said he had friends and threatened to have me followed home and my whole family stabbed. 'Get wetted up with a shiv,' to recite his slang.

This wasn't the first or the last time I have been threatened in my career, but it felt particularly personal and visceral. I didn't pull the mandatory alarm strapped to my belt, assuming that he would calm down as he always had done in the past. Another patient heard the yells from Jordan's bedroom and alerted the nurses, who summoned the Emergency Response Team. They surrounded Jordan and gave him a sedative. Being screamed at by a patient can feel very emasculating, as I cannot argue back. How dare he accuse me of bias against him? I'd bent over backwards, vouching for him to be granted leave against some resistance from my own team members. There was so much I wanted to yell at him. But de-escalation of the situation trumped my desire to have the last word. I had no choice but to shuffle out of his room under his scowl and a few more glancing insults.

I didn't tell anybody about the death threats or the shove. Maybe I should have. Some of my peers would even have reported it to the police. Death threats are technically criminal offences and if push came to shove (pardon the pun), him ramming me into the wardrobe technically constituted an assault. But I felt more hurt than scared. I'd thought we had some kind of (admittedly warped) understanding. In all honesty, another factor that prevented me from contacting the authorities was a lack of time. It was getting into the early evening and I still had several hours of typing and editing that pesky court report ahead of me. I knew from experience that calls from our psychiatric unit were not high priority for the police (which I suppose is logical, given that the perpetrators of any threats or assaults were already in detention) and I might have to wait several hours for the officers to arrive. Perhaps my subconscious favouritism, despite all that had just happened, also made me reluctant to put another blemish on Jordan's criminal record and further jeopardise his elusive discharge. He did mumble something like an apology a few weeks later. I dismissed it with a token shrug. In retrospect, I should have used the opportunity to discuss the incident thoroughly. Not so much to watch him squirm but to allow him to process the consequences of his actions, and recognise his capability of damaging relationships and alienating others.

Several months after Jordan had pushed and threatened me, I was due to take two weeks of paternity leave for the birth of our second son, Rayaan, who'd blessed the lives and cursed the sleep of Rizma and me once again. This creature had far wispier hair than the first, and dragon-like nostrils.

Obviously, the staff knew about my leave, but the detainees did not. We were actively discouraged from sharing our personal affairs with our patients. Although far more common in prison, the more antisocial patients in hospital could try to use this information to their advantage, for instance to blackmail staff with compromising information (or even photos), or to get their associates to contact staff outside to either bribe or intimidate them into bringing in contraband, such as phones or drugs. Also, maintaining professional boundaries strengthened the necessary patient-professional dynamic. The week before my paternity leave, Jordan said 'Congratulations on the baby'. Obviously, there had been a leak in our staff group. It wasn't a huge deal and I'm pretty sure it was meant as a pleasantry as opposed to a threat. However, I could not help but remember his ominous dark words several months earlier, threatening me and my family. 'Get wetted up with a shiv,' as I recalled.

Jordan eventually played ball. He engaged with therapy, behaved himself on the ward and (as far as we know) did nothing dodgy during his leave. The admin involved in discharging patients can be a nightmare, depending on the efficacy of the Community Mental Health Team responsible for the patient in the outside world. It is often a classic case of too many chefs ruin the stew. When the system succeeds, there might be one point of contact who has good communication with their colleagues. When it fails, there tends to be an excess of healthcare professionals involved, all with different ideas of what the patient requires, and their own requests, demands and expectations on the precise form of rehabilitation and follow-up (all involving excessive paperwork).

Jordan's discharge was particularly convoluted and prolonged. After finally sorting out which community team was responsible for him, Jordan was not happy with the series of hostels he was offered. Each time a new offer was

made and rejected, this involved identifying more placements, liaising with more staff, numerous phone calls,
filling out more forms and arranging a couple of visits
(which had to be accompanied by one of our nurses, taking
them away from supporting other patients).

The worst was yet to come. When there were literally
no more hostels left in the area, the plan changed to Jordan
living with his mother. Hardly ideal, not least because he
had tried to kill her two and a half years earlier. He was
also expected to attend a day centre every other day, so professionals could monitor his mental state. Our team social
worker, Mary, arranged for him to stay with his mother
for a trial weekend in mid-2016, during which time he was
supposed to visit the day centre a couple of times. Jordan
turned up to the first session three hours late, and sat in a
corner, scowling. He was a no-show at the second appointment. When the nursing staff came to pick him up from
his mother's house on Monday morning, not only was his
mother nowhere to be found but there were remnants of a
party that had been thrown in the house for the entire weekend. There were, I was told, people passed out everywhere,
condoms on the floor, cider bottles strewn and a stench of
weed. Jordan was driven back to the ward and clearly had
barely slept the entire weekend. Jordan could be accused of
many things, but tedium was not one of them.

All discharge plans were cancelled. The house of cards
came tumbling down. Back to the drawing board. To com-
plicate matters, Jordan even managed to impregnate his
girlfriend during his weekend away. Yes, girlfriend! Jordan
revealed that he had been in a relationship with a young

woman from his home area, and that he had neglected to mention it to us. This had lasted for the entire hospital admission (over two years at that point). He had apparently whispered sweet nothings to her over the phone regularly. This may have explained the shifty calls, huddling over the phone receiver. I knew she had never visited Jordan on the ward but perhaps she had travelled down to see him during his leave. Perhaps she was even the mysterious brunette? Maybe she was the one topping up his bank account and keeping him in 'peng garms'.

This was a minefield for us. Could Jordan have access to this child that he had fathered while he was still technically sectioned? Would social services need to be involved? His partner lost the child early in pregnancy. I suspect she had a termination, though Jordan would never share this with us. I expected him to be upset and possibly act out. But he seemed completely indifferent. Just like his entire rehabilitation process, I was more bothered by it than him. It was exasperating. But I had to swallow my bitter disappointment. My job was to support, not judge.

It took another six months of Jordan being settled on the ward before I could approach the commissioner to consider discharge planning again. His last few months were his quietest. He kept his head down. It didn't feel like we had broken him, rather that he'd finally realised that he was wasting his life with his defiance. It had been almost three years. In that time, I had released several patients with more severe mental illness who were just willing to play along with the game. A game that I was starting to lose faith in.

Jordan's discharge from hospital was bittersweet and

unceremonious. It was a Monday and I had back-to-back meetings all morning. Therefore, we arranged to rendezvous at 8 a.m. to say a final goodbye. There was torrential rain on the drive into work. I remember watching the thundering rain globules on the windows and hearing the incessant clacking of the windshield wipers, while wondering if Jordan, a notoriously late riser, would have woken up early to see me. No way, I thought. But I was wrong. He was up and dressed in a shirt, no less. Once again, defying my expectations, showing me in our last encounter that he was fully capable of organising himself and engaging, although only on his own terms.

I felt a loss when Jordan left. I suppose I missed him. He was a character and a half. I also felt a connection. It was the end of a relationship, albeit a dysfunctional one. And I mourned it. He was a slippery character with many faces, and I was not deluded enough to think I had seen them all. But I certainly had seen many versions of him: psychotic, petrified, rebellious, charming, witty, generous, cheeky, defiant, sneaky, angry, hostile, racist, threatening, settled, compliant. Even shirted. And, here on his last day of this admission, I saw him as a worthy adversary. As I shook his hand, I used a phrase that I often used to say goodbye to my patients. A phrase I'd nicked from a previous boss: 'I mean this in the nicest possible way: I hope I never see you again.'

And I didn't.

Chapter 12

Holding the Leash

Around the time of Jordan's departure, I noticed a tiny, niggling feeling in my chest. Ineffective antacids told me that this was worse than indigestion. This was doubt. I once wondered if I was built for this career. Now I wondered if it was suitable for me.

My colleagues and I, the whole system, definitely did help some patients. This I knew. We strived to give them the best chance to be re-integrated into a society that often wished to sweep them behind bars or lock them under the carpet (or was that the other way round?). Nevertheless, once I left behind the nomadic role of a specialist registrar for the more prestigious but also more stagnant position of a consultant, I came to some uncomfortable realisations. Firstly, just how high the proportion of revolving-door patients was. As a trainee, I had of course noticed that many patients had previously been admitted to forensic psychiatric wards and had already been through the gruelling rehabilitation rodeo.

But it was only once I owned responsibility for them as a consultant that I stopped to ponder *why*. I concluded two potential answers, neither of which sat well with me. Either the previous psychiatrists and their teams had failed them, in which case, why should I think we could do better? Or that some (though to be fair, by no means all) patients were beyond help. That's not to say we don't have a laudable role. We could still relieve their acute symptoms and improve their quality of life while they were in hospital and set them up with the best chances to thrive once they left. But maybe we were just plastering over the cracks and delaying the inevitable.

My rollercoaster ride with Jordan hammered home that our medication, our therapy, our boundaries and our rules were all enforced from our perspective. We might alter some, probably most, patients' trajectories. But for others, it felt like we were simply forcing them to behave while they were under our care, then allowing them to float back into their previous lifestyle with their previous destabilisers and vices after discharge: particularly the ones that were more 'bad' than 'mad'. Having grown up with stricter parents with more traditional values than my peers at school, I went a bit wild at university, once the shackles were off. Was it the same for some of our patients? I had always considered myself to harbour a healthy balance of cynicism and optimism, yet the relapsing and re-offending patients brought me more frustration than the success stories brought me satisfaction.

Other uncertainties loomed. Forensic psychiatry quenched my morbid fascination with criminality, but the payoff was having to be the bad guy. Many of our strategies were

restrictive: lengthy admissions, forcing medication (sometimes via restraining and jabbing), and rationing leave, not
to mention the dreaded seclusion room. I understood that it
was important to enforce boundaries on the ward, especially
for individuals who'd had little discipline in their formative
years. Despite this, I couldn't help feeling that a lot of my job
involved chastising and controlling fully grown adults. From
telling Reggie to turn the music down, to scolding Jordan for
drinking alcohol on leave and demanding details about his
romantic partners. Another constrictive practice, although
rare, was sedating very acutely disturbed, very aggressive
patients, sometimes beyond recognition. They became overweight, dribbling, shuffling and slow, just like the Hollywood
stereotypes of psychiatric patients that I loathed. I knew these
were all necessary evils to prevent agitation and violence, but
I didn't know how comfortable I felt with holding the leash.

One patient cemented in my mind how restrictive the
system was, particularly for the small but significant minority of my flock who might never improve. Those who would
spend most, if not all, of the remainder of their lives within
the 5.2m fences of a secure psychiatric forensic unit.

Mr Lenny Mariam was a man in his mid-fifties who suffered from chronic mania. He had an unruly beard, fluffy
white hair and a gut that had seen many beers. He wore a
leather jacket and had a weathered face, like a mixture of
the Fonz and Santa Claus. He claimed he used to be drinking buddies with The Kinks. We never had any objective
evidence and Lenny was full of bizarre, delusional beliefs.
Yet personally, I believed this particular assertion. He just

seemed like the kind of person who had done that kind of thing. I inherited him from my predecessor around the same time as Jordan in April 2014, when I started my first permanent consultant post in Essex.

The index offence that had led him to be arrested and eventually find his way to our ward happened in a quiet country pub in Suffolk. Lenny had been drinking for three days straight. He hadn't slept (common in acute mania), and was singing and swearing loudly in a corner, unnerving the families who had come to dine. The barman, who had known Lenny for decades, tried to quieten him down which resulted in shouting. They would not serve him any more alcohol. I actually read in the witness statements that the staff had a whispered conference in the corner of the bar and decided to put a couple of drops of pineapple juice and vinegar in a Coke hoping that he would think it was rum. Their choice of ingredients baffles me and I would love to have been privy to that conversation. After his very first sip, Lenny spat out the concoction, grabbed the logs from the open fire and started throwing them at the bar. Although the barman got away with a few small cuts, Lenny ruined a lot of lunches, caused around £1,000 worth of damage, and murdered a dozen innocent bottles of spirits. When the police arrived, Lenny collected ornaments from around the country pub and started throwing them at the police cars. The officers called for backup and eventually managed to restrain him, cuff him and drag him to the station, kicking and screaming, effing and blinding.

Although Lenny's intractable bipolar affective disorder tragically left him in a permanent state of mania, the way this presented itself was as variable and unpredictable as the British weather. He could be pleasant and charming, with a booming laugh that penetrated the whole ward and its occupants. At times he would be singing and dancing. Yet he could also be very irate and threatening. Unlike Jordan, he had not mastered the art of cheeky flirting. He was outright sexually explicit towards nurses at times but he literally couldn't help it. His mania gave him disinhibited and at times sexualised thoughts, and it also made him blurt them out without any filter. Luckily, the female staff mostly rolled their eyes. He was seen as more of a Benny Hill than a Harvey Weinstein. His manic energy was infectious and was a source of great pleasure and amusement on the ward, although I was always conscious of the fine line between others laughing with or at Lenny.

The first time we met, I was visiting my new ward a week before I started working there, and sat in on the daily morning patient community meeting. This was their opportunity to discuss any issues about living together on the ward, such as noise levels, the state of the communal toilets, and votes for the Friday night film and takeaway. Lenny was fascinated by me, his future psychiatrist. He constantly interrupted the meeting in his raucous voice to ask me questions. Where did I previously work? How old was I? Was I married? At first, I tried to answer politely and offered to speak to him separately afterwards, but with his lack of filter, the enquiries were incessant and unintentionally disruptive. He also seemed transfixed by my ethnicity. He kept making loud statements.

'I don't have a racist bone in my body.'

'You're probably as English as I am!'

And the classic: 'I have lots of Asian friends.'

I knew his intentions were affable, but he was just draw-ing attention to me in a room full of strangers. I was unsure if I should challenge him publicly and potentially send a message to my future patients that I would set boundaries when needed. By not doing so, was I coming across as a walkover? Or would confrontation be a bit rude? Would I be embarrassing him as much as he was embarrassing me? Again, I tried to fob him off politely. Again, it had no effect. He definitely stood out among this new group of detainees I was about to take charge of, a couple of whom didn't even acknowledge me at all. I knew right away that Lenny would be a handful.

Lenny's mood was the most labile of all the patients I have encountered. He would burst into tears when he saw starving children in third-world countries or news reports of wars on TV. He would donate his money to charitable causes (he'd inherited a tidy sum and was receiving disabil-ity benefits with almost no outgoing expenditure, except cigarettes and takeaways). This happened to the point where staff had to intervene. Lenny was not materialistic and rarely wanted any possessions, but it was hard to know where his personal values ended and his mental illness took over. For example, he would spend twenty quid to buy a takeaway for a new patient, yet not replace his own threadbare clothes. He once bought a pair of Air Jordans and showed them off spectacularly. His mania neutralised any subtlety, as he did his own flaccid, uncoordinated rendition of *Riverdance* in them the next morning during the patient community meeting, as the others clapped and cheered him on. Yet a week later, he'd given them away to a patient he barely spoke to. I was worried that he was being exploited. I wanted Lenny to hold onto at least some of his savings, and forbade him from donating any more of his belongings.

'It's my fucking money, my trainers, and my fucking feet! You don't own me,' he yelled at the next ward round. Once again, I was the bad guy.

On a good day, Lenny was almost pathologically jovial. In his thunderous voice, he would ask disinhibited, personal questions about my wife or about fatherhood or even about my sex life, before telling me some unsavoury anecdotes about his own. I would politely attempt to steer the conversation away, often to the amusement of my colleagues. The mischievous twinkle in his eye made me suspect that perhaps a tiny proportion of his mania was under his control and he was doing it for entertainment value. Fair play. He even used to call me Mowgli (from *The Jungle Book*): a bit racist but actually quite funny. The countertransference I felt was like that I had experienced with Josef, who also had mania. I felt invigorated and just plain cheerful after some interactions. It felt like banter with a mate. A very unstable and unpredictable, vulgar, sex-obsessed mate, who possibly used to drink with The Kinks.

On a bad day, Lenny would scream the entire unit down. Even the mischievous and sometimes intentionally provocative Jordan would give him a wide berth. Lenny would call me every name under the sun. He would accuse me of conspiring to kill him with medications, because I was jealous of his extreme intelligence, as he had an IQ of three hundred. For around a fortnight in the summer of 2015, he even waited by his bedroom window every morning to shout expletives at me as I walked through the courtyard to enter the ward. This vitriol was very public. Like me, the other hospital staff were used to dealing with hostility and verbal abuse from unwell patients. They were sympathetic and reassuring towards me. I had mixed emotions. To a degree I felt like a kid ducking the verbal assaults of a persistent bully. I didn't really believe I was in physical danger, but it was highly embarrassing. However, if I'm being honest, a part of me felt slightly amused, in part due to Lenny's surreal vocabulary. 'You rottenness psychiatry mass-murdering tanned bastardous barbarian thorn in my side!' was one of his more colourful phrases.

I did try to decrease Lenny's medication on around three occasions during the few years that he was under my care, from 2014 to 2017. I would cringe at seeing him so sedated and felt responsible to a degree. He looked how I felt. Constantly yawning, unsteady on his feet, and falling asleep so frequently in the threadbare armchair in the corner of the patient lounge that he practically became part of the furniture. But around a week after each lowered dose, Lenny would become extremely agitated. His eyes would redden, he would snarl, hunch his shoulders forward and prowl around the ward. Other patients would joke about whether there was a full moon. He would run up to visitors and scream at them, demanding to know who they were, would pull off their ID lanyards and accuse them of being sent to assassinate him. He would shriek at other patients for changing the channel and challenge them to a fight to the death. Most laughed it off, but a couple of times this escalated and needed urgent intervention from staff. On one occasion, he kicked a nurse hard in the leg, resulting in a nasty bruise and extra sedatives. I've always admired how stoic some nurses are, absorbing insults and assault as part of their daily routine. This should not be acceptable, but it was the reality, no matter how many patronising posters on the wall discouraged abuse. Each attempt to reduce his meds resulted in a trip to the seclusion room. Beyond the utter rage in his face, I could see confusion and pain. Lenny didn't want to be like this, but his mental illness was uncontainable without considerable chemical management. I felt responsible for each trip he made to seclusion. I had wanted to release him from his phlegmatic prison of chemicals but had only made matters worse.

It felt like I wasn't really treating Lenny. I failed to rescue the nice guy buried deep inside, who I knew was there. Numerous combinations of mood stabilisers and antipsychotics, all at maximum doses, might have taken the edge off his rage, but hadn't thwarted his symptoms to an acceptable degree. In fact, I might have been slowly killing him (ironically perpetuating his exact delusions about this). Or at least bringing forward his expiration date, by using medications which potentially cause a whole range of side effects, some of which can directly or indirectly reduce life expectancy, including arrhythmias (irregular heartbeats which increase the risk of heart attacks and strokes). I could see no light at the end of his tunnel. We were merely containing Lenny and it never sat right with me.

Like all doctors, forensic psychiatrists sign the Hippocratic

Oath upon graduation, the first tenet of which is to *do no harm*. Yet, arguably, some of our acts are to the detriment of our patients, albeit for very good reason: restraining and forcing them into a seclusion room, stopping their leave if they test positive for cannabis, or in our roles as expert witnesses, writing court reports refuting mental illness, leading to imprisonment. One could say these exploits are more akin to the strong arm of the law, rather than the gentle caress of the doctor. It is a moral conundrum that I struggled with the more I thought about it.

Unlike most patients, Lenny had nothing to lose. He liked it on the ward. He had regular meals, medication and 'beautiful nurses to ogle at' (his words). On some level, I believe he was aware of how intolerable and assault-provoking his words and behaviours would be in the outside world, so he must have also felt a degree of protection. Those same hospital walls that were a prison to so many, were his warm blanket. He was too unstable for leave, which meant I had no leverage to make him behave or to engage in the available therapy that he rejected.

Out of frustration, I found myself taking risks with Lenny. Calculated risks, but still. Although not a legal requirement, the general consensus was that patients needed to be settled for months before leave could even be considered. The hospital's policy was that if there were any outbursts or aggression, leave should be suspended for two weeks. Despite his regular untoward conduct on the ward, I granted him escorted trips outside, telling the staff that he had to be free of any incidents for only two days. We found that Lenny coped if he went to a tranquil environment such as a park or a zoo, away from crowds and away from stimulation (e.g. being driven in the hospital mini bus as opposed to taking public transport) with staff members he was familiar with. He would rise to the occasion, precariously, but only if the conditions were exactly perfect, like a soufflé. Allowing Lenny out in public was definitely a risk. If he shouted at a stranger, the hospital might get complaints. If he attacked anybody, the hospital could get sued, and although my job would be safe, my reputation would take a hit. This maverick move raised a few questions and a few eyebrows from some of my colleagues and the hospital managers. It led to discontent and accusations of favouritism from some other patients. I had improved his quality of life, but the very fact that I had to bend the rules and justify my decisions repeatedly made me question the effectiveness of the system.

One sunny afternoon in 2016, Lenny's leave had to be cancelled. Staff shortages meant a lack of nurses available to escort him. This was highly frustrating, though not uncommon. When Lenny was informed, he screamed with rage, then tore down a couple of framed pictures (of foliage, the ubiquitous theme in most secure units) from the wall and stamped on them. Staff approached him gently and tried to convince him to take a time out in his room. He picked up segments of the broken picture frames and brandished them, cutting his hands and bleeding all over the floor. Nobody else was hurt, but the Emergency Response Team had to restrain Lenny and frogmarch him to the seclusion room, a place he was becoming increasingly familiar with.

Chapter 13

The Dreaded Seclusion Room

The seclusion room is a dark presence in the world of secure psychiatric units. Another necessary evil. When patients are too disturbed to be contained on the ward, and there is an imminent risk of violence, they are taken there, if necessary, using the restraint techniques we are retaught annually. To puncture some common misconceptions about barbaric practices, contrary to popular belief, we do not use any physical restraints such as chains or strait jackets (even though other countries like Japan do). We also don't have big burly men with bulging biceps bursting out of their white shirts, as I have often seen depicted on TV programmes and films. All restraint is done by nurses with varying, but mostly average, physiques.

The seclusion room is equivalent to the antiquated concept of a padded cell. It isn't actually padded but it is designed to minimise the inhabitant's risk. It is a small, bare, escape-proof room with only a mattress, made of thick vinyl which cannot be torn, and a rip-proof blanket, which cannot be made into ligatures. There is a lack of furniture or other items that could be used either as a projectile or weapon, or to self-harm. There is a separate bathroom with a steel toilet, an unbreakable metallic mirror, button taps and a steel sink with no plug, to prevent flooding. The room usually has Perspex windows and some of the more high-tech ones have cameras in case patients hide in a corner. Staff are reluctant to use seclusion and do so only as a last resort. Unlike for some stereotypical dastardly movie characters, seclusion is *never* used as a form of punishment. Not only because it would hugely violate the patient's freedom, but also, on a more practical level, it is a big drain on resources. One member of nursing staff has to sit outside of the room and observe the patient at all times. This often puts a strain on already stretched nursing numbers.

There are regular nursing reviews every few hours, not only to check that the patient is physically well, including taking their blood pressure and pulse, but to offer food and drink (cold or tepid, but never hot beverages) and medication. Extra sedatives are usually offered in addition to routine daily medication, with the aim of getting the subject calm enough to leave ASAP. Medical reviews by doctors have to be carried out a few times per day, to prescribe medications, to deal with the rare medical emergency and to decide if and when seclusion can be terminated. Serious physical emergencies are extremely rare, but one particular disastrous incident cannot be forgotten. The horrendous tale of Rocky Bennett occurred before my time, though its reverberations were felt for decades within the world of forensic psychiatry. Although not related to seclusion, it involved over-zealous restraint by staff. Bennett was a thirty-eight-year-old African-Caribbean patient, who had suffered mental illness for eighteen years and had a diagnosis of schizophrenia. He died on 30 October 1998 in a medium secure psychiatric unit in Norwich, after being manhandled by staff. The physical restraint was protracted, and he was given a dose of medication that was above the recommended limit (which may have decreased his breathing rate and contributed to his demise). The inquiry into this death concluded that this was due to institutional racism within the mental health services. This included the fact that there were no repercussions at all for the white patient with whom Bennett had had an altercation, which had led to nurse intervention in the first place, even though it seems he was the one who'd provoked the fight.

The government agreed to hold an extended inquiry after the inquest on Bennett's death recorded a verdict of accidental death aggravated by neglect. The report, titled 'Independent Inquiry into the death of David Bennett' was published on 12 February 2004. It found many institutional failures in the treatment and care of Bennett in the mental health system, including that there was no real attempt to engage his family in the treatment and management of his illness during a period of seventeen years. He was not treated by the nurses as if he was a rational human being, but as a 'lesser being'. There was no indication that his racial, cultural or social needs were adequately attended to and there was a highly insidious form of racist abuse which likely contributed to his desire to retaliate, particularly as it seemed that no action was taken to prevent it. Further, Bennett was receiving three anti-psychotic drugs daily in excessively high doses, when only two anti-psychotic drugs were authorised. The inquiry also found that the restraint was mishandled by the nursing staff, who were 'pressing onto his body' until his capacity to breathe adequately was restricted, and carried out their actions substantially longer than was safe. There was no central training for control and restraint (though a national system was set up directly as a recommendation from this inquiry). A more menacing fault was uncovered, possibly stepping outside the realms of mere incompetency. That members of the family were not given a 'reasonably full disclosure of the relevant facts was not only inhumane but also bound to lead the family to suspect that there was some cover up going on'. Bennett's family were not informed of his death until the following morning, and then they were told he had died from 'breathing difficulties'. I think even the slipperiest politician would baulk at this level of dishonesty.

To look at broader racial injustices within mental health in the UK, an independent review of the Mental Health Act was undertaken to understand and make recommendations about 'the disproportionate number of people from Black and minority ethnicities detained under the act'. Its final report was published in December 2018; this revealed that Black people are 40 per cent more likely to access treatment through a police or criminal justice route, less likely to receive psychological therapies, more likely to be compulsorily admitted for treatment, more likely to be on a medium or high secure ward and more likely to be subject to seclusion or restraint (56.2 per 100,000 population for Black Caribbean people as against 16.2 per 100,000 population for white people). Follow-up studies by the Sainsbury Centre for Mental Health found that Black people have a strongly grounded fear and mistrust of health services, which they perceive as inhumane. This leads to them resisting seeking help and only presenting at the point of crisis.

Personally, I have not seen any overt racism from staff within the services I work for, but perhaps this is reflective of the majority of my career being based in or around London, where the ethnic mix of both patients and staff is far more diverse than in places like Norwich, where Bennett was killed.

Despite this tragic case, I think we need to appreciate that staff in secure units (especially nursing staff) have to deal with infrequent yet serious eruptions of violence. By not reacting with physical force swiftly or being lax in restraint techniques, they risk suffering serious injuries. It happens. I've seen broken bones, black eyes and bruises, some even caused by Lenny. Indubitably, any force used should be necessary and proportionate, an issue some cops seem to be struggling with in the States, especially with their ethnic citizens. It's just hard to measure this in the heat of the moment. The fact that these events occur is a reflection of the risky and unpredictable patient cohort we deal with. The fact that they occur so infrequently, when hundreds of restraints occur without incident in psychiatric units across the country every week, is an indication of the bravery, empathy and professionalism of our staff.

*

Patients are nursed in seclusion for the shortest period possible. It can be as brief as a few hours and rarely more than a few days. However, I do remember once carrying out a review as a specialist registrar on call one weekend, on a young man with schizophrenia who was admitted to hospital after the attempted murder of his nephew's babysitter. On the ward, he had fashioned a weapon out of a toothbrush and a razor blade and severely injured another patient, seemingly randomly, almost certainly due to psychotic delusions that he refused to disclose. Other makeshift weapons were found stashed in his room. He was deemed too high risk for our medium secure unit, and so was kept in seclusion for around two months, until a bed became available for him at Broadmoor Hospital.

There is a palpable tension before a seclusion review. With Lenny, his mental state fluctuated so wildly we would have no idea which version of him was lurking behind the door when we unlocked it. Sometimes, he was incandescent, screaming, and would even charge at us. Other times, he was making jokes or apologising profusely about the incident which led to seclusion in the first place. All staff members going in for every review know there is a risk of assault. I have always been impressed by how effectively and meticulously these events are planned. It almost feels like we are about to commit a bank heist. Four or five nurses enter in a pre-determined order, have their own spots to stand in and have their clearly defined roles if, and only if, the patient indicates that they might attack: one to restrain the head, one per arm and one or two for the legs. Occasionally, if the individual is very muscular, strong or dangerous, there are extra nurses for the limbs. A carefully orchestrated exit plan is also essential to prevent everybody in the cramped space from colliding with each other, while quickly leaving. Credit to the nursing staff I have had the pleasure of working with over the years; the vast majority of the time, these reviews have gone smoothly and even when risk of violence has been stark, this has been mitigated.

However, there are two incidents that stick out in my mind, which still send tingles down my backbone. Both were again during my specialist registrar training, a good two or three years before I took on the responsibility of treating Lenny. Once, a young paranoid man on an acute ward was secluded after he slapped an occupational therapist who had banned him from gym visits due to suspicions of him dealing cannabis in the toilets. Although there was a degree of 'mad' (he had schizoaffective disorder and some conspiratorial delusions about Scientologists brainwashing him), there was also a significant element of 'bad' (he had antisocial personality disorder and a problem with authority). He had somehow managed to sneak a lighter into the seclusion room. Patients are searched and given hospital tracksuits with no pockets, so I can only assume he had used a more, ahem, *intimate* internal pocket to sneak it in. He kicked and screamed during his forced entrance, and a staff member even had to prise his fingers from the doorframe to get him inside. Once the door was locked, he held up the lighter to the window. He took off his sweatshirt, flexed his wiry muscles and paced in front of the window with what I can only describe as a maniacal grin on his face. He then set his top on fire. Obviously, this could not be tolerated. He was gesturing through the Perspex window to a couple of the nurses he had taken a particular disliking to, running his finger across his neck. He explained in graphic detail how he would hurt them. Although his words were dampened by the thick metal door, we got the gist. We radioed for backup and summoned seven nurses from other wards; the optimum number within the limited space. They went in, took a few big punches, managed to restrain the young man and gave him a sedative injection. It took two staff members and several tense minutes to wrench the lighter from his bony, remarkably brawny fingers. The nurses sustained some scratches, a few bruises and a cut on a cheek. But no broken bones, head injuries or trips to A&E. An excellent outcome given the circumstances, in my opinion. As a doctor, I didn't get involved in the physical restraints. Even though I only observed from a distance, I remember my heart pounding throughout. This incident made getting punched on my first day feel like a picnic on a pleasant spring morning.

The other incident had a more horrendous conclusion, unfortunately. The culprit was a petite but deceptively strong middle-aged woman with more skull tattoos than teeth, and so many self-harm scars across her forearm you could barely see unscathed skin. She was clearly responding to voices and spat at the ward manager when he knelt down to speak to her during a seclusion review. Throughout the subsequent restraint, she wriggled one of her arms free and started punching out, indiscriminately. A member of staff panicked and broke formation, freeing another limb. Dominoes fell as more nurses let go and tried to run out of the door. In the ruckus, the sedative injection clattered across the room. The patient grabbed one nurse by her ponytail. The last person out didn't realise and slammed the heavy, solid seclusion door behind him, locking his colleague in with this deadly woman. It took two minutes for staff to reorganise themselves, draw up another tranquilliser injection and go back in. Two minutes, I think it's safe to say, that were probably the worst in that poor nurse's life. She was punched and stomped on repeatedly and left with a black eye, two broken ribs and chunks of her hair pulled out. And, I suspect, some nightmares.

The nurse was thankfully rescued, and the patient was restrained and injected. However, a few minutes after the door was locked again, she found the previous syringe and needle which had been left unaccounted for in the turmoil. She wielded it at the camera, slashing it through the air as a threat for the next seclusion review. The ward manager and I tried to negotiate with her via the intercom system, but her reply was a big ball of phlegm.

She wouldn't listen to reason or give up the weapon. We decided that it was far too dangerous to go in unaided and called the police. Several officers showed up with another squad with riot gear on standby. After several minutes of nail-biting negotiation, the woman left the syringe by the door and allowed staff to retrieve it as she sat in a corner. The multiple looming policeman, as well as the tranquilliser kicking in, seemed to have pacified her.

I wish there was a happy ending to Lenny's tale, but alas, he was repatriated nearer to his home area of Surrey. This was a financial decision by his NHS Trust, not a clinical one.

He was moved to a similar ward where he could continue to befuddle, amuse, threaten and ask inappropriate sexual questions to another forensic psychiatrist (although I do hope the nickname Mowgli was only reserved for me). I couldn't help ruminating that Lenny left my ward after my supposed treatment in worse shape than when he'd arrived: fatter, more dishevelled, and angrier, physically ravaged by the very medications that were supposed to cure him. Prescribed by my pen.

Logically, I knew that there was nothing more my colleagues or I could realistically have done for him. I was very aware that without our containment, Lenny would have been a serious danger outside the hospital. And there were far more success stories from my time as a hospital consultant forensic psychiatrist. But my heart ignored my head and I still could not shake off the feeling that I was, in some cases, detaining instead of healing. Turning the key in the lock in the wrong direction. Surely I hadn't grafted through all those years of gruelling training to feel like a prison warden with letters after his name?

Chapter 14

Niggling Doubts

In the odd pockets of calmness within my manic and intense hospital post in Essex, usually while sat at my desk or during my long commutes, I started to ponder on my creeping doubts. I realised that I felt somewhat empty. Earning my consultant stripes was thus far the pinnacle of my career. Our team discharged a respectable number of patients, some of whom had been particularly hard to treat. So, why did it all feel so . . . anti-climactic?

Another fear that danced around my psyche and occasionally into my nightmares (along with turning up to my ward round naked) was the statistically inevitable risk of one of my patients committing serious violence, including murder. For forensic psychiatrists, this can happen while the patient is in hospital, on leave or after discharge.

A shocking tale that illustrates this, which gave me goosebumps during my training, was that of a French psychiatrist who ended up in court as the defendant rather than an expert witness. Dr Danièle Canarelli was given a one-year suspended sentence and a €7,000 fine because one of her patients with paranoid schizophrenia, Joel Gaillard, killed somebody. The gruesome slaying occurred around February 2004, but it came to my attention when my good friend Jenny (another junior psychiatrist) and I created a poster presentation about this case to educate our peers at a conference. This was in 2013, a few weeks after Dr Canarelli was chastised in the dock, and about a year before I specialised in forensics.

Dr Canarelli had sectioned Gaillard several times in the past. However, more recently she had allegedly failed to establish the correct diagnosis, and ignored her colleagues who recommended hospitalisation to a specialised facility, choosing to continue with her ineffective therapy.

Mr Gaillard had apparently escaped during a consultation. Despite Dr Canarelli contacting the police, her patient killed his grandmother's eighty-year-old partner with an axe around three weeks later. He was thought to be psychotic at the time, not responsible for his actions, and therefore exonerated. The French courts found that Dr Canarelli had been negligent by underestimating the risk, and not taking into account previous episodes of violence. Her peers, including the union for French state psychiatrists, had her back, proclaiming that the profession was being scapegoated in a complex and unpredictable case.

In all fairness, it does appear that there were shortcomings in Dr Canarelli's treatment. However, in many other cases, as unpalatable as it may seem, the risk is not always predictable; even experts can't prognosticate the future.

Psychiatrists are not psychics. There aren't always signs or behaviours that are a harbinger to future violence. It would be completely inhumane, insensible and unacceptable to indefinitely detain somebody who has committed violence just because they suffer from a psychiatric disorder. Logistically, it would constipate the system, by preventing treatment for the next floridly mentally ill offender waiting in prison. Therefore, the best that we can do is to treat symptoms as far as possible and rehabilitate patients by utilising a variety of medications and psychological therapy. Eventually, a decision about discharge needs to be made. The bullet must be bitten.

None of my ex-patients have gone on to commit serious violence to my knowledge, probably more to do with my relatively short time as a hospital forensic psychiatrist than my medical acumen. Nevertheless, I have seen the toll it has taken on some of my peers. Interviews with police, debriefing and counselling the treating team, speaking to family members of the patient and possibly of the victim, a grilling by the hospital managers, and being scrutinised for internal serious incident investigations. This has dealt a blow to the ego, self-esteem, confidence and sanity of many competent psychiatrists. I've seen colleagues age rapidly over the space of a few weeks while this pandemonium occurred in the background. The possibility of it happening bothered me. Did I want to be part of a system that was at least partially culpable and occasionally blamed for discharging patients who went on to hurt others? I already had two major reasons for losing sleep at home, though to be fair, the older one was gradually snoozing through the night and leaving his bed dry for the majority of the time.

Another fly in the ointment of my job satisfaction was always having to be the bad guy. It took me some time to truly understand that while psychiatrists should be friendly with our patients, we are not their friends. With such a risky cohort, we frequently have to medicate them against their will, suspend their leave and enforce boundaries and rules as well as sometimes pressurise them into partaking in rehabilitation. We have to say no to people who already have issues with rules and boss around people who already have issues with authority. To be the bad guy, there needs to be a degree of detachment. Being overly affable can make it much harder to later establish professional boundaries, and thereby paradoxically damage some relationships. All the exams I sat and observed assessments I endured could not teach me this. Only challenging interactions with patients like Jordan and Lenny could.

Atop these insidious reservations, the straw that frac-tured the donkey's spine was ultimately the paperwork. A major contributory factor to this is litigation in healthcare, which has been increasing exponentially in recent years. The NHS paid £2.4 billion in clinical negligence claims in 2018–19, about 2 per cent of its entire budget in England. This has forced a culture of 'covering your own arse'. This might seem like a glib phrase, but I've heard it more than a hundred times in my career. Sadly, because of this defensive practice, excessive documentation had become the norm in the hospital that I worked in. Not only within medical notes, but there was a proliferation of forms for seemingly every pedestrian task and decision. Not to convey clinically useful information, but to document our basic competence in order to dodge potential blame.

From MOTs to tax returns, just as life is full of unwanted dull administrative chores, so are most jobs. There is no reason why mine should be different, but as far as I could tell, it was rarely for the betterment of the patients. We would be chastised by management for not having our myriad of often meaningless forms and paperwork up to date. Yet there seemed to be minimal focus on the *actual* progress of the detainees.

I knew we actively helped rehabilitate patients. But this increasingly felt like an afterthought to our enforced targets and administrative tasks. I seemed to be swamped with and sometimes ambushed by Gestapo-like management-driven metrics. I realised that I had to get out. I considered moving to another hospital. But the core issues – paperwork, having to occasionally over-medicate, revolving-door patients, indefinitely detaining the incurable, and of course having to be the bad guy – would follow me. I should mention that many of my peers were relatively content in their work. My complaints, although not unique, did not bother most of my colleagues as much as me. I guess tolerance has never been one of my virtues.

I still wanted to work with mentally disordered offenders. Not only did their back stories fascinate me, not only did I question why certain people committed certain appalling acts, but I still felt there was an honour in caring for the doubly stigmatised, those whom society had turned their back on.

As well as the system, my impatience also played a large part in my dissatisfaction. I craved a quicker pace of work, with a snappier turnover of cases than I was getting in hospital. I needed an intellectual jolt to defibrillate my brain. I knew that to truly taste the nexus of violence and mental illness, I had to dive into the belly of the beast.

Part Two

Prisons

Chapter 15

A Shrink Behind Bars

After I decided to move on from my role in secure hospitals in early 2017, I found a part-time job in Europe's largest female prison, which was located in the outskirts of Ashford in Middlesex. The job itself was relatively easy to obtain, as most of my peers wanted to work full time, rather than dedicate some of their working week to freelance private medico-legal work, like I did. Also, generally, there is a dearth of psychiatrists within many mental health teams, especially in the more challenging environment of the penitentiary. It was a buyer's market.

Around this time, my younger son, Rayaan, was developing from a tiny wrinkly dragon-nosed ball with wispy hair into a shrieking, incredibly cute toddler, who had an exceptionally labile mood; he would change from fits of giggles to outbursts of rage at the drop of a hat (or more often the drop of a biscuit). He was walking and babbling, though would prefer to communicate by blowing raspberries, egged on by the hysterical laughter of his older brother, Kamran, who was approaching four.

The first year of Kamran's life was a tough time for me and my wife, Rizma. My boys' company is an absolute pleasure now (notwithstanding the occasional bedtime protest). However, as babies, they needed relentless attention. Both would wake frequently and only stop crying if we rocked them for hours. Literally, hours. It was a nightmare. Worse: at least I would be getting some sleep during an actual nightmare. To be fair, Rizma took the brunt of it. But my shoulders still get flashbacks. The returns felt somewhat diminishing during the early years: tears, destruction of property, and poos of various, sometimes unfathomable and occasionally scientifically impossible smells, consistencies and colours. On a good day, perhaps a brief smile.

The first year of my second-born's life was paradoxically more difficult and yet easier than the elder one's. Harder, because as well as the constant feeding, nappy-changing and incessant rocking, there was also a toddler in the background needing attention and entertainment. Both of our kids were sensitive babies (which is a polite way of saying they would cry relentlessly for no discernible reason). At the age of six months, the elder one, Kamran, once burst into tears just at the sound of me shutting the door when I came in from work: not slamming, shutting! But Rayaan's earlier years were easier because I had already made an internal shift in resilience and sacrifice. I had learnt the hard way from Kamran exactly how much our freedom would be restricted. We couldn't go out on a whim. Trips to the pub were possible, but never spontaneous. I and my friends, most of whom had kids at roughly the same time, had to balance the complexity of aligning schedules and permissions from partners with the dexterity of an acrobat. Even raves and festivals were possible, I realised, though they took several months or more of pre-planning. Lie-ins were out of the question (both of our boys were and still are unconscionably early risers). Even basic plans such as going out for lunch or a gym class, let alone weekends away, became chickens I learnt not to count; they could be thwarted at any moment by child sickness. The first time around, the responsibilities of fatherhood punched me in the face harder than that patient did on my first day. I was more ready for *fatherhood: the sequel*. One could even postulate that it was a case of 'learned helplessness', a psychological construct that represents a sense of powerlessness arising from a traumatic event or persistent failure to succeed. It's the cognitive state where victims passively allow themselves to be targeted repeatedly. Or perhaps I'm being a tad melodramatic. Regardless, another resurgence of overpriced brunches invaded my life once again. Over a tenner for scrambled eggs mixed with crème fraiche and chives, served on a bed of smashed avocado and sourdough bread. Thrown on the floor in a tantrum. Again.

Inside the penitentiary, as well as giving advice to the non-medics on my team, my main tasks were to hold psychiatric clinics and oversee patients within the healthcare unit, which is like a hospital ward inside a prison. I was also tasked with the fiendishly bureaucratic struggle of transferring the most psychotic prisoners to the type of secure hospital I had just left. With massive waiting lists, a shortage of beds, and glacial response times from some (though, to be fair, not all) of the gatekeepers of these units, the words 'running', 'through' and 'treacle' came to mind.

The prison was relatively new and privately owned. Despite the standard dreary exterior of red brick and huge grey gates decorated with barbed wire, the interior was reasonably congenial. The many noticeboards and pictures along the walls gave it a kind of high-school vibe.

Of course, the environment of penitentiaries was not completely novel for me, but being able to simply show my staff pass and saunter through the gates was. During my previous visits as an outside psychiatrist, the degree of pedantry to enter some of these institutions was crippling; the wrong ID, a misspelt letter of introduction from the solicitors' firm and even the wrong combination of clothing were all potential reasons to be turned away at the prison gate after interminable queueing. Some establishments didn't allow watches or belts through their doors, whereas others did. Woe betide the psychiatrist who arrived with overly baggy trousers and had their belt confiscated. Assessments are never effective when one's pants are falling down. 'It's bloody well harder to get in to prison than to get out,' as I've heard many a miffed barrister say as they are being turned away at the gate.

A question that I frequently got asked (mainly by anxious family members who shouldn't be watching documentaries about murderers) was whether I felt safe in prison. To be honest, I felt safer there than when I worked in secure forensic psychiatric hospitals. For a start, if anything did kick off, the average prison officer is several stone and many more protein shakes and bicep curls ahead of the average nurse. More importantly, in psychiatric hospital I was often withholding something the patient wanted (for good reason), whether it was leave, discharge or permission for certain visitors. I was in charge of their treatment, therefore there was a rationale to confront or intimidate me. For the convicts, screws and governors were in charge of their overall management. I was a visitor who only oversaw their mental health. Also, hearing antagonistic voices and other active symptoms of mental illness ramped up the possibility of sudden agitation and unpredictable outbursts. These were far more frequent in hospital, as the patients had been sectioned for this very reason. Insanity was present in the prison population, but it was diluted.

During the prison clinics, I functioned like a GP for the psyche. I would see eight to ten patients a day with a whole range of psychiatric presentations. Severe disorders that would be rare in the community, such as schizophrenia or post-traumatic stress disorder, came through my door as often as common disorders, such as depression and anxiety.

One of the first clinic cases I had was a skinny emo Caucasian woman with cornrows and facial holes (like many hapless psychiatrists' belts, her piercings had had to be removed at the gate), and swollen arms from years of heroin abuse. I'm not saying all people of a certain skin complexion who have cornrows need psychiatric attention, but let's just say they put me on heightened alert. Chantelle had been arrested for armed robbery, which she had committed to fund her drug habit. Her third one, or at least the third that the law knew about. She and her boyfriend had used an imitation handgun, and were apparently caught because his very distinctive tattoo of Homer Simpson on the back of his neck was picked up on CCTV. I have no idea what he said upon arrest, but I really hope it was 'Doh!'

Chantelle had the classic symptoms of anxiety. These were both cognitive (racing thoughts, uncontrollable over-thinking, feelings of dread and heightened alertness), as well as physiological (heart palpitations and shortness of breath).

'I don't think it's madness, doc,' she said, after I proposed the potential diagnosis to her. 'It's just the way I am. Plus it's much worse every time I get banged up and have to go cold turkey from smack.'

For the uninitiated, this is a slang term for heroin. Other street monikers include dope, smack, junk, skag and H (not to be confused with the hair-highlighted, over-enthusiastic, annoying singer of the same name from Steps).

'Maybe. But you've been in prison for almost a year now. You haven't been using, yet you are still getting the symptoms,' I said.

Chantelle nodded slowly as she eyed the clinic room.

'You haven't been taking anything, have you, Chantelle? Do you think I don't know what goes on in your houseblock?'

'No, doc. Scout's honour,' she said raising her hand in what I was pretty sure was a Vulcan greeting.

Although relatively well contained in the prison I worked in, drugs are generally rife and it's getting worse. A survey from HM Inspectorate of Prisons in the UK found that the proportion of inmates developing a drug problem inside more than doubled to 15 per cent between 2014 and 2019. Substances are smuggled in by visitors, staff and, in the spirit of modern technological entrepreneurialism, even drones. For users, addiction and boredom are mighty motivators to get high in prison. For dealers, extortionate prices and a large captive customer base are potent persuaders. This influx of substances, along with overcrowding, crumbling infrastructure, low prison officer numbers and attention all contribute to the chaos inside prisons and the subsequent dire mental health of the inmates.

Chantelle twisted a braid of her hair for a while. 'That anxiety, isn't that like all those stressed-out housewives from the seventies who just popped Valium?'

'Not really. It's quite common even nowadays,' I said, reaching into my desk drawer shuffling through piles of papers, to find a patient information leaflet. 'About 5 to 10 per cent of the population suffers from it, and it's twice as common in women. And before you ask, I'm not going to prescribe you Valium.'

'Please.'

'No.'

'Pretty please,' she said with a grin.

'Actually, it's banned from this prison. From most prisons. It's addictive. And if you become hooked, coming off it would make your anxiety far worse. But I can give you propranolol which will deal with the palpitations. And I can refer you to the 'shared anxiety' therapy groups we have here, run by our psychologists.'

Chantelle grilled me on the side effects of propranolol, then chewed her lip for a while.

'To be honest,' I said, 'it's far safer than the heroin you put inside yourself for over ten years.'

She smirked at this. 'I'm sold.'

As she walked out, she spun around. 'I wasn't sure about telling you about my symptoms. My cellmate told me that psychologists like you always nutted us off to a loony bin at the first whiff of anybody being, you know . . . ' She whirled a finger next to her head, ' . . . one sandwich short of a packed lunch'.

'Psychiatrists.'

'What?'

'Doesn't matter.'

Scanning the prison medical records before I saw each patient made for despairing reading. Like superhero-film villains, it was their back stories that were fascinating to me. Almost every inmate had suffered some form of childhood abuse: homelessness, poverty, neglect, drug addiction or domestic violence. Often it was like a pick 'n' mix of tragedies. From my experience, even more than their male counterparts, female prisoners had a clear set of reasons and circumstances that carved out their path to eventual incarceration.

It is only fair to mention that from my observations, camaraderie and compassion also appeared to be more prevalent between female inmates. They would often offer overt support to each other, such as accompanying each other to appointments and generally showing concern over each other's psychological well-being, such as when a comrade had had a bad day or received sorrowful news from the outside world. I'm sure this benevolence must exist to a degree in male prisons, but it's probably expressed more subtly due to the machoism and possibly even paranoid homophobia.

Often, the psychiatric diagnoses were fairly standard but had been camouflaged by the convicts' chaotic lives. For a drug addict in a violent relationship, it can be hard to differentiate clinical depression from the general vicissitudes of their existence. Often misunderstood and appropriated by people who are feeling a bit miserable, clinical depression is more than a bog-standard low mood. It is a far more persistent beast, and has associated symptoms, which can include loss of motivation and energy, insomnia, poor appetite and concentration, negative cognitions (such as pessimism and low self-esteem) and a lack of pleasure in previous activities (anhedonia). It was very common within the female prison population.

I didn't see Chantelle again for another two years, indicating that the propranolol that I prescribed for her had helped. When she did eventually pop back through my clinic doors, she wanted to undergo gender reassignment. We supported women who requested this. It occurred more often than I was expecting: around once every four or five months. I remember wondering if this was a random spike within the time I was working there, or if there was perhaps a correlation between gender dysphoria and offending. My role was to undertake a basic mental health screen, mostly to rule out that this was their genuine intent and not driven by undisclosed psychosis. Voices telling you to change gender can be eliminated with medications. Surgically grafted male genitalia, not so much. If I was satisfied that the inmate was legit, I would make a referral to the appropriate clinic based in Charing Cross, which had an eye-watering two-year waiting list. I helped Chantelle get on the list, but she withdrew herself a couple of months later. I never found out why, but I'm just glad she had this change of mind *before* the transition.

As well as the unexpected regularity of inmates wanting gender reassignment, another issue that initially befuddled me was the proportion of non-attendees for my clinics. Prisoners frequently disappeared. Not, I hasten to add, by patiently chipping away at their walls with a small rock hammer and then crawling through a sewer pipe during a thunderstorm. Sometimes they would be suddenly transferred to another penitentiary. Sometimes their cases were dropped at court (perhaps due to lack of evidence or a witness also no-showing their appointments) or they would be released if they had short sentences with time already served on remand. The psychologists from our team may have started to make progress with therapy or I may have changed their prescription and we would never get to see the results. I would hope that their new medication regime would follow them, though I knew that with a whole host of destabilisers, as well as more intoxicating and less legal forms of self-medication on the streets, the reality was bleak. A huge handicap in prison psychiatry was the lack of nursing observation, which I had perhaps taken for granted in the hospital environment. Prison officers were not able to compensate. With drugs and violence, including gang beefs, particularly in men's prisons, the officers were perennially overstretched and struggled to contain the pandemonium. Sometimes their own safety hung in the balance. Asking them to observe their flock for signs of mental illness was often fruitless. They also lacked the necessary training and experience to differentiate the occasional psychotic man responding to voices and threatening to stab the shape-shifting alien in the next cell from the dozen other inmates responding to each other's voices and threatening to stab the snitch in the next cell.

The lack of surrogate eyes on the prison wings was a major handicap for me in distinguishing genuine psychiatric presentations from the many fraudsters who were fishing for medication. Another consequence of absent nursing scrutiny was one that Yasmin almost fell foul of: not being the proverbial squeakiest wheel. Patients who were quietly psychotic could often fester inside themselves, drowning in their own insanity, under the radar of the prison mental health team.

One such case that I came across a few months into my part-time prison job, in mid-2017, was an indignant middle-aged Brazilian woman named Ms Adriana De Silva.

Chapter 16

When Psychosis Festers

Ms Adriana De Silva had been charged with stalking and then assaulting a man who worked in a local clothes shop. She had apparently sent him more than thirty texts per day, oscillating between declarations of love, threats of beheading him and marriage proposals. Talk about mixed messages! She followed him into a bar one night in disguise, wearing a wig and sunglasses, and sat in a corner watching him drinking with his friends for several hours. When he chatted up a young woman at the next table, Adriana threw a bar stool at them both, accused the man of cheating and started scratching at his face. He managed to push her off and nearby drinkers restrained her until the police arrived. This must have been bewildering for the victim. It was in a swanky Soho bar, too: the type with craft ales, cocktails inexplicably served in jam jars, quinoa crisps and definitely not accustomed to bar brawls.

Adriana chose to represent herself in court proceedings.

This scenario indicates one of two possibilities to me: the accused is either a legal genius or is delusional. I'm yet to see the former. Adriana refused almost all contact with others, which was reminiscent of Yasmin and Jordan when they were both behind bars. She refused to see the barrister whom the court had assigned and barely spoke to the prison officers. Hearing this, my psych spidey-sense started tingling. She had almost no medical notes on the system. It wasn't even clear when she had come to the UK. She didn't appear to have any previous offences or contact with mental health services. I offered Adriana two appointments at my prison clinic, though perhaps predictably, she did not attend either. This left me no choice but to go searching for her in the main prison. Adriana was a tall, plump, tanned woman. Her scraggly black hair framed a suspicious face with a notable scar across her cheek. She was extremely dismissive and evasive. In fact, when I first approached her on the prison landing outside her cell, she denied her identity, meaning I had to double check with the nearest guard that it was actually her. When I returned, she then talked about herself in the third person. 'She already told you that she will give you no conversation,' she barked over her shoulder. 'Leave her alone.' I gave her space, then returned to the landing an hour later.

I have learnt to adapt psychiatric assessments to the subject in front of me. If they are lucid and cooperative, I will carry out a structured and ordered evaluation. As I'm asking them directly about symptoms, all the while I'm analysing their demeanour, looking for clues. Diagnoses can be telegraphed by the subject's appearance. For example, somebody in an acute manic episode like Josef Jefferson (who kidnapped that poor defenceless mannequin) might be wearing loud, bright clothes or have a curious hairstyle (like his reverse mohawk) and might be speaking rapidly and energetically. Somebody suffering from an anxiety disorder is likely to appear nervous, stutter, not be able to focus on the conversation and might have an increased breathing rate and pulse. Somebody with an acute psychosis might be suspicious and paranoid, not only in their defensive answers, but in scanning the environment and possibly even whispering to the voices they are hearing.

During the conversation, I first enquire about several aspects of the subject's history, from potential genetic mental illnesses in their family, to their upbringing and adolescence, to their academic ability, to their relationships: romantic and platonic, historic and current. I explore their social circumstances. I specifically elicit details of their previous mental health history, like if they've ever been diagnosed, medicated, sectioned or tried to commit suicide. I also ask about past indiscretions with the law and substance abuse. Each of these areas could potentially reveal nuggets of information that help me form the diagnosis and aetiology (the attribution or cause of the disorder) and crucially within forensic psychiatry, to help me formulate the subject's risk of violence.

With patients like Adriana, all of the above goes out of the window. Sometimes, I can sense that the patient is not going to cooperate, due to hallucinations, delusions, confusion, agitation, paranoia or simply because they don't like the look of me. I am aware that I have a small window of interaction, and therefore I adapt my approach to elicit as much as possible as subtly as possible, as quickly as possible. The trick is to look non-threatening and casual, the opposite of a scorpion deimatically raising its tail and pincers. I put my notebook away, avoid direct eye contact and slip in some minor enquiries into polite conversation.

My nonchalant probing worked for a few minutes with Adriana during my second approach. She refused to enter a clinic room with me, but I did convince her to sit with me on a small sofa in the corner of the prison wing. It wasn't ideal as other prisoners could walk past, though it was a relatively quiet morning, with the majority attending work or education. We were only interrupted once when another prisoner told me that she liked my waistcoat. Unsure how to respond, I grinned inanely until she left. I managed to establish that Adriana lived in Slough, and a little bit about her social circumstances before prison. She told me that she used to work as a pet therapist and that she had never drunk as her father was an alcoholic. She continued to speak about herself in the third person. I may have flown a little bit too close to the sun, because as soon as I tried to slip in clandestine questions about her mental health, she jumped at me with a raised fist.

'Look, she's already told you she's not insane. Just go away and leave her alone before she shoves your beard up your arse,' she snarled.

Message received. That did not sound like a pleasant makeover.

Our interaction left more questions than answers. Was

Adriana's third-person reference a sign of psychosis? Did she have any friends or family in the UK? Could she have previously been psychiatrically unstable in Brazil? How did she get that scar? Does a pet therapist give therapy *to* pets or *with* them?

When I asked the prison officers for their input, they did not describe any overt symptoms of mental illness, such as Adriana responding to voices or expressing delusional beliefs. However, they highlighted odd behaviour, including her staring into space for hours in her cell and putting a sheet over her head. I believed that she was psychotic. The challenge was to persuade my forensic psychiatrist peers working in her home area of Slough to admit her. After all, Adriana could simply be choosing not to engage and wasn't necessarily mentally ill. With the constant pressure on beds in secure psychiatric units (even more so for women, whose wards are a rarer breed) and an extensive waiting list of blatantly unwell and agitated prisoners, it was a hard sell. Her offence was far less serious than a patient like Yasmin's and therefore garnered less concern. If at first you don't succeed, refer, refer, refer. After batting back my weekly letters for around four months, the hospital in Slough finally admitted her. Clinically, they justified that over time such a prolonged period of non-engagement from her indicated a possible underlying mental illness, but I also think they were fed up of dealing with me. Persistence overcomes resistance: a lesson I had learnt from courting my wife.

In the interim period before she was transferred to hospital, I did try to convince Adriana to take anti-psychotic medication to speed up her recovery journey. She would swear at me in her own language. At least, that is what I assumed by her tone and the gestures. My Portuguese profanity vocabulary is somewhat limited.

In contrast to Adriana, I soon discovered how common medication-seeking behaviour was amongst the other inmates. Whereas food seems to be the vice of choice for patients sectioned in hospital, many prisoners sought particular tablets to give them a buzz or to help them sleep. They were also used as currency. For this very reason, several known intoxicants were under a blanket ban in prison. Benzodiazepines (addictive sedatives like the Valium that I had refused to prescribe for Chantelle), sleeping tablets and particular anti-epileptic drugs were all forbidden. Every week, I would have two or three women beg, plead, demand or threaten for one prohibited medication or another. Sometimes they had been prescribed these previously by a colleague in the community, often inappropriately in my view. Which made me wonder if my peers had been hoodwinked into reaching for the prescription pad or had caved under pressure, making them complicit.

As Christmas of 2017 was approaching, the first during my new role, a fairly weak anti-psychotic which can give the user a mild buzz, named quetiapine, became all the rage. One morning, having driven through heavy snow, I arrived late and flustered. My first clinic patient was a young woman who complained of hearing a voice coming from the toilet in her cell and seeing vampires in the clouds. To test the intensity and authenticity of her symptoms, I asked her how real they felt and how she could differentiate them from actual experiences (very and she couldn't). I made other enquiries about the voices: what they were saying, who they belonged to and whether they were inside or outside her head. I wasn't fully convinced by her vague answers but gave her the benefit of the doubt. As a trial, I prescribed a low dose of quetiapine, which she had requested by name. The next woman in my clinic had almost exactly the same story. And the next. My suspicions were raised further when I found out over lunch later that week that my consultant forensic psychiatrist colleague who ran clinics in the same prison on different days had encountered the same repeated presentation. The problem was that among this flagrant drug-seeking behaviour, there may well have been genuine cases. I had to sharpen my clinical senses and be extra pedantic in enquiring about symptoms. I also emphasised the side effects of quetiapine, including weight-gain and constipation, which deterred a couple of the chancers. This included one woman who said, 'On second thought, I don't think it was the toilet speaking to me. I think it was my cellmate mumbling in her sleep,' as she comically bumbled out of the room.

Of all the fields of medicine, psychiatry is the vaguest. We don't have scans or blood tests to confirm diagnoses. Patients' symptoms are open to a high degree of subjectivity; many of them are extreme versions of normal human experiences and the point at which they cross over to being pathological is hard to define. Just as cooks with the same ingredients might concoct different dishes, or children with the same Play-Doh might concoct different degrees of mess, even with the same set of symptoms, psychiatrists can arrive at different diagnoses. Arguably, mentally disturbed prisoners are even more complex. They often have multiple intertwined previous traumas as well as more pressing social issues. For these reasons, there was room for misinterpretation. Perhaps predictably within the criminal cohort, this also meant room for exploitation. A small but significant proportion exaggerated or fabricated symptoms of mental illness. As well as in attempts to finesse tablets from me in prison, I would see this quite frequently in the accused during their criminal trials. They would either hope that their case would be dropped, or they could wring out some drops of sympathy and leniency from the judge.

Early in 2018, I was involved in a curious case for which I gave evidence in court, where I'm at least 90 per cent sure that a con-artist managed to use mental illness to dodge her charges, despite my best efforts to expose her.

Chapter 17

Ousting the Chancers

Ms Daryna Boyko was a recently divorced woman in her mid-thirties from Ukraine, who used to be a model. She was facing multiple charges related to a convoluted multi-million-dollar swindle. She had allegedly mis-sold carbon credits and was in cahoots with her cousin and her ex-boss, with whom she'd had an affair for over a year. This was sophisticated fraud and Daryna had, allegedly, assumed a false identity, attended numerous meetings with 'marks' and fabricated documents. She received more than £2.5 million in corrupt payments across six bank accounts, over three years, which she syphoned off to her co-defendants. The evidence against her was overwhelming. The bank statements were black and white, figuratively and literally.

This was an independent fitness to plead assignment I was asked to do as an expert witness on behalf of the Crown Prosecution Service, which wanted a second opinion on a previous assessment. The trial was at the Old Bailey, which by now had become more familiar and less intimidating for me.

This type of offence is relatively rare within the world of forensic psychiatry. In a Venn diagram, the overlap of fraud and serious mental illness would be a tiny sliver. To put it bluntly, symptoms that often include hearing voices telling you that you deserve to die or suffering paranoid delusions that the CIA are trying to kill you, might cause the sufferer to commit impulsive or violent acts. But they very rarely drive people to rip others off. Complex fraud, which requires focus and attention, as well as elements of planning and research, is even rarer. Skulduggery requires clarity of thought. Every time such a case comes across my desk, my natural scepticism is tickled.

According to the first court report, Daryna was privately educated and culturally nurtured. She was forced into piano, ballet and Latin. She informed the other psychiatrist that her parents were overbearing and critical: hardly the gritty upbringing of abuse and poverty that most mentally disordered offenders have endured. Daryna obtained an economics degree at a prestigious university and had thrived in a six-figure-salaried, highly pressurised job in trading. Again, highly unusual within my patient cohort. She had married a multi-millionaire CEO twenty years her senior and had two children. They lived in Mayfair, a very exclusive area of London, home to the odd billionaire oligarch and A-list celebrity, its ostentatiousness reflected by its extortionate price on the Monopoly board. Even before the divorce, her husband seemed disconnected from the family, spending weeks at a time abroad or in their second home in the south of France.

Daryna's cousin, a self-effacing but well-respected businessman, had originally been arrested and the police followed the financial breadcrumb trail to her. A criminal trial had started the previous year, though was stopped short due to her five-year-old son developing a rare form of leukaemia. The court had adjourned her case in the hope that, not to put it indelicately, this situation would resolve itself one way or another. Both of her co-defendants were tried, found guilty and incarcerated.

When Daryna's trial resumed, she flat-out refused to engage with the court process. She ignored all legal letters, including those from her own solicitors. On the odd occasion that her legal team did manage to speak to her, her floods of tears would wash away any attempts to discuss her trial. Daryna claimed to have developed depression due to the situation with her son, exacerbated by the recent breakdown of her marriage and also post-traumatic stress disorder after a relatively minor car accident. According to her medical notes, her GP did not seem particularly concerned about her mental health. However, a private psychiatrist had written a remarkably brief letter confirming the diagnoses she had proposed. If I was cynical (which I am), I might suspect that some people pay private psychiatrists to write spurious letters for their personal gain (which they do). Some even use them as dodgy evidence for criminal trials. I can't say for certain that this was the case for Daryna, but the letter did not appear to be professionally written to me. It conveyed very little clinical information and contained no description of the symptomatology. Like in maths exams, psychiatrists are supposed to show their working as to how they reached a certain diagnosis. These gaping omissions made it tricky to corroborate this doctor's conclusions. Further, the letter contained emotive and loaded terms, like 'I have nothing but pity for this poor woman, whose life just keeps taking one horrible turn after another' and 'she clearly needs a break from the vicissitudes of existence'. What? This was supposed to be a neutral, objective formal clinical evaluation, not slam poetry.

Daryna's previous fitness to plead assessment was undertaken by a senior, very experienced forensic psychiatrist on behalf of the defence, who had found her unfit to plead. His name was on the spine of many of the textbooks I had read (or purchased with the genuine intention to read eventually).

The Crown Prosecution Service clearly found his conclusion to be dubious, which is why they instructed me for a second opinion. I was sent the first report before I assessed Daryna, and I have to say that in my opinion, and I need to stress that this was only my opinion, she had duped this doctor. Her dramatic, tearful presentation had evoked so much sympathy that I think it may have clouded his judgement.

When I assessed Daryna, she presented as a very smartly dressed woman. Her pristine suit and designer handbag appeared incongruous in the slightly grotty office I had hired in the back of a library in north London. She even mumbled a snooty comment as she walked through the door about how she was 'expecting a more professional setting for such a serious assessment'. Her blonde hair was tied up and her striking features were betrayed by bags under both eyes. She was extremely tearful throughout the interview. She cried heavily, often for minutes at a time. She was also incredibly passive-aggressive. After I introduced myself, I asked as is standard, 'Do you understand why the court has asked me to assess you?'

'Those bastards want to separate me from my children. And you want to help them,' she replied, dabbing at her eyes with a hanky.

I felt that Daryna was being deliberately obstructive during the interview. She was extremely touchy, guarded and evasive when speaking about the alleged offences and her court case. 'How many times must I tell you, I never kept track of my incomings and outgoings. It was pocket change for me.' Yet she was able to discuss other topics, such as her childhood and previous employment, in detail, without the waterworks.

Other elements didn't add up. She claimed to have a debilitating disorder, yet her GP had not felt the need to escalate her management with a referral to an NHS psychiatrist for a second opinion. She seemed to have made no efforts to engage in any recommended treatment, declining anti-depressants her GP had offered and the psychotherapy that the other forensic psychiatrist had suggested. Another disparity was Daryna's level of functioning. She was able to take her children out to the park on a daily basis, drive to medical appointments, attend the odd spin class, go for runs and cook most days. Although we were both encumbered with small children, I did not have a nanny like she did, and her lifestyle sounded more exciting and fulfilling than mine!

Daryna's tears elongated the entire interview to almost two and a half hours. After some verbal jabbing and weaving, she realised early on that I would not allow her to shirk discussion of the fraud allegations. Other dubious cracks started appearing. She was apparently incapable of remembering even the very basic elements of the case. She forgot the name of the co-defendant with whom she had had an intimate relationship for over a year and had worked for for more than three. She told me that she could not remember if there were any other co-defendants (i.e. her cousin), even after some prompting from me. To ascertain her understanding of the court process (one of the Pritchard Criteria, the legal test that defines fitness to plead), I asked specific questions about the roles of courtroom inhabitants (the judge, a barrister, a solicitor, the jury). But this well-educated, erudite, successful ex-trader was not even able to give me a ballpark guess.

My conclusion was that Daryna's profuse crying, dodging questions, ignoring legal letters, avoiding her solicitors, declining psychiatric treatment and seemingly selective memory loss were all deliberate attempts to evade her trial. Taking all of the above into consideration, in my opinion, on the balance of probabilities, Daryna was *capable* of all the elements of the Pritchard Criteria, even though she chose not to address them. Therefore, I concluded that she was fit to plead. This is what I proclaimed in my court report and also on the witness stand at the Old Bailey, as I ignored the death stares from Daryna who sat in the dock in an even sharper suit (though interestingly, with far less sobbing). During cross-examination, the defence barrister's main argument was that my assessment was limited, as I hadn't properly elicited all the elements of the Pritchard Criteria.

I agreed, but countered that I'd done the best I could, as Daryna wouldn't cooperate.

He counter-countered. 'The best that you can do surely falls short of the standard of evidence required for such a major case, where the imprisonment of a woman and separation from her children is hanging in the balance, wouldn't you say, Dr Das?'

I couldn't really argue with that and, perhaps sensing a chink in my armour, the barrister kept returning to the same issue. I had expected the judge to step in and ask my aggressor to move along, kind of like a boxer repeatedly getting hit below the belt, waiting for the referee to intervene. For some reason, I felt obliged to change the wording of my answers even though I was essentially being asked the same question, which left me a little flustered. Maybe I should have stuck to my guns and repeated my response verbatim to hammer home the ridiculous pointlessness of this repetition.

To engage in some retrospective damage-control of my personal image, to be clear, I am a father and I have a heart (even if it is somewhat calloused by years of analysing horrific acts of violence). I fully appreciated that Daryna was going through a traumatic period with the illness of her son. Yes, she probably did have a degree of depression and anxiety. I accept that there might have been humanitarian reasons why the court might not wish to put Daryna through a criminal trial. In fact, I specifically asserted this in my report. If the judge wished to drop the charges on compassionate grounds, I had no qualms with that. What I objected to was her using mental illness as a smokescreen.

In the end, the judge discarded my opinion, and adjudged Daryna as being unfit to plead. I was (and still am) fairly certain that this was an incorrect call. But I also knew my place. My role was as an advisor only. The judge has the ultimate say. Personally, I think the image of the courts dragging a grieving mother with a sick child over the coals was too unpalatable. Also, I believe that having the two main perpetrators behind bars was a concession of sorts. Compassion overruling justice in this particular case was not unreasonable, in my view, but it should have been a legal decision, not a clinical one. Otherwise, the system *itself* is at risk of also using mental illness as a smokescreen.

To me, the case had echoes of Anna Sorokin, who committed fraud around the same time as Daryna and was arrested in 2017. She was a Russian-born German who moved to New York City in 2016 in the guise of a wealthy German heiress named Anna Delvey. In 2019, she was convicted of multiple counts of attempted grand larceny, theft of services and larceny in the second degree for defrauding New York hotels and wealthy acquaintances. Her biggest score was defrauding City National Bank. In November 2016, she submitted a falsified loan application purporting to show that she had access to around €60 million stored in Swiss bank accounts and convinced the bank to give her a loan of $100,000 to cover legal expenses. When I read about this, I had to remind myself that crime is a crime, even if it was against a bank. Like Daryna, Sorokin seemed to use her confidence and charm to hoodwink professionals. Her mental state was never in question. To me, she seemed to exhibit the classic personality traits of a fraudster: narcissism, lack of empathy and entitlement. Bad, not mad.

My dealings with Daryna also forced me to consider how many other legal proceedings might be unjustly swayed by the presentation and the amateur dramatics of the accused. Would the judge (and the other expert psychiatrist who graced my books' spines for that matter) have been so lenient towards another defendant who was not so white, pretty, female, educated, eloquent, credible, grieving and tearful?

Daryna's case helped me solidify the notion of how a forensic psychiatrist needs to be adroit at spotting the diamonds from the cubic zirconias among those we assess. The Rolexes from the Rolllexes. I made a concerted effort to sharpen the many strategies I personally use. It is relatively easy to fake some symptoms of psychosis (such as pretending to hear voices or acting paranoid), but hard to do so convincingly and consistently. It is especially difficult to fool a frontline professional who has spent many years working extensively and closely with severe mental illness and with criminals. Nevertheless, there are a few high-profile cases when the defendants have tried their luck. Few were as dramatic as the Hillside Strangler, a case that I read about during my training.

Kenneth Bianchi, the Hillside Strangler, was apprehended for a dozen murders of young women in California between October 1977 and February 1978. He buried them in the surrounding hills. It transpired that these heinous acts were carried out by two criminals working together: Bianchi and his cousin, Angelo Buono Jr. They were convicted of kidnapping, raping, torturing and murdering ten women and girls ranging in age from twelve to twenty-eight years old. The first victims were three sex workers who were found strangled and dumped naked on hillsides northeast of Los Angeles in late 1977. It was not until the deaths of five young women who were not sex workers, but girls who had been abducted from middle-class neighbourhoods, that the media attention and subsequent 'Hillside Strangler' nickname was created. There were two more deaths in December and February 1978 before the murders abruptly stopped. After some barren months of investigation, the arrest of Bianchi in January 1979 for the murder of two more young women in Washington and the subsequent linking of his past to the Strangler opened the case back up. This was the most expensive trial in the history of the Californian legal system at that time. Bianchi and Buono were eventually sentenced to life imprisonment.

Bianchi managed to persuade several respected experts that he had an unpleasant (but rather timidly named) alter ego, Steve, who had committed these heinous crimes. A diagnosis of multiple personality disorder was being considered until the investigators brought in a psychologist, Martin Orne, who tricked the trickster. Told by Orne that multiple personality disorder patients usually had at least three personalities, Bianchi promptly invented another one, 'Billy'. He was also pulled up on obvious exaggeration of his confusion at seeing the actions committed by Steve. A police search of Bianchi's house turned up a pile of textbooks on psychology, behavioural science, hypnosis and police procedure law. There was also evidence that he had viewed a couple of films dealing with multiple personality disorder, including one named *Sybil*. In the end, cornered, he admitted that he was faking it and pleaded guilty to avoid the death penalty. Sentencing Bianchi, the judge said: 'In this Mr Bianchi was unwittingly aided and abetted by most of the psychiatrists who naively swallowed Mr Bianchi's story hook, line and sinker.' I must admit, when reading about this case, I thought that my brethren involved sounded like schmucks and would have benefitted from a healthy dose of my scepticism.

The very existence of multiple personality disorder, known now as dissociative identity disorder, is a contentious issue. Characterised by the existence of at least two distinct and relatively enduring personalities and by huge memory gaps, it is associated with overwhelming traumas, or abuse during childhood. Many psychiatrists don't believe in it. I would classify myself as a dissociative identity disorder *agnostic* rather than atheist. I've never seen a credible case, though I've had a few chancers blatantly faking the symptoms. If I ever do encounter it, I will repent my sins and believe.

I've always approached my evaluations with a hint of cynicism, especially when a potential psychiatric defence for alleged criminal acts is on the cards. Firstly, I take all available evidence into consideration, including school reports, social services documentation, GP records and previous correspondence with other mental health practitioners. Generally, mental illness develops progressively, as highlighted by Yasmin's prodrome of psychosis. I'm scouring for signs of gradual deterioration. As well as overt symptoms,

I'm looking for subtler clues about declining function or change in personality. Have they been withdrawn? Avoiding social engagements? Ducking their friends? Underperforming in their job? Although rare, some psychiatric disorders can appear suddenly and spontaneously, such as drug-induced psychosis, or brief reactive psychosis (the psychiatric equivalent of spontaneous human combustion).

Next, I scrutinise the legal evidence, which outlines the culprit's mental state at the time of the alleged offences. This includes case papers, which contain witness statements; police interview transcripts; and CCTV footage or pictures of the actual crime, as well as the aftermath. This can all serve as a window into the accused's mindset at the time. Paranoid ramblings or clear delusions can jump off the page. For the occasional mild glamour of being a forensic psychiatrist, trudging through evidence is definitely the antithesis. I have been sent over a thousand pages for a single case on a couple of occasions and have had to spend more than a full day and a large cafetière of coffee to get through it all. Finally, if the relevant evidence is available, I also try to get an objective perspective on the defendant's mental state more recently, since the crime took place. This can be from interviewing prison officers, healthcare professionals or family members, if the subject has been remanded, sectioned or bailed, respectively.

Finally, I am ready to assess the defendant in person to ascertain the quality and validity of the symptoms they are reporting. Certain symptoms tend to follow established patterns. For example, in true psychosis, visual hallucinations are relatively rare and more often result from organic causes, such as a brain tumour (which would also present with specific neurological symptoms) or even magic mushrooms. Auditory hallucinations are more common and tend to be external, so it's not the voices *in* your head, but the voices heard *outside*, that are likely to tell you to kill, kill, kill. They typically give a running commentary on what the sufferer is doing or bark simple commands at them, as opposed to, for example, full conversations with opinions. I have had numerous defendants try to convince me that they have an evil entity lurking inside them which has its own complex personalities, views and outlooks (like the Hillside Strangler's false alter ego, Steve). Real psychotic experiences are far less sophisticated and blunter. Other relevant factors which help distinguish genuine from fabricated cases include the age of onset of symptoms; bipolar affective disorder, for instance, tends to surface in early to mid-twenties.

I am not saying that anybody who reports seeing visions of ghosts for the first time in their forties, or hearing voices inside their heads (with whom they have detailed debates about the geo-political uprisings in the Middle East) is automatically lying. There are exceptions for pretty much all of the above archetypes, and the entire presentation needs to be weighed up holistically. What I am saying is that anomalies might lead to an increase in beard-stroking and might evoke the spirit of a very sceptical Columbo inside me. 'There's just one last thing I don't understand . . . '

As well as all of the above, like any decent psychiatrist, as I listen to the subjects' words, I also undertake clandestine evaluation of their general countenance. Is the man who claims to be petrified of strangers and tortured by suicide-goading voices, goofing around with other inmates in the corridor before my interview? Is the woman who shrieks at the corner of her cell in terror, asking me if I can also see the floating baby-eating ogre, miraculously calm and coherent when later describing her alibi? Does the alleged rapist who claims he is too distressed to follow legal proceedings manage to correct me when I drop in a deliberate mistake about his previous offending history? Another consideration is the defendant's agenda. Those who are genuinely psychotic usually lack insight. It typically takes a while to tease their symptoms out of them. If I was truly suffering from paranoid thoughts, I would be more likely to mask them from a stranger than blurt them out. Contrast this with somebody faking mental illness who wants to be sectioned to a psychiatric hospital to dodge prison. They tend to try too hard to convince me. They are usually overdramatic and implausible. You don't find many leading Hollywood actors in prison. Actually, a quick Google search tells me that Robert Downey Jr, Mark Wahlberg, Sean Penn, Christian Slater, Kiefer Sutherland and Wesley Snipes have all done time. I take that back!

To me, of possibly greater significance is the intuition that all decent psychiatrists develop after seeing hundreds of cases. As well as giving me a few grey hairs, years of working regularly with offenders has helped me nurture a healthy scepticism. An intangible quality, a bit like the ability to sense that your partner is in a bad mood (but she doesn't want to talk about it), or when your four-year-old son is lying to you about who opened the packet of chocolate digestives (to pick two completely random examples).

Psychiatrists worth their salt develop a 'bullshit radar'; being around genuine psychopathology for such a long time allows us to pick up on little nuances when something is off.

Despite all these bold claims, I must admit that I have been hoodwinked. One case left me professionally embarrassed and made me the target of mild mockery from my colleagues.

Chapter 18

Hoodwinked

Around a year into my prison job in early 2018, I met Ms Stella Lawrence, the hoodwinker. She had racked up over thirty offences by her mid-twenties, mostly minor assaults as well as a litany of theft and shoplifting. Her life before prison was tumultuous and frankly tragic. After years of social service intervention due to a mother who prioritised booze over parenting, she had bounced around foster care. There were whispers of her being sexually abused by a step-brother but this did not appear to have been confirmed. She had garnered the attention of mental health services several times and had had more than a dozen assessments over the space of a few years, to ascertain whether she was ill enough to require sectioning to a psychiatric ward. Despite some conflicting views, the overriding opinion was that she had 'no acute mental illness'.

Reading through her notes, it was clear to me that everything about Stella's life was hectic and much was uncertain or unexplained. Mentions of being pregnant during one recent assessment, yet none two days later, during a follow-up review. Had she lost the baby? Did she fabricate carrying a child? She missed most appointments and was notably challenging to assess, either turning up drunk, refusing to engage or being very aggressive. There were also glaring inconsistencies in her presentations at times and suspicions that she was seeking medication.

Two months before our paths intertwined in prison, she was cowering in fear in an accident and emergency department one night, claiming she was hearing voices and seeing werewolves in the shadows. She was inches away from convincing a young, naive doctor to prescribe her some Valium (an addictive sedative which, as Chantelle pointed out, was the tipple of choice for housewives in the seventies), when a more senior doctor who knew Stella's previous shenanigans intervened. She immediately transformed into a gnarling angry beast (ironically, almost fulfilling her bogus claims of turning into a werewolf). When her demands for medication were rejected, she shouted at staff, kicked a door and left. Minutes later, she was seen laughing and joking outside the hospital with some well-known nefarious characters who had just brought in a friend who had been stabbed. The majority of assessments on Stella led to a conclusion of borderline (also known as emotionally unstable) personality disorder. Sufferers of this ailment often have impulsive, self-destructive behaviours, commit self-harm and use drugs. They are renowned for having unstable relationships. As I found out the hard way many years later, they are also not particularly pleased about having YouTube videos made about their diagnosis.

Stella was under my care for a few months in prison, serving a sentence for theft of a £4 bottle of wine from Morrisons and assault. A security guard saw her tuck the bottle under her jumper and confronted her. She responded by punching him in the face. As I had learnt on my first day on a secure unit, being thumped is never pleasant. I appreciated that the victim had every right to want justice, especially as it seemed that Stella was not mentally ill. Although her personality traits might have led to extreme emotional swings and explosive anger, there was no psychiatric reason that she wasn't in control of her actions, unlike the young man who punched me who was labouring under a Fregoli delusion and was convinced that I was an old school bully in disguise. But sometimes what is fair isn't always what is right. I couldn't help feel that regardless of what Stella may have deserved, repeated short prison sentences were not breaking the cycle. Arguably it was barely punishment, given that her life was probably more pleasant and definitely more structured in prison.

After the custodial officers had concerns about Stella laughing to herself, I invited her to my psychiatric clinics several times, though was snubbed. I saw her on a few occasions when she would curtly tell me to leave her alone, not unlike her Brazilian counterpart, Adriana, had done in the same wing of the same prison around seven months earlier. When she did engage, Stella asked odd questions and seemed fixated on irrelevant details. Once, she insisted that she wouldn't see me without first being sent an appointment letter and would not listen to my explanations that we didn't send these out in prison. Another time she asked me what the date was, then argued that she would only follow the lunar calendar, refusing to continue the conversation. This oddness was not barn-door psychosis, but my gut told me that something was awry.

Over the next few weeks, Stella's behaviour on the wing became increasingly concerning. From minor boundary breaches, such as not showering and intentionally running over her allotted phone time, to more serious infringements, like frequent arguments and fights with other inmates. As she refused a proper assessment, I was unable to determine if her cantankerous nature was a grumbling psychosis or just her natural personality or both. I was loath to prescribe an anti-psychotic unnecessarily.

Around two months into her incarceration, Stella spat at an officer and was promptly transferred to what was called the 'Separation and Care Unit' in our prison. This is also known formally as the segregation unit, in popular media as solitary confinement, and colloquially by the inmates as 'the hole'. A rose by any other name. The segregation unit is not too dissimilar to the seclusion room in secure hospitals, though as it's conceptualised as retribution rather than an extreme variant of treatment, there is less of an impetus to release inmates promptly. A prison inside a prison, solitary confinement lacks the usual hum of conversation, hustle and chatter of the main wings. With far smaller cells that are often locked for around twenty-three hours a day or more, and a ban on most possessions, there is nothing to do and very little contact with others. They look like bright off-white boxes with a huge door and big windows and have minimalistic décor. For some reason, they always conjured up images of futuristic hotel pods in a dystopian, vastly over-populated world. But maybe that's just me … Segregation is usually used to contain extremely violent inmates, but occasionally for their own protection. Some convicts are known to kick off with the guards intentionally to 'hide' in segregation, if they want to avoid others, due to gang beefs or drug debts.

In the segregation unit, Stella constantly rang her buzzer, yet when prison officers arrived she would either ignore them, shout at them or make demands for objects she knew she would not be allowed, such as a pen and paper. Again, this didn't make sense to me. It was purposeless and random.

I spoke to some colleagues in the Mental Health In-Reach Team (the prison equivalent of the hospital multi-disciplinary team), which was made up of a few nurses, numerous psychologists and another forensic psychiatrist. A few of the staff members who had worked there longer than me had had the dubious pleasure of looking after Stella in the past. They were convinced that she was not mentally ill and that her behaviours were all in her total control. I started to doubt them as Stella deteriorated even further. Her shouting became more frequent and had a sharper, animalistic, guttural edge to it. She stopped showering altogether and started throwing food around her cell. Yet she remained almost impossible to assess. She was placed on a 'two-man unlock', meaning I could only see her through a one-inch gap in her door, while flanked by two prison officers. She would speak so quietly I could barely hear her. I was convinced she was doing this intentionally, as her vocal cords had evidently surpassed functional expectations at other times.

My bullshit radar buzzed when Stella apparently began to hear voices. This is because she was having full-on conversations with another entity, in an exaggerated and obviously forced manner. Also, this only ever occurred when she knew I was in her vicinity and not when I was covertly observing her. I was clinically befuddled. The game was afoot. As well as my colleagues' admonishments, her fake voices and selective whispering all suggested that Stella was faking mental illness. Then her behaviour degenerated even further. After a fortnight in solitary confinement, she was shouting incessantly. She barely slept for two hours per night and was yelling the entire rest of the time. It was actually quite impressive. On the thankfully increasingly rare rough night when the kids woke me up with tears or nightmares (and once asking if I wanted to play Scrabble), even with four or five hours of sleep, I was a zombie the next day. I would feel like I needed a triple espresso and would look like I needed a defibrillator. I couldn't fathom how Stella could survive on two hours per night for weeks on end.

'You scoundrels will never take me alive!'

'My baby can never see me like this.'

'I won't tell him anything he doesn't already know.'

These were some of the nonsensical phrases she would repeat, often over and over again for hours, at times breaking into a melodic chant.

Stella had also taken to smearing faeces around her room.

As well as terrible feng shui, this was a classic sign of some-body being 'one sandwich short of a packed lunch', to quote Chantelle. Surely, this behaviour couldn't all be within her control? If it was, it begged the question: why was she doing this? When people manipulate, they have an objec-tive. Stella seemed indifferent to being admitted to hospital and much of her behaviour seemed totally pointless. In the end, I relented and prescribed her an anti-psychotic called olanzapine to take every evening, partially from clinical judgement and partially from desperation. Stella did take the medication but seemed indifferent to it. On a couple of occasions when her dose was accidentally omitted due to staff changeovers, she did not request it, suggesting that this wasn't drug-seeking behaviour.

Over the next fortnight, Stella's screams became increas-ingly more blood-curdling. I moved her to the healthcare unit where she could be observed by nurses. This in itself was a battle, with segregation unit staff feeling she needed to be punished, healthcare unit staff believing it was a waste of their oversubscribed resources, and my colleagues telling me that Stella was faking it. The medication made absolutely no difference, indicating that this was likely not mental illness.

One Monday morning, I was informed that her sentence was about to end and that she would be released in a mere two days. Stella was about to become one of those disap-pearing prisoners. I was flabbergasted that this woman who screamed for twenty-two hours a day, constantly banging, unwashed for weeks and with poo for wallpaper would be let out into the wide world. Surely it would be barbaric, negligent even, to release her in this state? Let alone her own potential for violence, I worried that she would be extremely vulnerable in the wilderness, particularly with the nefarious company she kept. I spoke to my colleagues again, including my more experienced forensic psychiatrist colleague in the prison and a senior psychologist. They insisted that Stella would be fine (well, at least by her standards) when the day came. Something niggled inside me. Against their advice, I arranged an assessment for her to be sectioned and wrote one of the two medical recommendations required. This involved summoning an approved mental health practitioner (a senior social worker who oversees detention under the Mental Health Act) and an independent doctor to meet Stella at the prison gates. As usual, this was a bureaucratic minefield with numerous NHS Trusts denying jurisdiction. After I finally pinned down the right service, they had to identify a free bed in a secure unit with only two days' notice. After several phone calls, emails, and a couple of mumbled profanities, I managed to organise the assessment. Getting it wrong would be professionally embarrassing as I had to convince the other parties that she was psychotic, despite numerous previous recent Mental Health Act assessments and my own colleagues concluding otherwise. I was very much going against the grain of medical opinion.

Stella was released on a day I was not working in the prison, so I was absent for the evaluation. I was told she was *absolutely fine*. She showered, dressed up nicely and had a completely normal, psychosis-free, sane, even pleasant conversation with the assessors. No chat of scoundrels or babies. I imagine the approved mental health practitioner and independent psychiatrist must have mumbled their own profanities about me for wasting their time.

I did get a gentle ribbing from my colleagues over lunch for the next few days. Maybe Stella had set the whole thing up just to mock and embarrass me. I never saw her again, so it has remained a mystery. I imagined her skipping away with a coy grin. Hats off to her and her commitment to the art of acting. She deserved an Oscar as much as I deserved the mockery.

Chapter 19

Deliberate Self-Harm and Burnt Bridges

The image of one face will always be etched into my memory, as well as pools of her blood. Ms Pamela Thorne was an overweight, unemployed woman in her thirties, with purple hair. She had severe borderline personality disorder and a learning disability. When provoked, her rage would erupt and she would internalise it by cutting herself.

Pamela spent her entire prison sentence in the healthcare unit. It was where the most severely mentally disturbed prisoners, such as the excessively vocal Stella, were housed. As there were more than five hundred women in the prison and only around a dozen spaces in the healthcare unit, the threshold to be admitted was high. The apex of insanity. Florid psychosis was the usual presentation. Around the same time that Pamela was there, I remember treating a woman who was convinced that we were all Russian spies, and another who believed that every time she showered, layers of invisible skin were shedding off her and she would eventually disintegrate. I also saw a couple of women with such severe disinhibition from acute mania, they would strip off in their cells. One even openly masturbated while laughing.

It was also where those who self-harmed horrifically, like Pamela, were placed for surveillance. This was beyond the bog-standard self-inflicted minor cuts and scratches to release frustration that were dealt with within the main prison. It was for those who were in real danger of death or life-changing injury. The healthcare unit was designed for treatment and observation, with regular nurses, visiting doctors and clinical equipment, unlike the segregation unit, which was for punishment. Nevertheless, they had stark similarities: the same wide empty corridors, the same blinking strip lights, the same eerie silence which would amplify the clapping of footsteps.

Naturally, many of the inmates there were the most disturbed in the entire prison and were potentially the riskiest. As in the segregation unit, many needed two or even three prison officers present to be allowed out of their cell. With staffing usually stretched, this meant that prisoners there often spent the majority of their days locked up. This contrasted with the main wings where the women in the prison I worked in were strongly encouraged to engage in education or work (in the café, garden or even the on-site call centre).

The first time I set foot in our healthcare unit, within a week of starting my prison job in 2017, I was struck by the sharp stench of detergent. I have since come to learn that dirty protests were not unusual, and some of the prisoners wouldn't shower. I was then struck by the familiarity of an inmate cleaner, mopping the floor. She was short, with a mousy pale face and darting shy blue-grey eyes. She smiled as I walked past. She looked eerily familiar. Over lunch I racked my brains. I must have assessed her before, but where? Then a colleague clarified that I had probably seen her in the newspapers. Mairead Philpott, who was jailed in 2013 for the manslaughter of her six children at her home in Derby in an intentional fire with her much-reviled husband, Mick, in a scheme to get a bigger council house.

I had dealt with the aftercare and support aspect of deliberate self-harm and suicide attempts ever since my psychiatry attachment at medical school. Risk-assessing people who may harm themselves is to a psychiatrist what dodging questions is to a politician, or avoiding tax is to a millionaire. But witnessing the immediate gory aftermath in prison was an eye-opener for me. I was already aware that there was a wide range of severity. Most inmates would scratch or cut themselves superficially, barely requiring a plaster. Sometimes, this was to relieve frustration or, sadly, in some establishments, a desperate attempt to propel themselves up the lengthy waiting list to see the mental health team. And then there was Pamela. Before her incarceration, she would carry around a Stanley knife and had, on at least three occasions, sliced her arm or her thighs so deeply that she needed blood transfusions and plastic surgery. In fact, she was imprisoned for waving around this very knife, which seemed a tad unfair as she had not seemingly intended to hurt anybody else. I suspect her repeated shenanigans in her hostel had left the carers who called the police at the end of their tether.

Pamela's borderline personality disorder cursed her with emotional instability, inappropriate anger, impulsiveness and frequent mood swings. It also led to explosive arguments with a number of strangers as well as people she knew well. Pamela's learning disability meant she couldn't process or express her frustrations in a healthy manner. This was already a lethal concoction, but in my view, a lifetime of being rejected had fanned the flames. This came from her family, who gave her up into foster care as a toddler, as well as society. Men would fool her with friendship and use her for sex. Mental health services were complicit too; she would frequently be turned away from the accident and emergency department due to her presentation being deemed 'secondary to social issues' (mental-health-professional coded language for 'go away, we're not able to help you'). When services occasionally relented and admitted Pamela to hospital, aside from containing her for a few days until her crisis had passed (usually an argument with her mother or her abusive on-and-off partner), there was little they could do for her in the long term. She also burnt her bridges on several psychiatric wards with her puerile behaviour, from absconding to stealing from other residents, to sneaking in cannabis and wine for the little night-time parties she assembled. This made arranging further admission even more arduous. The nurses didn't want her. This likely added to her sense of rejection and her inferiority complex.

Borderline personality disorder is notoriously difficult to treat, but was nigh on impossible with Pamela's low cognitive ability and, crucially, her refusal to engage. On our healthcare unit, she would use any means available to harm herself and had resourcefulness that would impress the A-Team. Obviously, sharp objects would be removed from her cell. She would somehow manage to hack away at her arms and legs with plastic cutlery and even a pencil. After being stitched up, Pamela would bite open her sutures and once even rubbed toilet water on her wounds so that they became infected. Triggers for this behaviour would include people telling her off or setting boundaries, not being allowed privileges such as attending an arts and crafts class within the therapy block of the main prison (which was withheld because other inmates there were bullying her) and upsetting phone calls to her damningly critical mother. Pamela would often frustrate and annoy staff with incessant demands and insults. 'Get that stinking basic bitch off the phone. It's my turn. My man needs to hear my sweet voice. He loves me,' I recall her once commenting. With her limited intelligence, I wondered what kind of environment she must have grown up in to pick up such insults and attitudes. Harsh responses from staff would trigger more self-harming. On one occasion, I was called out of a meeting for an emergency, after Pamela managed to cut herself particularly brutally because a prisoner had made fun of her by stuffing pillows up her blouse and doing an impression. By the time I got there, Pamela had already been carted off for stitches in an ambulance, and a few prison officers were literally mopping up blood from the floor of her cell and wiping splatters off the wall, dressed in hazmat suits. The scene looked like a gritty remix of a Beastie Boys video.

'I don't need a babysitter, I'm thirty-four. Leave me the fuck alone,' Pamela said during a particularly tense session with me and the psychologist, Tracey, the next day. 'And you cretins better let me onto A-block for my session this afternoon or I'll tear this bloody place up,' she added, raising her bandaged forearm. 'I'm gonna bleed all over the floor and my mum says she'll tell the newspapers that you left me to die.'

I looked over at Tracey. She rolled her eyes.

'Listen, Pamela, maybe we can think about a compromise,' I said. 'Perhaps you could earn an arts and crafts session next week if you could just have a look at this plan we agreed with you yesterday. Look, I've even printed it out for you. You could just . . . ' She snatched the paper out of my hand, screwed it up, popped it into her mouth then started rocking back and forth with her hands over her ears. It was going to be a long day.

In the end, we managed to contain Pamela's risk but it was a fraught and turbulent process. We had to challenge the attitude of some of the staff members dealing with her. They struggled to conceptualise her needy, hostile nature as a mental health issue that needed cotton-wool-wrapped warm words. Instead, they saw it as an insult to their authority, that needed razorblade-wrapped cutting insults. To be fair, this wasn't an unreasonable perspective, considering the aggressive microcosm these prison officers worked in, where bullies would rule the playground if given half an inch. To me, Pamela's cantankerous attitude was almost a form of deliberate self-harm in itself. She knew her stinging words would be reciprocated. She provoked others to punish her. By killing her with kindness we took away that power. Other strategies included allowing her occasional visits to creative therapy classes escorted by a nurse and limiting the length of phone calls to her mother, which also had to be observed. Tracey managed to form a trusting bond and had to hold psychotherapy sessions with Pamela at least once a day, sometimes twice, to talk through her accumulating emotions and frustrations, thereby allowing a cathartic dissipation.

Credit to Tracey, who not only came up with the entire plan, but opened my eyes. Busy and distracted with other prisoners and focused on the practicalities of Pamela's self-harm, I had barely considered *why* Pamela was acting out until Tracey encouraged me to. Pamela was depressed at times. That was a given. But I also ruminated on Pamela's position in life; she had been ignored or rejected by so many (parents, partners, accommodation staff, doctors, nurses) and harboured an inferiority complex fuelled by her learning disability. In this context, it seemed like hurting herself was her way of escalating behaviour so she could no longer be invisible. She was also upping the ante for a sense of control. All those decisions by authorities had been made without her input, knowledge and possibly to some degree, given her pathologically low IQ, her understanding. She had been moved in and out of foster homes, and in and out of psychiatric wards. Her Stanley knife was a tool to show others she was in charge.

I think we did a great job considering the circumstances. We reduced Pamela's self-harming behaviour from almost daily to once or twice a month. The cost, however, was an unprecedented and perhaps unjustifiable proportion of time and manpower. This removed me, Tracey and her psychologist colleagues, nurses and officers away from being available to support many other very unwell patients within the prison. Predictably, this led to discontent from many of Pamela's peers and even staff members.

I shudder to think how Pamela fared after her release back into her chaotic and unsupported life. Especially as she had also alienated herself from community services (such as hostels, shelters and benefits offices) due to her exceptionally insolent behaviour. We could barely manage her when she was contained behind bars and under our almost-constant supervision. I still half expect to see an article about her suicide in a newspaper, some day. Perhaps it would be intentional, or perhaps she would continue to tempt fate and eventually take it too far. If and when that article ever comes, I imagine it will be riddled with criticisms of how she was failed by mental health services.

Although usually far less dramatic, self-harm is a colossal problem in prison. In fact, it is a leading cause of morbidity in inmates; the annual prevalence has been estimated in England and Wales to be 5 to 6 per cent in men and 20 to 24 per cent in women, which greatly exceeds the less than 1 per cent of adults in the general population.* This is by no means a problem isolated in our fair island. A recent international study conducted on suicide rates between 2011 and 2014 in twenty-four high-income countries in Europe, Australasia, and North America concluded that this risk

---

* https://www.thelancet.com/journals/lancet/article/PIIS0140-6736(13)62118-2/fulltext

increased at least three-fold for male prisoners and at least nine times for females, compared to the general population. Interestingly, the countries with the lowest rates of prisoners taking their own lives were the USA, Poland and Canada, and the countries with the highest rates were Norway and France.[*]

Relevant influences include psychiatric diagnoses, particularly major depression and borderline personality disorder, as well as prison-specific environmental risk factors such as solitary confinement, and experiencing sexual or physical victimisation. In addition to the psychiatrists, psychologists and nurses, we recruit inmates to address this dire problem. Senior prisoners are trained as 'listeners' by the Samaritans to give counselling to their particularly distressed peers. For my YouTube channel, I interviewed Chris Atkins, a reporter who was found guilty on two counts of 'conspiracy to cheat the public revenue, theft and fraud' and sentenced to five years in jail in 2016. He left me flabbergasted with tales of his experience as a listener. He was often placed in a cell with extremely disturbed inmates, some floridly psychotic, who clearly should have been in hospital. Chris has described the grisly, tragic and sometimes amusing anecdotes from his time behind bars in his book, *A Bit of a Stretch*.

Another safeguard in the UK is the Assessment, Care in Custody and Teamwork (ACCT) process, which involves regular one-to-one sessions, heightened observation of the subject, regular support sessions and reviews by a large

---

* https://www.thelancet.com/journals/lanpsy/article/PIIS2215-0366(17)30430-3/fulltext

multi-disciplinary team. Although this is a welcome step, it does have weaknesses. Inmates who truly wish to kill themselves will mask their true despondency to prevent interference. Also, many prisoners are embarrassed about the stigma of being seen to be mentally ill, especially in the hyper-macho prison culture where the weak are easy prey.

Incidentally, threatening deliberate self-harm or suicide was a common tactic for many defendants I saw for psychiatric assessments on behalf of the court during their trial. 'If you don't section me, I swear I'll kill myself, doctor,' is a phrase I still hear at least once every couple of months. This is very rarely a successful ploy to dodge prison for a number of reasons. Firstly, prisons are actually equipped with the aforementioned (admittedly imperfect) systems for dealing with self-harmers. Secondly, if it worked, the floodgates would open with a huge proportion of those facing trial worming their way out of prison into hospital on false pretences, potentially blocking beds for those who genuinely needed them. Also, there is potentially no end in sight for somebody who is suicidal in the long term, so the savvy prisoner could claim this for the entirety of their sentence.

Having said that, underestimating suicide risk can also have disastrous consequences. A case that sent shockwaves through the world of forensic psychiatry was the suicide of thirty-two-year-old Sarah Reed in Holloway Prison, north London in early 2016. Reed had a history of mental health issues and purportedly suffered from bulimia, paranoid schizophrenia and substance abuse. Her problems stemmed from the death of her baby daughter in 2003. In 2012, Reed who was mixed-race was the victim of a severe attack by a white police officer, and suffered two broken ribs. She was waiting to be assessed in prison to see if she was mentally fit to plead after being charged with assaulting a nurse in a secure psychiatric unit. She had been waiting in prison for nine weeks for an assessment, but it never came. On 11 January 2016, Reed was found to be unresponsive on her prison bed with strips of linen around her neck. The inquest found that a series of failures such as not treating her in a timely manner, an unacceptable number of cancelled visits by staff, not being allowed to have baths or showers and at times not even being provided with food or water because staff felt she was so mentally unwell that she couldn't be approached. This was obviously big news within our female prison, and hammered home to me how essential thorough risk assessments are.

Another more recent and more controversial prison suicide was Jeffrey Epstein's. He was charged with sex trafficking in July 2019 and while awaiting trial, facing a potential forty-five years in federal prison, was found dead in a jail in New York. In the UK people are remanded in prisons along with sentenced inmates, whereas in America they are held in jails, and sent to prisons if found guilty. Epstein, who had been on suicide watch after being found unconscious with marks on his neck three weeks earlier, was deemed no longer at risk a few days before his death. An attorney general severely criticised his management in jail. It is alleged that guards failed to check on him every thirty minutes, as protocol requires. That would make even Prince Andrew sweat. It is well known that jails in America are often understaffed, overcrowded, and plagued with mental illnesses. A third of deaths within jails are caused by suicide, a rate far higher than that in prisons. Every year, more than three hundred people die by suicide in jails in the States. A quarter of these people kill themselves in the first twenty-four hours of incarceration, and half die within two weeks. A 2010 study from the Department of Justice showed that 38 per cent of those who die by suicide in jails are mentally ill and 34 per cent have a history of suicidal behaviour. Yet the study revealed that regular suicide prevention training for staff wasn't provided in two-thirds of the jails examined. Even when treatment is available in theory, it tends to be hard to access and inadequate.

One fairly harrowing case of mine and possibly the most extreme version of non-suicidal deliberate self-harm that I can imagine, was a man who removed his own eyeballs in prison. This was never on my wish list of scenarios entering medical school as a fresh-faced eighteen-year-old. It was a breach of duty assessment for a civil court case that I was instructed for (as opposed to a criminal case). Mr Rex Peterson was serving a relatively short sentence for arson. While drunk, he started a fire in his ex-girlfriend's garage, which was empty at the time. Apparently, some false rumours spread around the inmates that he was a paedophile and that an innocent girl was killed in the blaze: neither of which were true. For a group of men who purportedly honour omertà (the mafia vow of silence), in my experience, prisoners gossip and rumour-monger more than teenage schoolgirls.

Rex was in his fifties with a side parting, thick specs

and a pronounced limp from polio as a child. He was not built for prison. He received some intimidating comments, suspicious looks and menacing threats once the rumours started spreading. For the first few weeks of his incarceration, he was also withdrawing from alcohol, which he had used daily for years. This didn't exactly help his paranoia and agitation. Rex became psychotic for the first time in his life, which is highly unusual for someone his age. Stress was clearly the trigger. He became convinced that the other inmates wanted to eat his eyeballs to release superhuman strength so they could smash through the walls to escape. He was in constant fear of being attacked, so he decided to pre-emptively remove them himself with a pen. He was locked in a cell in the segregation unit when this happened. The nurses called for backup but by the time the officers arrived and 'kitted up' with riot gear, the deed had been done. When I assessed Rex two years later, my evaluation focused on whether the standard of assessment and treatment offered by the mental health team had been adequate and whether this had led to the gruesome outcome (it is far more complex than that, and several strict medico-legal tests need to be applied, but that is perhaps for another book).

When I interviewed Rex, his presentation was unexpected. He'd been released from prison and had been living in a care home due to his blindness. His psychosis had fully resolved. He came across as an intelligent, articulate and highly capable man. And yes, he wore sunglasses for the whole assessment. According to him, not only had the nurses intentionally delayed going to his cell to restrain him when he was gouging out his eyes, but they were actually goading him and calling him a paedophile. With the evidence provided to me, including various witness statements by staff, this seemed to be untrue. I could only presume they were delusional beliefs.

I found that there were certainly some inadequacies with the care Rex was provided behind bars, including a very rudimentary, seemingly rushed assessment by a nurse (the timing, late on a Friday afternoon, was probably a contributory factor), which lacked a deep exploration of all his risk factors. One area I was critical of was that Rex had been banging his head against his cell door a week before the event, causing some bruising. There was no consideration of why he did this or if anything had changed to reassure staff it would not occur again, thus falling short of the basic standards of a risk assessment, in my opinion. Despite all of this, I concluded that Rex's psychosis escalated so rapidly and he had masked his intentions so effectively that his extreme actions could not have realistically been predicted or prevented.

Chapter 20

Hurdles for a Prison Psychiatrist

Working in this prison role, I couldn't avoid pondering about why mental illness is so rife in those incarcerated at Her Majesty's pleasure. The obvious connection is the environment of prison itself. Restricted freedom, isolation, being separated from friends and family, bullying and the constant threat of violence would affect most people's mood, regardless of whether they suffered from mental illness or not. But there are other factors at play. Firstly, there are demographics which work as confounding factors. As was clearly laid out within the inmates' records I would read before I assessed them in clinic, many of the same disadvantages in life (poverty, joblessness, homelessness, previous trauma, felonious peers and drug abuse) that lead people to crime also predispose to a whole host of mental illnesses.

It shames me to say this as a forensic psychiatrist, but another contributory factor which cannot be overlooked is the abysmal access to psychiatric care in some (though not all) UK prisons. My comrades are simply overburdened. The large female prison I worked in was exceptionally well resourced and the majority of the psychiatrically disturbed were assessed and offered treatment, promptly. However, most of the others that I visited for external assessments on behalf of the court painted a much bleaker picture. I would see dishevelled, desolate, extremely ill men who had been waiting weeks to see a doctor. The kind of mumbling, agitated, disturbed individuals that many of us would give a wide berth on the street would be roaming around in penitentiaries with alarming frequency. Not only was there a deficit of mental health staff to deal with the caseload and continuous flow of fresh inmates, but in some establishments, officers were so sparse that prisoners were barely allowed out of their cells. Psychosis would fester. Out of sight, out of mind. I may have been working in a free-range prison, but I felt uncomfortable visiting the battery-cage equivalent.

I once met an Albanian man named Flamur, with long hair and potholed skin, in a prison in Oxfordshire for a one-off assessment in the autumn of 2018. He was facing a charge of possessing a blade in a public place and common assault. It is alleged that outside a Tube station, the victim, a stranger, walked past, and with no warning, Flamur punched him multiple times in the chest. A passer-by provided a statement, which corroborated this account. CCTV footage showed the attack and also revealed that he punched a second random member of the public, also in the chest. The case papers reported that when Flamur was arrested, a knife was found on him, which thankfully he didn't use. When interviewed by police, he reportedly made some odd comments. He stated that he carried a knife for protection and had 'not one single regret for punching those guys. They were talking about drilling me in the head. They think they can just threaten me and there will be no consequences.'

When I saw him, Flamur was gaunt and pale, with huge bags under his eyes. He was hyperventilating, nervous and sweaty. Even his pulse was raised (almost impossible to fake, unless you are David Blaine). He was suspicious that his food was being poisoned by the FBI, though these ideas were not quite fixed enough to be delusions. He had a level of insight and could be reasoned with.

'Yeah, you're probably right, doctor. Poisoning me does seem a little far-fetched.'

'And it doesn't really make sense that the FBI would be investigating you here in Oxfordshire,' I proposed.

He rubbed his cheeks and nodded slowly. 'When you put it like that, fair point.'

In my court report, I opined that Flamur was developing a gradual psychosis on the background of a severe anxiety. I explained he was fit to plead and did not quite meet the criteria for hospital transfer, though should be offered anti-psychotics and followed-up regularly by the prison mental health team should he deteriorate further.

Almost a year later, his solicitor asked me to re-assess him. Flamur was barely recognisable. He was emaciated, paler, haggard and scruffier. His head was shaved. He seemed to have been largely ignored in prison, and as a result, his psychosis had intensified. He could barely follow my words due to pronounced thought block (a rare symptom, when the person's speech is suddenly interrupted by silences that may last around a minute, after which, they will speak about an unrelated subject). I used the words 'skeletal' and 'ghostly' in my second court report: phrases that had not previously entered my psychiatric vernacular. When I relayed my concerns to the prison mental health team, they seemed convinced he was malingering. He was under their jurisdiction. Aside from alerting the team and the court, there was little I could do. I had to accept that as I had only two snapshot assessments of Flamur, and they had the benefit of assessing him longitudinally, their observations trumped mine. The words of a great philosopher rang through my head. *Let it go.*

Another crippling disadvantage was that even when prisoners came to the attention of mental health teams in prisons like ours, we were limited in our arsenal of treatment. Medications cannot be enforced in injectable form under the Mental Health Act as they can in hospital. So, if patients without insight refused tablets, all we could do was refer them on to secure psychiatric units. In fact, we were often at the mercy of our counterparts in hospitals. The healthcare unit functioned like a holding space for the numerous floridly psychotic women who were on a long waiting list to be transferred. To paraphrase the Bible, it was easier for a camel to go through the eye of a needle than to admit these patients under the various criminal sections of the Act. This process was by far the most frustrating aspect of my job. It was a postcode lottery. The leafy counties generally had shorter waiting lists: perhaps a week or two. But for major cities, especially London, these were longer and there was often resistance from the services that I made referrals to. For starters, there were frequent concerted efforts to denounce patients as belonging to another jurisdiction (a depressingly recurring theme in mental health organisations, reminiscent of my struggles in discharging Jordan). 'Not our problem,' was the message I would read between the lines of the responses I received. I quickly learnt that even when the catchment area was clear, it could be a challenge to find the contact details to make the referral in the first place. Whereas the various NHS Mental Health Trust websites all had an excess of photos of patients and nurses smiling and staring off into the distance, very few had relevant contact details. On a few occasions, I had to send the required information by fax. I once sent a referral by email along with around two hundred pages of the inmate's medical notes, only to be asked to print everything and fax it over. What next? Referral via carrier pigeon?

Another hurdle in providing psychiatric care for inmates who desperately needed it, it must be said, was the attitude of some (though not all) prison officers. For some offenders, particularly those with more contemptuous offences, the prison guards seemed to discourage or even actively prevent mental health intervention. I remember arranging an assessment of a suspected paedophile in a prison in south London only to be told in the visitors' hall that he had refused to leave his cell to attend our appointment. I was later told by his solicitor that this was simply untrue; he hadn't been informed of my arrival. I re-booked my visit two weeks later and the same thing happened. In the end, the judge had to adjourn the case and speak to the prison governor to quash any further hiccups. Aside from the inconvenience this caused me in wasted journeys, London traffic, parking-meter fees and time getting through prison security, this must have meddled with justice by the forced rescheduling of his court case, which would inevitably have had a knock-on effect for other trials. The irony was that my eventual conclusion (that the prisoner didn't have significant mental health problems and therefore didn't need hospitalisation), was probably what the prison officers wanted anyway. Although obviously, my conclusions were objective and based on the alleged paedophile's clinical presentation and not on the nature of his crimes.

Being non-judgemental is an essential characteristic of a decent forensic psychiatrist. It is an area that some of my peers struggle with more than others. When it comes to assessing and treating mental illness, we should approach the predatory paedophile with the same level of professionalism and integrity as the victim of domestic abuse. I was able to demarcate and separate the prisoner's mental health needs from the potentially hideous nature of his or her crimes. To do this, I had to have faith that the criminal justice system would fairly adjudge and punish the individual. If this was the case, then as a doctor I shouldn't want to add to the perpetrator's misery by withholding or minimising psychiatric treatment or writing an overly critical court report. I occasionally saw my colleagues do this, or the opposite, like the experienced senior consultant forensic psychiatrist who, in my opinion, allowed Daryna's dramatic, tearful presentation to cloud his judgement. I had heard of prison officers intentionally leaking the nature of perpetrators' crimes (usually sexual assault, sometimes against children) or even their profession (like an ex-policeman), so that the individual would be subjected to a supplementary form of justice from the other inmates.

Outside of my part-time role in this prison, I was being regularly instructed to carry out independent assessments in others. Perhaps unfairly and even a little smugly, I would compare our relatively high standards to these other establishments. A case that jumps out from my memory is of visiting a prison in Nottinghamshire. This was for another civil, not a criminal, court case. The person I was assessing was already fifteen years into a twenty-five-year stretch (for killing a man when their two rival football hooligan firms clashed) when I interviewed him. He was suing the prison estate for not keeping him safe and my assessment was for potential clinical negligence, that is, evaluating the standard of the treatment he received. He was a thin, wiry, bald man with an unfathomably thick Scouse accent (I genuinely thought he was speaking another language, possibly Klingon, for the first minute). His name was Mr George Spriggs and although I have no intention of perpetuating a Scouse stereotype, he literally asked me to call him Sprigzy.

There was apparently a gang of youths on the landing of his wing who pedalled Spice to other prisoners then demanded extortionate payments from them into an external bank account. Spice started off as a 'legal high', a laboratory-engineered substance that claimed to mimic the effects of cannabis, though within its short existence of less than a decade, it has perpetuated pandemonium within the prison service. It gained popularity because it is cheap, evades most standard urine drug tests and can be easily snuck in. One form exists in a spray and has been found on children's paintings that have made it through security. I've never understood the appeal of Spice. I'm no stranger to festivals and raves, and have seen many a gurning stranger prance around topless. But they look like they're having a great time. A little party for one in their heads. Prisoners that I've witnessed on Spice have always seemed tremendously agitated, and some have become floridly psychotic.

According to Sprigzy, this gang regularly beat up their prey and had even shattered an eye socket. Sprigzy felt compelled to intervene and therefore told a visiting rabbi. This rabbi arranged a meeting with a prison officer to pass on information about the culprits and their operation. Apparently, after the meeting, another prisoner in the chapel had overheard the officer asking the rabbi to clarify some things Sprigzy had told them both. Sprigzy was labelled as a snitch and a campaign of hate started against him. He was moved to a different prison wing for his own protection, but the aggressors apparently put a bounty on his head. 'Three grams of Spice for anybody who would smash me up. Bonus two grams if they put me in the hospital,' as he put it, a little indelicately. He moved prison twice and was even transferred to a vulnerable prisoners' wing, usually reserved for sex offenders. But his reputation as a snitch and the lust for revenge followed him like a rotten stink.

Sprigzy was punched on around six separate occasions and had his face slashed, actualising that common phrase in the criminal world, 'snitches get stitches'. When he was locked up all day for his own protection, he had urine, faeces and boiling water squirted through the hatch of his door. I couldn't help feel a pang of pity when he reported this to me. He may have taken a life, but he was already paying his debt to society and seemed to be being targeted due to his own altruism. Though I also caught myself wondering about the ergonomics of how one would load up said bottle with faecal matter, and the consequences of making a mistake. I suppose in some places you can never have too much detergent. Sprigzy even needed to have his food delivered pre-packed by prison officers as excrement was once found in it (shepherd's pie, which I suppose was quite an effective camouflage). From my assessment, I concluded that Sprigzy had developed an adjustment disorder, which can be thought of as an acute period of depression or anxiety caused by certain traumatic circumstances. In addition, I deemed that he was suffering from a specific phobia. This is a persistent and excessive fear of an object or situation. In Sprigzy's case, he had a phobia of being assaulted. This could be differentiated from the average person's reluctance to being hurt (kinky masochists aside) by Sprigzy's constant obsession and rumination over this and the immense effect it was having on his daily functioning.

By the time I saw Sprigzy, he was a paranoid nervous wreck. He was barely sleeping or eating and was in a state of pathological terror. Once again, as I was undertaking a one-off assessment on behalf of the court, he was not under my jurisdiction. I gave the prison mental health team advice on medication options. Thankfully, unlike in Flamur's case, they were open to my recommendations. Aside from this,

I was powerless to improve Sprigzy's situation or offer him any protection. I just hoped that my evidence advancing his civil court case would be some consolation.

Ethics, fairness, retribution, justice, the balance of power and misuse of authority were thoughts that would preoccupy me in a way I had never considered before my prison job. Was I part of a system that abused its position on occasion? Or was I overthinking things?

Working behind bars certainly quenched the thirst I had developed. I was seeing a large caseload with numerous new and disparate presentations every week. The pace kept me stimulated and the paperwork was far more manageable than in hospital and didn't make me fantasise about slamming my head through my computer, to the same degree.

Another pleasant benefit was the volume of medico-legal work. Solicitors and courts approached me to write court reports on some inmates who were on remand in my prison. As much as diagnosing and treating offenders was interesting, the more of this expert witness work I took on, the more I explored *why* people committed crimes. What drove them to take what didn't belong to them. To inflict pain on strangers and even those they supposedly loved. I already had a morbid fascination with crime and I found myself drifting towards the recent spate of true crime and serial killer documentaries. I was also dabbling in opinion pieces for various newspapers and magazines, commenting on the crossroads of mental illness and offending. Analysing what leads to violence was a natural progression for me.

When I started my two-year stint of working in a prison in 2017, I was taking on one or two medico-legal assignments per month. By the time I had finished, that had increased threefold. And with it, my confidence blossomed. Chasing the first high from my Old Bailey experience giving evidence in Yasmin's trial, I gravitated to the more complicated, uncertain and gruesome cases, that I had previously been apprehensive about. A schizophrenic father who beheaded his own baby. A man with drug-induced psychosis who broke into a stranger's house, urinated in the bedroom then jumped out of the window. A serial rapist who claimed to have post-traumatic stress disorder.

With my natural pathological impatience, I wanted to sink my teeth deeper into this type of work. The most straightforward way to do this would have been to continue my gradual ascent. However, to be a real player in the expert witness field usually takes years or even decades. Instead, I opted for the bolder option of changing jobs to work in a court psychiatrist role for the NHS for two days per week, to free up even more time for my medico-legal reports. This was a risk because whereas the NHS work was contracted and secure, medico-legal work was ad hoc and unpredictable. If for some reason the work dried up, my wallet would emaciate.

I tried to seek advice from psychiatrists experienced in this arena, but I hit a wall. It's a well-known secret that experts are somewhat cagey about their work. It's a competitive field and my rivals wouldn't want a young, gold-toothed whippersnapper swooping in and potentially under-quoting them to solicitors. To them, the pool of experts was already spilling over, especially around London. When I did get advice from seniors who didn't take on expert witness work, it was unequivocal. Medico-legal work is too unpredictable. By all means, continue doing it alongside your permanent role, but you cannot rely on it as a source of income. I did the opposite. I categorically believed that they were giving me what they considered the best advice, but I just saw things differently. Although it was a turbulent market, if I dedicated my time and efforts (via textbooks, courses and qualifications), I believed it was possible to dominate it. I've always understood that big risks in life are fine as long as they are calculated. I ignored the advice of my colleagues and I bet on myself.

Part Three

Courtrooms

Chapter 21

Cowboy Experts

The stabilisers were off and I finally felt ready to be a dedicated freelance expert witness. Instead of fitting in the odd case around other work, from now on this would be my jam. With my two and a half years within a secure psychiatric hospital as a consultant and another two years in a prison, on top of more than a decade of working and training since graduating medical school, my teeth had been sharpened. As well as my part-time NHS court diversion role, I had set up my own limited company, Sigma Delta Psychiatry Expertise, at the beginning of 2019. I even had business cards printed out – what could be more legit than that? Taking the plunge to carve this niche out for myself has been one of my best career moves. It has gifted me some of my most extreme, mind-blowing, heart-breaking and bizarre cases.

As an expert witness, I advise the courts of law on specific medico-legal issues for individual defendants during their trial. As well as assessing the accused and reading their medical notes, this work often involves sifting through evidence, which sometimes amounts to hundreds or even thousands of pages. Caffeine-fuelled, I trawl through witness statements, police interview transcripts and CCTV footage. I search for clues to ascertain the culprit's mental state during their alleged offences and whether this correlates with psychiatric illness. As well as diagnosing, I recommend the most appropriate and safest environment for the individual to be treated in (community, prison or hospital). I advise on how to reduce their future potential risks of violence and offending. I also distil the genuinely mentally ill from the exaggerators, the fabricators, the chancers, the time-wasters and the hustlers. I am occasionally thwarted, like in the case of Daryna.

For my first case under the umbrella of my limited company, the defendant was an ex-soldier, named Mr Jake Gove. He had developed post-traumatic stress disorder from witnessing two of his squad members being blown up by a landmine in Afghanistan. Seven years later, he was charged with racially aggravated assault. Jake was refused alcohol in his local corner shop because he was stumbling around, knocking items over. He swore at the shopkeeper, shouted some racial slurs, grabbed a bottle of vodka from behind the counter and smashed it over the victim's head. Another psychiatrist had carried out a previous assessment on behalf of the defence team. A poor effort, in my view (two stars). He claimed that Jake's PTSD could have triggered a flashback which made him agitated and lash out. Sure, that's *possible*, I thought, but did it *actually happen*? They barely explored the accused's mental state and did not elicit a detailed depiction of his specific experiences at the time. What constituted this supposed flashback? Was Jake actually re-living the trauma of the bomb? Was there a trigger that reminded him of the incident? What was his reality at the exact moment of the offence? Did he, for example, genuinely believe the shop-keeper was an Afghan rebel and his own life was in danger?

The psychiatrist omitted to mention that the defendant was drunk, despite the arresting officers commenting on the stench of alcohol in their witness statements and the custody sergeant deciding to wait two days before the police interview to allow Jake to sober up. Therefore, disinhibition, impulsivity and poor judgement could have driven the offence. To me, this was a far more logical and likely explanation for the assault than mid-flashback lashing out. Not even considering it proved that this was not a balanced and objective opinion. I expressed this in my own report. The judge agreed and threw out the other expert's evidence. As per my recommendation, Jake narrowly avoided a custodial sentence and had to attend alcohol rehabilitation as a condition of his community order. I was satisfied that justice had been served, but also felt uneasy. What would the outcome have been if the Crown Prosecution Service had not smelt a rat and asked for a second opinion? Or if the judge had accepted the first expert's evidence at face value, not appreciating the clinical intricacies of PTSD? This was my introduction to the concept of the 'cowboy expert'.

The expert witness game can be quite lucrative and I have heard of highly decorated medical veterans being paid upwards of £10,000 for a single case (though I myself have never reached these dizzying heights). Like flies to faeces, this remuneration can attract dodgy experts. To qualify in every sub-specialty of psychiatry in the UK, and indeed in every faction of medicine, there are years of focused training, multiple assessments and more hoops to jump through than at Crufts. However, much to my initial surprise, the medico-legal expert witness field is almost lawless. Courses and qualifications do exist, but the former are voluntary and the latter are often meaningless. Perhaps because this work is not seen as providing care to the sick but rather as greasing the wheels of justice, there is no overriding governing body, such as the Royal College of Psychiatrists and the General Medical Council in the UK, whose professional standards I am held accountable to (and whose extortionate annual membership fees I am privileged to pay). There is therefore no enforced quality control. This leads to some 'cowboy experts' who twist the evidence of their cases to reach spurious conclusions. These charlatans always deduce findings that would benefit the party who instructed them, which happens to be the same party who signs their cheques. Experts are supposed to write neutral, objective reports only for the benefit of the court, and not to unilaterally advantage the prosecution or defence (in a criminal case) or the claimant or defendant (in a civil case).

When making my transition into expert witness work, I read about a couple of high-profile cases where experts had been chastised by judges. As a modern-day equivalent of being trapped in stocks and having rotten veg thrown at them, these culprits and their blunders are widely publicised in various professional blogs and websites. I must admit a smug satisfaction in reading these. A kind of vindication for justice. Not only do these embarrassments bring the whole field into disrepute, and make a mockery of the system, but more importantly, they hurt the individuals who are involved in the court cases, both perpetrators and victims. As well as being yelled at by a stern figure in a wig, the potential consequences of gross incompetency include having to pay wasted court costs, which could easily reach tens of thousands of pounds. In more serious cases, there might be a claim of professional negligence against the expert. The culprit may even be referred by their judge to their professional body for investigation. One widely promulgated case was that of Dr Asef Zafar, whose professional misdemeanours went even further and resulted in a charge of contempt of court in 2018.

Dr Zafar was a GP, based in Surrey, who had a successful medico-legal practice, specialising in low-value personal injury claims. He was able to streamline the process of examining a patient and producing a report to within fifteen minutes: an indication to me that he had either achieved superhuman speed or was cutting corners. He purportedly produced around five thousand reports a year, earning him a staggering income of £350,000. Dr Zafar's downfall transpired when he examined a whiplash victim and in his court report proposed that the patient had made a full recovery. The victim complained to his solicitor, stating that he had ongoing symptoms of neck, shoulder and wrist pain. The solicitor apparently wrote to Dr Zafar asking him to review his notes and produce an amended report, nudging him to opine that recovery was likely to take six to eight months, which would have fattened up the compensation heading towards the victim. Dr Zafar produced a revised report with the requested changes, without even undergoing a further examination of the client and with no clinical basis. This document had the same date as the original and gave no indication that there had been a previous version, despite the substantial changes. A paralegal accidentally included the original report in the trial bundle, which made its way to the judge, who now had two conflicting reports. It appeared that Dr Zafar tried to wriggle his way out of this tangled web by lying, stating that the original report was correct and the revised version had been produced without his consent, though he later retracted this. The insurance company that was due to pay the compensation issued a claim for contempt of court against Dr Zafar and the instructing solicitor. The High Court found that the doctor had gone way beyond negligence and this was compounded by his dishonest cover-up attempt. Dr Zafar was sentenced to six months in prison, suspended for two years. The Court of Appeal thought that his sentence was unduly lenient, though they did not impose a more severe one. He's no Harold Shipman, but for a supposed pillar of the community, overseeing the health and well-being of the masses, it's not a good look.

Another cautionary tale, which sent reverberations across expert witness circles and made it into a few of my textbooks, was that of Professor Sir Roy Meadow. His errors were seemingly driven by misplaced confidence rather than greed. In 1999, a solicitor named Sally Clark was tried at Chester Crown Court, in northwest England, for allegedly murdering her two babies. One died at the age of eleven weeks and the other at eight weeks. Expert medical opinion was divided; several leading paediatricians testified that the deaths were probably natural, though experts acting for the prosecution diagnosed that the babies had been shaken to death or smothered. Professor Meadow, who was a renowned and highly respected paediatrician, claimed to have uncovered eighty-one apparent cot deaths which were in fact murder. He testified that the odds against two cot deaths occurring in the same family was one in 73 million and was only likely to occur once every hundred years in England, Scotland and Wales. He went way beyond his expertise to make a glib statistical analysis, comparing this to successfully backing an eighty to one outsider at the Grand National for four successive years. The jury returned a guilty verdict and Sally Clark was sent to prison.

Afterwards, Professor Meadow received criticism from professional statisticians over his calculation. Some said that he had made the assumption that cot death cases within families were statistically independent, thereby not taking into account other factors, such as the potential existence of conditions specific to individual families (e.g. a hypothesised 'cot death gene' which would make some offspring genetically vulnerable). He had also not considered that some families might have specific conditions that would increase the probability of this. Some mathematicians even estimated that taking these factors into account, the true odds may have been greater than two to one in favour of the death not being murder, thereby demonstrating Clark's innocence. To the shock of many public figures, including expert statisticians, as well as some legal professionals, a Court of Appeal case in 2000 did not overturn the murder conviction. However, shortly afterwards a campaigning lawyer obtained new evidence from another expert witness in the original case, a pathologist, who had failed to disclose other evidence from medical tests. This indicated that the second child had died from a bacterial infection and not from smothering as the prosecution had claimed. A second appeal was launched and Sally Clark was vindicated. Tragically, she died in March 2007 from accidental acute alcohol intoxication. She apparently never recovered from the psychological trauma from the experience of her two babies' deaths and then being unjustly convicted of murder and imprisoned, which led to her also being separated from her third infant. The repercussions of this bled into a backlog of Professor Meadow's previous cases, including other mothers previously convicted of murdering their babies on his evidence being freed on appeal. Eventually, Professor Meadow was effectively barred from court work and investigated by the General Medical Council (an impartial public body that regulates all doctors in the UK) for alleged professional misconduct. This case became even more convoluted as the General Medical Council initially struck off Professor Meadow, though he appealed to the High Court which in February 2006 ruled in his favour. The General Medical Council appealed to the Court of Appeal but in October 2006 the court upheld that Meadow was not guilty of those charges. Unsurprisingly, it damaged his reputation irreversibly, and he never shook off the stench of the devastating consequences of his professional arrogance. When I first heard about this, the thought of calamitous Sally Clark, who had spent over three years in prison, moved me. Over a decade later, I made a YouTube video about her to educate and warn the public. To date, it remains one of the most viewed episodes on my channel.

Although the majority of the medico-legal reports I come across are decent, or at least acceptable, occasionally I see some that frankly blemish the profession. This may be rare, but as Professor Meadow's case illustrates, the potential consequences can be devastating: sending an innocent person to prison, seemingly the exact opposite of letting someone get away with murder.

Another pet peeve of mine that I would see with alarming frequency was psychiatrists who literally 'cut and paste' vast swathes of other reports into their own, instead of absorbing and summarising information to help guide the court. Their resultant documents would read like a very dull, rambling biography rather than a helpful psychiatric opinion. Another common blunder was the overuse of psychiatric jargon without explanation for the layman. These reports were inaccessible to non-medically-trained court professionals and negated the whole point of recruiting an expert in the first place. I have even seen, on one occasion, a second expert being brought in to translate the findings of the first. This is a monumental waste of time and money. To me, this is as absurd as paying a second interpreter to interpret an interpreter.

Chapter 22

An Inept Psychobabblist

One trait that makes me thrive in my field is my ability to separate the offender from the offence. Whether they have killed a family member, gravely injured a stranger or even sexually abused a child. No matter how horrific the deed is, I consider it a separate entity from the perpetrator's psychiatric needs. Not only do I not know why I have this ability (if you can call emotional detachment an ability) but I didn't even realise until others pointed it out. My wife was gobsmacked at how I could cold-heartedly eat cereal while we were watching The Mountain pushing his thumbs through the eye sockets of the Red Viper of Dorne (*Game of Thrones* reference, btw). My friends are perturbed at how I can act like Dr Spock, speaking logically and emotionlessly about a mother I have just assessed who drowned her baby. It's taken a few bewildered facial expressions of those around me to realise that I am ... different inside. The irony isn't lost on me that some of these features are the building blocks of diagnoses I make on my defendants. Antisocial personality disorder leads to callous indifference. Psychopathy involves not recognising distress in others. Autistic spectrum disorder is associated with defects in some areas of empathy. I'm not proposing that I'm an antisocial psychopath who is on the spectrum, but let's just say I might share the occasional trait.

This emotional inertness helps me to remain objective in my assessments of defendants and gives me equanimity on the rare occasion that I'm being threatened. I have never felt physically scared of a defendant in person, but there was one occasion when an assessment made me reflect more carefully upon the damage an aggrieved patient, and even his father, could pose to me.

I was driving in to meet Mr Ralph Reilley at his solicitor's office on a dreary Wednesday afternoon in the winter, towards the end of 2019. Darkness was already looming when I got a phone call from the lawyer informing me that they had arrived an hour early and warning me that 'they're both quite a handful'. I had thought this a tad odd.

'Don't worry. I have experience in dealing with challenging defendants,' I replied.

'Good. You'll need it,' he scoffed.

'By the way,' I hastily added, 'what do you mean by "both"?'

He had hung up.

Alarm bells should have started ringing when I read the case papers earlier that morning. Ralph was in his early forties, same as me, though he was single and lived with his father. His mother had apparently committed suicide when he was a toddler. He had received treatment around three years previously for some problems inside his nose (his nasal septum and his turbinates) which resulted in trouble breathing. He was not happy with the outcome and after exhausting the usual NHS complaints procedure, he launched a campaign against doctors and staff at the hospital. He had written letters to the medics personally, expressing his displeasure and claiming clinical negligence. He then started covertly filming them at various meetings and appointments and used still pictures to make newsletters and pamphlets, calling for the execution of the doctors who he believed had harmed him. He had been distributing these leaflets in the local community, including posting them through the mailboxes in streets where the hospital was located and also where the doctors resided. Ralph caused significant distress, damaged reputations and made his targets fear for their safety, proving that the inkjet printer is mightier than the sword. He even created a website and a blog and founded the 'British Rainbow Party', a political organisation which, according to the Crown Prosecution Service, was not properly incorporated and therefore did not exist. Also, he hadn't printed business cards like I had, which in my mind proved he wasn't for real.

By the time I had been asked to assess him, Ralph had already been convicted of two counts of harassment without violence and two counts of sending communications conveying a threatening message. He had already received a community order and a restraining order and was made to pay court costs, though he appealed against the decision. His next hearing was postponed due to the bizarre statements he made during his trial. This raised some concerns about his mental health, which prompted my evaluation. I think the judge overseeing the case, Judge Whitaker, very perceptibly felt that Ralph's crimes were not serious enough to warrant prison, but that he still might be unhinged enough to need hospitalisation.

As I drove into the car park behind the solicitors' firm, I saw a man in a trench coat standing in front of the entrance. He seemed to be noting down my car registration. I assumed he was a security guard and waved at him. He shook his head and walked back into the building. How strange, I thought. Ralph was a very overweight man with thinning, scraggly brown hair and huge thick spectacles which looked like magnifying glasses, with tape between the lenses. His elderly father was a fraction of his size, though had the same beady eyes and wore a permanent scowl. He sported fingerless gloves and bared yellow teeth through his sneer, which gave him a look I can only describe as 'urchin-chic'. He had taken off the trench coat. The office that the solicitor gave us to use was a large conference room downstairs, which looked discarded, with tables and chairs stacked across the walls and old law textbooks in a heap in the corner. Having carried out work for this law firm before, I knew there were more modern, swankier rooms upstairs, next to the main solicitors' offices. Perhaps they were undergoing refurbishment?

The interview was gruelling. 'Both quite a handful' was an understatement. The father insisted very loudly that he should attend so he could be a witness in case of discrepancies in what I wrote about the assessment in my court report. Before I even had a chance to introduce myself, he stated that they would refuse to cooperate if I didn't allow his presence. The threat was unnecessary; like all clients I assess, I was happy for family members to attend. Although Ralph shook my hand, his father refused to do so. They both chastised me for being late (I was fifteen minutes early). Before I could respond, Ralph's father asked me if I was a doctor and when I replied that I was, he barked at me that this was untrue because I was a psychiatrist. He referred to me and all other psychiatrists as 'inept psychobabblists'. They then unleashed a barrage of complaints about the various doctors who had tried to treat Ralph.

I attempted at several points throughout the interview to explain that I could not make any recommendations for physical healthcare and that I was not undergoing a clinical negligence assessment. Despite this, they kept returning to the topic of their perceived medical maltreatment. They teased me with occasional morsels of a wider conspiracy, which was what I was really interested in. But they refused to answer any questions directly and shouted over me. The flow of the conversation was disjointed as the angry pair had a tendency to switch topics frequently. About ten minutes into the interview, Ralph stood on a chair, uncrumpled a piece of paper and announced that he had a statement that he insisted on making. 'As part of the British Rainbow Party health charter, I henceforth proclaim that I have been commissioned to research the extent and causes of medical negligence. Psychiatry is a tool to commit and cover up medical negligence and also to control society and suppress freedom of thought and speech, classing mad people as sane and vice versa,' he boomed.

I looked over at Ralph's father who was clutching one hand to his chest and had the other arm raised, close to tears with pride. Ralph continued: 'You and your ilk create fictional diagnosises [sic] while true mental illness, such as royalism and paedophilia, are ignored. Henceforth, I do not recognise you or your speciality. You originate from Nazi Gestapo culture. I declare that when the British Rainbow Party comes to power, all psychobabblists such as yourself will be removed from civilised society and sectioned to a safe place. Those who do not conform will be executed and this country will be cleansed of psychobabble.'

I had mixed emotions. I did not feel physically endangered. Their animosity was so surreal, I couldn't suppress a sliver of amusement. But I was also aware of his charges, which made me nervous about his potential future actions against me. Mostly, I was trying to figure out how to subtly steer the conversation to elicit the relevant clinical details for my assessment without invoking a diatribe.

'Any attempt to place me in any kind in prison will result in the following—' Ralph cleared his throat. His father cackled. 'All covert video recordings that I have not yet leaked will henceforth be flooded into the internet,' Ralph continued. 'Fifty thousand policy sheets with our manifesto will flood the borough of Westminster. Election ballot boxes in all of Kent will be wrecked by my party. A further three hundred thousand sheets will henceforth flood the relevant parts of London, exposing Judge Whitaker, who oversaw the mockery of my court case, and her role in suppressing my manifesto to protect unscrupulous doctors, the judiciary and psychobabblists.' He folded the piece of paper, peered over at me with his dark eyes, and then ended with the ominous phrase: 'You may think surely you can hurt me but my people and my party can hurt you far worser.' I was not sure what astounded me the most: the sheer paranoia behind his statements, the prospect of his photocopying fees, the overuse of the term 'henceforth', or the reprehensible grammar. It then dawned on me why we had been given this derelict room. The solicitor probably wanted to distance himself, metaphorically and literally, from the chaotic couple.

I asked if there was any chance that I could have a copy of his statement. Ralph seemed genuinely pleased and handed the page over to me with a flicker of a smile. I suspect he thought his declaration had swayed me towards his belief. In reality, I had black-and-white proof of his delusions for my court report and also a threat against the judge. After an awkward minute of silence, I thanked Ralph for his statement with all the sincerity I could muster. I explained that I needed to ask questions about his background in order to write the court report. He nodded, though barely answered my enquiries. 'I don't see how that's relevant' and 'It's none of your business,' were his more polite answers. He seemed deeply offended when I asked about his employment history, bog-standard background material for any psychiatric assessment. He shouted: 'Christ almighty! Haven't you been listening to a single bloody word I've been saying? How could I possibly work? I've been sick, you cretin! My nose is malfunctioning, I can't breathe and these doctors have done sod all about it. Exposing them *is* my job'.

Although I had obtained an excruciatingly detailed

narrative from Ralph about his previous doctors and their apparent negligence, I struggled to elicit much about his behaviours and intentions when distributing the hateful material. Extracting this and teasing out specific instrumental psychiatric symptoms would form the crux of my risk assessment. With every attempt, I was repeatedly interrupted by Ralph's tirades against the medical profession and his father's guffaws of encouragement. One specialist who had attracted a lion's share of the hostility had suggested that as Ralph had undergone a couple of successful minor procedures, there was no corporeal explanation for his ongoing breathing problems. So, they needed to entertain the possibility that symptoms might be caused by a psychological element. This is known as 'somatisation', experiencing emotional distress in the form of physical symptoms. Ralph screamed, 'Instead of taking my nasal issues seriously, this retard had the nerve to start asking me bullshit psychobabble questions about my mood. Was I depressed? Any stresses at home recently? I made a mental note to forgo my routine questions about his mood as part of my own assessment.

They both seemed absolutely convinced that the British Rainbow Party would eventually come to power and they spoke of revolution. They conveyed their policies, including free CT scans for everybody and that '90 per cent of those doctors who are crooked will be replaced by homeopaths' (which arguably might have been the craziest thing they said). Another policy was that anybody who killed a judge or a member of the Crown Prosecution Service would be pardoned. Ralph made even more derogatory statements against Judge Whitaker. 'If she dares put me in prison she will feel the wrath of my organisation. She is an immoral and illegal buffoon. If I am incarcerated my disciples shall rise up and there will be havoc to pay.' What did concern me was the pair repeatedly specifying that these apparently negligent doctors should be 'hung up naked and flogged to death publicly'. But I knew that their barks were worse than their bites. They had been distributing their hateful material for years, but their targets had remained un-hung and un-flogged.

The entire interaction lasted almost two hours, although I had made my diagnosis within the first few minutes of Ralph's speech. His ramblings indicated an intricate paranoid delusional system, which involved the police, the judiciary and doctors all being in cahoots. There was also a sprinkling of delusional grandiosity regarding his own authority, his martyrdom and the power of his non-existent political party. There was no indication of him or his father believing that his harassment was in any way wrong or that his legal proceedings or the restraining order would curtail this behaviour. In fact, this all seemed to have reinforced their ideas and motivated Ralph to continue his attempts to uncover this supposed conspiracy. There were some menacing hints of derogatory material being disseminated, but no direct threats of actual physical harm, at least none that I personally considered to be credible.

It was only after discussing this bizarre interaction later with Rizma over dinner that I considered that my reaction at the time could be seen as atypical. She pointed out that she and 'most sane people' would be frightened, or at the very least unnerved, by having two complete strangers screaming at them. She even had a tongue-in-cheek jab at my previous mildly psychopathic *Game of Thrones*-viewing lack of emotion. In all honesty, I found the consultation somewhat invigorating and more exciting than my usual assessments. And I must admit, I couldn't take a man with fingerless gloves seriously.

I concluded that Ralph had developed a delusional disorder. This is characterised by either a single delusion or a set of related delusions that are usually persistent and lifelong. This illness differs from schizophrenia in that other psychopathology (such as hearing voices) is absent and there is less of a functional or cognitive decline. There are also no negative symptoms, like a lack of energy and motivation. This actually makes the sufferer more determined and therefore potentially more dangerous. Onset is commonly in middle age, again unlike schizophrenia, which tends to occur in the late teens or early twenties.

This case exposed me, for the first and only time in my career, to *folie à deux*, a very rare and unnecessarily French psychiatric phenomenon. Also known as 'shared psychosis', this is when delusional beliefs are transmitted from one individual to another, usually a close family member, and classically when both sufferers are isolated from society. This is probably a mixture of shared genetic predisposition (psychosis runs in families) as well as the secondary sufferer being brainwashed with delusional ideas over time, without any contradictory voices of reason. To me, this is akin to extreme fanatic religious beliefs spreading across marginalised communities. Although of course, those are not technically delusions.

As a trainee psychiatrist, I spent so much time learning about bizarre syndromes that the average psychiatrist might not ever see in their career, that when I did come across such a presentation, there was a perverse pleasure in having 'collected' the disease. It was equivalent to the joy I felt obtaining the special gold stickers in the ThunderCats sticker books I had as a kid.

Deep-rooted conspiratorial delusions of treachery and persecution are certainly not rare in my line of work. But it felt different coming from the Reilleys for two reasons. Firstly, and selfishly, I was one of their potential targets (as was the judge). But perhaps more importantly, this dastardly duo had actually been quite successful. Their campaign of vitriol had lasted over two years and had caused unwanted public attention, serious distress and embarrassment for some innocent doctors. I had been a little dismissive about all of this initially, but as I collated my report and after a mini chastisement from Rizma to 'take this more seriously', I imagined the potential reputational damage they could cause.

I decided that I had no option but to contact Judge Whitaker directly to warn her of the imminent threat. A little part of me was tempted to suggest to the judge that she remand Ralph to prison and perhaps even consider arresting his father on a charge related to threatening behaviour. Scanning her a copy of Ralph's threat-filled manifesto strengthened my case. But the judge had a more robust and fairer plan. She made some very clear bail conditions which Ralph had to sign off on, including that he was specifically prohibited from making any form of contact or threat to myself or Her Honour. If he broke this, he would be immediately arrested and incarcerated. This extended to any literature from their website or any menacing leaflets, thereby hindering his maniacal father from taking over the reins of hatred. Although I suspected, given his age and scraggly appearance, he was not capable of updating the website or printing literature himself. Fingerless gloves and technological prowess do not go hand-in-hand, in my experience. It must have worked as I didn't hear a peep from either of them, much to my relief. I heard from their solicitors that Ralph was later transferred to a psychiatric unit, which was one of the recommendations that I had made in my report. I imagine he would have been quite a handful for the unfortunate forensic psychiatrist who had to treat him there. Delusional disorder is notoriously difficult to treat, and responds far less successfully to anti-psychotic medication than its cousin diagnoses, such as schizophrenia. A lack of insight and reluctance to engage in therapy is fairly common for mentally disordered offenders sent for rehabilitation. But this degree of vitriol and disdain for the medical profession is not.

Despite my initial, possibly immature, response to Ralph and his father, I am minded that occasionally forensic psychiatrists can be the victim of disgruntled patients. Between 30 May and 4 June 2018, a spree killer sought out and fatally shot six people in Scottsdale, Arizona, United States. The shooter was identified as fifty-six-year-old Dwight Lamon Jones, who killed himself as police closed in. One of his victims was fifty-nine-year-old Dr Steven Pitt, a well-known forensic psychiatrist, who had examined Jones in connection with a bitter divorce and was shot and killed outside his office on 31 May. The other victims included two paralegals and a counsellor, all shot within twenty-four hours of each other and within a ten-mile radius. Two other victims were discovered on 4 June. Reflecting upon this tragedy, I realised that Rizma was right (as usual). I did need to 'take this more seriously'.

Chapter 23

Semi-Detached

Of course, I'm not completely void of emotion towards my defendants. More semi-detached. On occasions when I have been moved by a case, it was usually not due to the heinous nature of the offence, but rather a degree of sympathy I felt for the accused. That's not to say I don't pity the victims and their families, and I recognise the immense devastation they have endured, but I am often removed from them. I rarely interact with them personally, except for when I was working in hospital and they were involved in the perpetrators' lives and recovery, like Yasmin's brother who participated in family therapy with her, or Jordan's mother who was an integral part of our initial (failed) attempt to discharge him. But in my work as an expert witness, I have no direct interaction with the victims. The only vicarious contact is through occasional victim-impact statements or pictures of injuries within the case papers.

Among the hundreds of offenders I have assessed in

person, Yasmin's case undeniably struck a chord with me, but I didn't feel such intensity of pity for many more years. Then I met Mr Cetin Burak. This was an assignment I was sent in early 2020, a couple of months after meeting the Reilleys, by which time I had recovered from the surreal interaction and stopped creeping towards my doorstep with trepidation, half expecting a defamatory pamphlet. Cetin's case was not for the criminal court, but rather for a first-tier tribunal immigration panel, an area I had been delving into through Sigma Delta Psychiatry Expertise. I was typically asked to assess the overall mental state of detainees who were about to be deported, either because they had entered the country illegally or were foreigners who were about to finish a prison sentence on English soil. I was asked to give opinions on whether they were too unwell and vulnerable to be moved. These institutions were not technically prisons (and some of the detainees had no criminal record). However, the big, locked gates and barbed-wire fences must have made the distinction purely academic for the residents. Most of my assessments in immigration removal centres have been near Heathrow Airport, where a cluster are located. Great for transporting foreign criminals, terrible for traffic.

Cetin was a man in his mid-twenties who was born in Turkey. He was young and athletic, with a baby-face, an immaculate Turkish beard and soft eyes which betrayed his clenched jaw and stern face. He had come over to the UK at the age of eleven with his mother to join his father who had already set up a life here. Both of his parents were in the police force; his father was an officer and his mother worked in a clerical role. He was a gifted footballer and played county-level as a teenager. His first year in the UK was difficult, having to adjust to the difference in culture and the language barrier. 'I was gobsmacked to see kids cuss out their parents here. Back at home, we'd get a slap to the cheek before we got to the end of the sentence,' he told me. Football was his way in and his skills gained him swift popularity. He dropped out of school and started an apprenticeship to become a mechanic, with a couple of unsuccessful trials at professional clubs. At seventeen, a very close friend, who had an undiagnosed heart abnormality, suddenly collapsed during a match. Three days later, he was dead.

This set off a catastrophic chain reaction which ultimately led Cetin to a failed stint as a criminal and the prospect of deportation. Grieving his friend, Cetin spiralled into a depression, which drained him of energy and left him tearful every day. Apparently, this was strongly discouraged by his father who used to grumble at him that 'a true man shouldn't cry'. He would ruminate about his companion's death and started taking cocaine as a distraction. His lack of energy bled into other parts of his life, and soon he began neglecting his friends and stopped playing football. His personality changed too, from being bubbly and gregarious to irritable and isolative. Like a see-saw, the more Cetin's bereavement deepened, the more his cocaine use escalated. He also drank heavily with his mechanic buddies after work every day and pretty soon he noticed that he was always the last one out of the pub. His weekend binges soon tumbled into the week until there were only one or two days when he was sober, usually recovering from previous benders. 'When I was high, nothing mattered,' he said. 'When I was on a comedown, everything mattered. Either way, his death was drowned out.' Cetin gradually lost contact with his old group of friends and made a different set of associates who shared his penchant for heavy drug use. Through them, he became indoctrinated into the clubbing scene. He lost his job after he called in sick one too many times. 'All my old mates from school were concerned. They told me to sort myself out. I said I would. I promised. But it was so much easier to just avoid them.'

During my assessment, Cetin told me of a poignant memory. He was in a taxi on a mission to score some crack with a bunch of clubbers with whom he had been out all night. They drove through Camden, right past a group of his old school friends playing five-a-side. He had a sudden urge to jump out of the taxi and join them. He suppressed it, put his head in his lap and distracted himself by imagining the sweet plasticky taste of crack that would be imminently flowing through his lungs.

Soon afterwards, Cetin's parents refused to support him financially and kicked him out. He sofa-surfed and reported sometimes continuing the party at friends' houses for days with the help of stimulants, because he literally had no place to sleep. His continued drug use pushed him into spiralling debt. He fell into the pocket of a particular drug dealer, Blimpy (which I hoped to God was his nickname), owing around £7,000. Cetin was roughed up on a couple of occasions and was once taken into an alley where he had a knife put to his throat and was stripped of his clothes. A memory which, I noted within intrigue, he conveyed to me with far less emotion than seeing his old friends play football. He was informed unequivocally that his family would be hurt if he didn't pay up. The dealer coerced Cetin into running errands for him, mostly picking up and delivering particular packages. He never looked inside them, though it didn't take a great imagination to guess what they contained. After a noise complaint, the police had gone to his friend's house, where he was staying on the couch for a few days. They smelt cannabis, searched the property and found a big package of drugs and cash which Cetin had been stashing there, to the utter dismay of his host. During my interview, he told me this was 'definitely the worse day in my life. Worse than losing my friend. This time, I couldn't blame God.' Cetin was potentially facing a long custodial sentence and had further disappointed his parents, who were already slipping away. His law-abiding and law-enforcing father screamed at him in the police station that he 'did not work my ass off to support a delinquent druggie son'. But mostly, Cetin was terrified that Blimpy would blame him for the drugs and money being seized. He was released on bail though he isolated himself, hiding in his one remaining mate's house. He engaged with the local drug rehabilitation service and managed to stay clean for around two months. He was also officially diagnosed with depression and given anti-depressants by his GP.

One day at the supermarket, Cetin was suddenly accosted and cornered in the freezer section by the drug dealer and his cronies. He described this as: 'first, a shock. I would never have pictured Blimpy in Aldi. Then it was kind of a relief, to be honest. I knew he would definitely find me eventually. London isn't big enough.' His captor demanded that Cetin run another errand. He had to hire a car and drive up to Glasgow to collect a huge package, then make three deliveries on his way back down to London. He was reluctant to do this but was persuaded by a quick flash of a blade. 'For your family's sake, you don't want to fuck this one up,' Blimpy said, almost serenely, as his thugs snarled at Cetin. One of them kicked him hard in the bum as he skulked out of the supermarket.

Cetin picked up the package from under a bench in a grimy playground in Glasgow. He described circling the park several times in the blistering wind. At first, he was paranoid that there might be undercover cops around. Then he was paranoid that 'I'd been lingering so long around the playground, I might start looking like . . . '

'Like what?'

'You know, a wrong-un.'

On the return journey, he got as far as Newcastle before the police pulled him over (presumably due to undercover intel). Already on bail, he received a three-year custodial sentence. In prison, he stayed abstinent from substances and undertook multiple courses, including peer mentoring, learning support groups and drug rehabilitation. He even became a 'listener', trying to pacify suicidal inmates. His plan was to eventually become a counsellor and drug rehabilitation worker. 'I've lived it. I might as well teach it,' he said to me with a sigh. He also focused on his fitness, working out in the gym most days.

Cetin was apprehensive about leaving prison. He had

reformed himself, but needed to mend relationships. However, the day before the end of his sentence, his offender manager dealt him a devastating blow. Cetin would be transferred to an immigration removal centre where he would await deportation to Turkey.

By the time I saw him, although he had barely been in the immigration centre for a month, Cetin had put his time to good use. He had managed to get a job as a wing cleaner, was still going to the gym almost every day and was even playing football regularly. Just like at school, his skill level afforded him instant popularity and dissolved any language barriers; though in an ironic reversal since his arrival in the UK, here he was one of the only detainees who spoke fluent English.

During my interview, I found Cetin to be polite, honest, open and engaging. He burst into tears several times, especially when talking about the despondency of his future. Although we were in a private interview room, the windows were huge and we were in view of numerous other detainees who were having legal visits. I remember feeling protective of Cetin and not wanting the others to see him as weak, vulnerable and a potential target. But what could I do? Tell him not to cry? Wouldn't that just reignite painful emotions towards his father?

'I can't believe I screwed up so monumentally,' he told me. 'It only seems like weeks ago that my mate died. After that, it was like I was possessed. The person making all those decisions was me, but it wasn't really me. I felt it. I felt a little voice telling me to snap out of it. I would even sometimes slap my cheek really hard in the mirror. I could've listened to that voice. I wanted to. But another drink or another line of powder or a blast from the pipe would shut it up. Shutting it up was so easy.'

For the conclusions of my first-tier tribunal immigration panel report, I opined that Cetin suffered from a mild to moderate depressive disorder. Although he was abstinent by the time I assessed him, he had previously satisfied the criteria for dependence syndrome for multiple drugs, notably ecstasy, cocaine, crack and ketamine. He also used cannabis, acid and GHB recreationally, though was not physically dependent on them. 'It would be quicker to tell you the drugs I haven't done,' he said with a hollow laugh when I enquired about this.

What is colloquially known as 'addiction' bears the psychiatric moniker of 'dependence syndrome'. This is a cluster of physiological, behavioural, and cognitive features. The use of substances takes on a much higher priority for a given individual than other behaviours that once had greater value. There is a desire (sometimes overpowering) to take the psychoactive drugs. Typically, returning to substance use after a period of abstinence leads to rapidly escalating use, quickly matching the previous pattern. In my report, I stressed that Cetin's drug use had adversely affected his life in a number of ways. It ruined relationships with family and friends, prevented him from undertaking previous hobbies, got him into significant debt, ruined his job and sporting prospects and exacerbated the depression he suffered after losing his best friend. It also appeared to drive his offending behaviour, though more indirectly (under duress from Blimpy and his goons) than directly (to fund his habit).

I was asked to consider Cetin's circumstances and give an opinion of the impact of deportation on his mental health. I explained that, according to him, he had very few connections in Turkey with no friends and only his elderly frail grandmother who spoke no English. I stated that, on balance, this would likely lead to a recurrence of his depressive disorder and due to his previously indicated poor coping mechanisms, this would in turn likely lead to a relapse of substance use. I also pointed out that support services for drug users were limited in Turkey. I highlighted the positive factors that would mitigate his overall risk of relapse into drug use and therefore into offending; he had reportedly disassociated himself from drug-using peers, had been abstinent from substances for almost three years and appeared well motivated in his ongoing recovery. Cetin had already made contact with community rehabilitation services ahead of his release and had made realistic and sensible plans for the future. I was careful not to give an opinion on whether I thought he *should* be deported, as this was solely the decision of the immigration panel and overstepping the boundaries could render my evidence biased and potentially inadmissible. I had to mention in my report that I could not be absolutely sure that Cetin was telling me the truth. Some aspects of his story were not confirmed by objective documentation, such as the death of his friend and the threats from the drug dealer. Nevertheless, even if elements were exaggerated, I felt sorry for the guy.

Unfortunately, I've had no closure for this case from his solicitor. Sometimes cases are not resolved until weeks after I've submitted my evidence, and fairly frequently the lawyers don't have the courtesy to update me when I ask, ignoring me once they have what they need, leaving me feeling like a one-night stand who has been ghosted. However, I found myself obsessing over Cetin's fate weeks afterwards, and I didn't fully understand why. Cetin wasn't naturally antisocial and he didn't have a criminal mindset. Perhaps my subconscious was perturbed by the realisation that he could be anybody. He could be *me*. I have made my fair share of bad decisions, including in relation to vices, as many people have. But it did seem that life had been particularly harsh on him. Although the wider consequences of his drug distribution could not be ignored, he hadn't physically hurt anybody, unlike the majority of the other individuals I had evaluated.

Cetin's case highlighted how rife drug and alcohol use was among the cohort I assessed. I would go as far as saying this was a salient factor in far more cases than acute psychiatric illness. The relationship between substance use and offending is complex and convoluted. A disconcerting coalition. The most common connection is that intoxication disinhibits people, who may consequently act out violently, like the ex-soldier, Jake, who smashed a bottle of vodka over the shopkeeper's head. Sometimes addicts commit crimes to fund their own habits, like the braided Chantelle, who carried out armed robberies. In other instances, particularly for drug dealers like the facially rosed Reggie, violence is a necessary requisite of business. All the more reason to be exasperated by recent funding cuts to rehabilitation services, social care and youth clubs as well as general mental health services and prisons. It's a perfect storm to lead more vulnerable people towards offending via the conduit of drugs and alcohol and to keep people like me busy.

With well over a hundred medico-legal cases under my belt, a realisation came to me. I acted as a sieve for the system. My role was more often about weeding out those *without* mental illness (such as habitual drug users) than identifying and sectioning those with. Of all the defendants I saw, many had mild background grumbling depression or anxiety, often related to the very factors and situations that led them to break the law. Only a small proportion had a *severe* mental illness and even fewer had reduced criminal culpability because of it. Of those who fell into this tight category, many didn't need to be transferred to a forensic unit for rehabilitation anyway, as they could be treated appropriately in prison.

As my confidence as an expert witness flourished after a few more immigration tribunal cases like Cetin's, I started branching out into disparate types of assessment for other courts. This included civil court cases and family court cases. Unlike criminal cases, in which the state prosecutes an individual, civil court cases arise where an individual or a business believes their rights have been infringed, such as companies trying to recover money they are owed or individuals seeking compensation for injuries (hopefully more impartially than Dr Zafar's bogus whiplash claims). Family courts deal with a variety of legal issues between relatives, commonly including parental disputes over the upbringing of children, local authority intervention to protect children and also divorce and adoption proceedings.

My most memorable civil court work outside of the

prison environment involved historical sexual abuse cases. I undertook around ten assessments on the victims of a man named Jon Styler. This ex-headmaster is alleged to have abused boys in schools in Newport and Worcestershire in the 1970s and 1980s. Had he been alive, he very well may have come across my radar as a defendant in criminal proceedings. But, some might say deservedly, he killed himself in Newport in 2007, despite having strongly denied the allegations. The civil claims were against Newport Council for not protecting the victims when they were children. Some solicitors believe Mr Styler may be one of Wales's most-prolific sex offenders, with more than a hundred suspected victims. From what the claimants, all now men in their fifties, reported to me, Styler would groom the boys and befriend their parents. He would cherry-pick some boys as 'gifted' and entice them into his office for private lessons. He would coax them into playing with his genitals and performing oral sex. As is all too common in sexual abuse, he gave them the illusion of being special and that these private activities were a secret privilege they had earned. Shockingly, it seemed that many of the other teachers knew, or at least suspected, that Styler was abusing children. They looked the other way, reminiscent of the many people who passively allowed Jimmy Savile to perpetrate his evil.

My task was to carry out detailed mental health assessments on the victims to ascertain the degree of injury they suffered as a consequence of the trauma. I had to be crystal clear in my findings as my diagnoses heavily influenced the level of compensation they were afforded. What struck me from these cases was the range of psychiatric outcomes of the victims, despite the abuse being very similar. On one end of the spectrum was a man who was reasonably well-adjusted, barely thought about the abuse and suffered from mild dysthymia; also known as persistent depressive disorder, this is associated with continuous feelings of sadness and hopelessness, though the symptoms are less severe and shorter lasting than clinical depression. Despite this, he functioned well and had a happy family life and a successful six-figure-salaried managerial position. At the other extreme was a severely damaged man who was plagued with memories and flashbacks of the abuse on a daily basis. I diagnosed full-blown severe post-traumatic stress disorder. It was heart-breaking to see how the demons from his ordeals infiltrated so many aspects of his life, including sexual promiscuity in his teenage years, drug-taking, thrill-seeking and violence towards strangers, landing him in frequent trouble with the police. Again, my spurious gift, my ability to emotionally detach from the graphic details of the abuse, when I think many of my peers would have baulked, made my assessments palatable and effective.

My venture into other court arenas provided me with the variety that was the proverbial spice of life I needed. It also kept me on my toes and ensured that my clinical and medico-legal skills stayed sharp. However, this work also helped me cement in my mind that my real passion was criminal law. My experiences of historical sex abuse cases, clinical negligence lawsuits and parenting assessments were undoubtedly intellectually stimulating (and perhaps warrant another book). But it is the lawbreakers and the vagabonds who inherently excite me.

Chapter 24

Murder on the Mind

I was getting a regular flow of work, but most cases felt a tad bland. The odd assault. Occasional destruction of property. Sporadic arson. I had seen it all before. That anti-climactic feeling started to creep in again, and my naturally impatient personality, inability to relax and childlike need for stimulation didn't help. In my career, murder cases have been like buses. After what seemed like an eternity, two came across my desk, merely days apart. The devastation behind this savage act cannot be overlooked, of course, but from a purely forensic psychiatric perspective, the degree of scrutiny and the gravity of the trials are more intense and the overall vibe of these cases is much more lurid.

Before me, Mr Arnold Davis's assignment had actually been accepted by one of my peers, the same renowned senior forensic psychiatrist who had given evidence in Daryna's case (and who in my opinion was hoodwinked by her tears). However, he had had to pull out after a skiing accident, leaving the solicitors scrambling around to find a replacement. They had approached some other more senior and established psychiatrists before me, but the deadline must have been off-putting: a mere seven days to carry out the assessment in a prison in Manchester, digest and summarise hundreds of pages of case papers and medical records, and write up a watertight report that would be put under a microscope with the proverbial extra thick lens reserved for murder trials. When I got the call, I looked at my own timetable and it wasn't pretty. But I found a way, by cancelling a couple of gym classes, escaping a kid's birthday party I really hadn't wanted to go to (not my own flesh and blood) and negotiating with my ever-accommodating wife, Rizma, to take the kids to their swimming lessons if I made up for it the following week. I couldn't pass an opportunity like this up. Approaching Rizma with this request was fraught, as I had already expended ample 'wife tokens' a fortnight earlier for three days at a techno festival in Amsterdam (and two days to recover). 'Wife tokens' was a term which had by now cemented itself in the vernacular of me and my friends and is met with eye rolls from our spouses.

As the prison officers wheeled Arnold in at the prison in Manchester one morning in late 2019, it was the unexpected smell that bothered me more than the sight of his disfigured face. Talcum powder over-compensated for some kind of fleshy stench. The flaps of skin where his jaw once was were a notably darker pink than the upper part of his face. Instead of a mouth was a hole within a halo of stitches. To be fair, I don't think there was much remaining for the plastic surgeons to work with. Arnold's breathing was also distracting.

Half wheezing, half sucking. The visiting room we were given was the only wheelchair-accessible one in the health-care unit. It was spacious with polished furniture. Although the thick dust on the shelves on the walls suggested it was used infrequently, and had just been spruced up for us.

I suddenly realised that I'd been staring at him for far too long, so I cleared my throat and introduced myself. I stood up, leaned across the table to shake Arnold's hand and sat back down, once again trying to pull my bolted-down chair towards the bolted-down table. With well over a couple of hundred assessments under my belt, you'd think I'd have learnt by now. The unthrowable furniture was to ensure my safety. But sitting across from Arnold, it was obvious I had nothing to fear. His body slumped in his wheelchair when he shook my hand, indicating hemiplegia (one-sided paraly-sis): an entirely foreseeable side effect of shooting oneself in the face with a shotgun.

My anatomy lectures at medical school taught me that people without mouths can't talk. When the solicitor sent me the letter of instruction, she forewarned me that Arnold communicated by typing on a tablet. What she hadn't mentioned was how slow he was. I suppose farmers don't develop much of a touch-typing prowess. After what seemed like a perpetuity of one-fingered clunky tapping, he showed me the screen which had the answer to my first question. 'Not too bad. Up and down really.'

It soon became apparent that with Arnold's glacially slow method of communication and generally taciturn nature, I would need to adapt my interview to extract what I needed as effectively as possible, while not ruining rapport by rushing him. Even though the solicitor had booked a double visit totalling two hours, I knew we'd be pushed for time. I would have to focus on the crucial matter first: his mental state at the time when the killing occurred. This would determine whether the legal criteria for diminished responsibility would be met to downgrade his murder charge to manslaughter. Once this was elicited, if there was time, I could circle back and enquire about his background.

Arnold openly admitted to the killing and appeared apologetic and remorseful. Though I imagine that this was little consolation to his in-laws. There was no doubt that the homicide was calculated. Arnold had clearly stated in police interviews that he believed his estranged wife was having an affair. There were several witnesses to him confronting her with her new lover in a restaurant only two hours before. He had openly admitted that he wrangled her new address from a mutual friend the previous week, had driven over and hid behind a gate with a shotgun, seething. Forensic crime-scene investigations corroborated the son's eyewitness account; Arnold ran up behind his wife as she was walking up the drive, carrying her shopping from the Land Rover, and shot her in the back from point blank range. He then apologised to their son, who was frozen, one leg still inside the vehicle. Arnold then put the shotgun barrel in his mouth and pulled the trigger. He woke up four weeks later in hospital with numerous tubes coming in and out of him, the bottom half of his face absent.

The facts of the killing were not under question. His mental state was. I knew going in to the assessment that a finding of diminished responsibility would be highly unlikely (though not impossible). From the medical notes and my chat with his GP, as well as studying the witness statements, the clinical picture was pretty clear. Depression and alcohol dependence in terms of psychiatric diagnoses. Breakdown of a relationship, feeling rejected, increasing loneliness, an escalation of drinking and jealous rage in terms of the context. The main issue for me was teasing out Arnold's thought processes during the killing. Deciding whether his symptoms constituted an *abnormality of mental functioning* and if so, was this to the degree that it affected his actions and his fatal decision? To his credit, Arnold took full responsibility. He didn't attempt to weasel his way towards leniency by exaggerating mental illness or try to suggest he was not in control. He had even discussed diminished responsibility with his solicitors and insisted that he was guilty of 'full-on murder', as he put it to me. Looking at legal criteria, I agreed with him. Forming the opinion was easy. Constructing the court report around this, outlining all the relevant material and weaving in all the legal jargon, in the minutiae expected for a murder trial, was far more onerous.

On the train journey back to London, I was lucky enough to have the whole carriage to myself, which meant I could start dictating the material for my report without worrying about prying ears. Patient confidentiality is taken very seriously in my line of work and public leakage has led to disciplinary measures. Every once in a while, I would look up through the window while considering how to formulate the next paragraph. As I watched the hundreds of trees swish by in a blur, I reflected on what Arnold had made me feel. Although his disfigured face and that sickly smell stuck with me, there was minimal emotional impact. Even the knowledge that Arnold was doomed to spend the rest of his life crippled and incarcerated evoked little from me. There was no pity, no smugness, no thirst for vengeance. I felt indifferent. It wasn't that I didn't recognise the horrific nature of his acts. Unlike most of my other cases, I was even able to put a face to the victim from the numerous online articles. I also appreciated the sheer impact the trauma must have had on the young boy. What could possibly top witnessing your mother being murdered by your father? I just couldn't feel anything *visceral*. Over the incessant clanking of train tracks, I watched hundreds of strangers zoom past. Some walking down the street, some chatting, others getting in and out of their cars. Would these people feel so unmoved? What was missing inside me? And had it shrunk further over the years since Yasmin's case? Was I turning into a psychopath?

When I got to King's Cross Station, I randomly bumped into my friend Jenny in the queue at Costa. We'd been pally during our days as psychiatry senior house officers on the same training scheme and had studied together for exams. We had written a joint poster presentation for a conference about Dr Danièle Canarelli, the French psychiatrist who was charged after her patient had taken a life, discussed in Chapter 14. Jenny and I had drifted apart after our careers diverged; she became a general adult psychiatrist and I had chosen forensics. I distinctly remember several conversations between us when we were both deciding upon our future sub-specialties as we applied for our higher training placements. I had been torn between general adult and forensic psychiatry and Jenny between child and adolescent mental health services and general adult psychiatry, eventually choosing the latter. We had even written out lists of pros and cons.

We caught up over extortionately priced coffees at the station. It turned out, like me, Jenny was married with two kids. She had chosen west London as her abode. As we sat down, I told her about the assessment I had just carried out in Manchester.

'Oh yeah! I read all about him.' Jenny grimaced. 'He killed himself, didn't he? Thank God.'

I stirred my cappuccino and stared at her, waiting for the penny to drop.

'What?' she said.

'Are you saying I just carried out a psychiatric assessment on a corpse?'

'Oh yeah. Of course,' she nodded slowly. 'So, what is he like?'

I described Arnold's disfigurement, his odour and his excruciating typing.

'Sure, but what was he like?'

'Oh, er . . . well, his affect was flat with little reactivity,' I said. 'There were no overt psychotic symptoms such as hallucinations or delusions. He had an appropriate level of insight into his actions and expressed remorse. He was able to acknowledge . . .'

'Yeah, yeah. I didn't mean a full mental state examination. What was he actually *like*?'

I shrugged. 'I don't know what you want me to say, Jenny.'

'Was he not kinda creepy?' She circled a finger around her cup. 'Did he give you that vibe?'

'What vibe?'

'You know what I mean, Sohom.'

I blew across my coffee and took a long gulp. I repressed the wince from scalding my throat. Jenny was prone to teasing. 'He didn't really give off any vibe. I'm not sure there is such a vibe.' I searched Jenny's eyes for a few moments. She did not blink. 'I never felt in any danger,' I said. 'I mean he was hemiplegic.'

'I don't mean danger, just a certain . . . '

'What?'

'Disgust.'

'I mean, the smell was pretty nasty.'

'Stop! You always used to do this,' she said, slapping the table. 'Why can't you ever open up about . . . '

'About what?'

She let out a long sigh. 'Never mind. I meant, didn't you feel disgusted at *him*? At what he did. At what he's capable of.'

I pursed my lips and gave a long hard blow over my cup. I took a trepidatious sip. 'Not really.'

'I couldn't sit in a room with someone like that. It would feel . . . I dunno, a bit dirty.' Jenny frowned. 'Don't you pity his wife's family? His poor son?'

'Of course I do,' I said. 'But it's not our job to evaluate the morality of the situation. That's for the judge.'

'Well, if I was the judge, I would lock him up for ever.'

'Now you sound like my barber.'

'What do you mean?'

'Never mind.'

I read in the newspaper months later that Arnold was sentenced to life imprisonment with a minimum of thirty years behind bars. It would then be up to him and his legal team to prove to a parole board that he was no longer a danger to society, though arguably this was automatic given that he could barely use his arms and legs.

Jenny told me about the psychiatric clinic she had been running that morning in Cambridge along with a junior doctor, whom she supervised. She saw seven patients. One had post-traumatic stress disorder and all the others had some form of anxiety or depression, or both. She mainly discussed the potency of various medications and the side effects and tinkered with the dosages. Not a single patient argued with her or lost their temper (I had to ask). Sitting there in King's Cross with the occasional muffled announcements, the din of commuters and the clacks and scratches of suitcases being wheeled around us, I realised something. There is, of course, a nobility in what Jenny did. She helped patients recover and live fulfilling lives. But it sounded so *dull*. Where was the danger? Where were the tragic background stories? The pictures of gruesome stab wounds? I'm fairly sure my success rate was much lower than hers, but I helped the most damaged and vulnerable. The doubly stigmatised. I thought back to a few general adult psychiatry clinics that I had observed as a junior psychiatrist, before I found forensics. I had even run a couple, under close supervision of a consultant, around eight years earlier. But I could never go back to that now. It would feel too tame.

A couple of coffees in, we realised that we both had

only admin scheduled for the rest of the day and no actual appointments. I had already planned to devote the weekend to Arnold's report, and besides, I couldn't make any headway until my dictation was sent back. We decided to write off the afternoon and head to the pub, reminiscent of numerous occasions while we were both supposed to be studying for our Royal College of Psychiatrists membership exams (Jenny scored 6 per cent more than me, despite studying around 20 per cent less – not that I was keeping count or anything). Over gin and tonics, we caught up on life and our expanding families. It turns out that not only did we have different opinions about judging murderous farmers but also about the enjoyment of toddler-driven brunches.

Then Jenny spluttered suddenly. 'George Hilton!' she said between coughs as she dried her chin with a tissue. 'Do you remember him?'

Around a decade earlier, I had rotated on to a six-month placement working on a psychiatric ward near Camden to replace Jenny, who rotated on to an eating disorder clinic. We were both supervised by the same consultant, whom we remembered well due to his devastatingly powerful floral aftershave. We also had both treated the same patients due to the overlap of the same role. George stuck out in my memory more than most. He was a pleasant man in his late forties with an infectious smile and soft voice. I remember having long chats with him in the ward office. They felt more casual and friendly than with other patients and his dry sense of humour (he picked up on the senior doctor's whiff and mocked him long before we did) was a welcome relief on days that were often crammed with morose conversations. At that time, George, or 'G-man' as he insisted I call him in private, had recently been made redundant as a personal trainer and then developed a muscle-wasting disorder in his arms, which crushed his future job prospects. He got into financial trouble, which prompted him to re-evaluate his life. He told me that he felt like a loser. Aside from his career, he had a failed marriage and was living in a house share with several young strangers 'who play thumpy repetitive music all night and eat smelly takeaways'. I encouraged George to focus on the abundant positives in his life. He was very popular in his neighbourhood; he was 'that guy' that everybody across every generation knew and respected. He had a new partner and was close with his ex-wife and daughter who lived a couple of miles away. George had been admitted to our ward after a failed suicide attempt. He'd tried to hang himself from a tree in a secluded spot in a forest but the branch snapped (which he added to his growing list of failures).

Once Jenny had become a general adult consultant psychiatrist, she had taken over that particular patch of London when the overly odoured consultant had retired. George was one of the patients she inherited. She told me that he had re-married, recently had a baby girl, moved into a new home and had been running a successful independent café. Jenny had been very gradually weaning him off anti-depressants (doing this too quickly would likely cause a relapse). Aside from the occasional temporary dip in mood once or twice a year, George was thriving. He had not considered suicide for well over three years. I felt a fuzzy happiness when I heard about George (perhaps partly thanks to a mild gin-induced buzz). I could clearly picture his huge grin. I promised myself to drop into his café soon. At that moment, I understood the trade-off. I realised that the price I pay for my white-knuckle cases was a lack of *this* feeling. If I'm lucky, I might get some closure from some solicitors about some of the individuals I see for my medico-legal work, but I never get an insight into their lives many years down the line, unless of course they have reoffended. Even my forensic psychiatrist colleagues who work in the community and follow-up patients in the long term have to drop the most stable from their caseload, to make room for the risky. These subjects are either discharged to the care of a general adult psychiatrist, like Jenny, or back to their GPs because they are deemed too low risk to need our specialist (and stretched) resources. Looking back, when I worked within forensic psychiatric units and prisons, the measure of success for me and my colleagues would be not seeing the patients or inmates again. Despite the myriad of social disadvantages, I'm sure many of them have gone on to find success and stability, but like an adulterous father who has disowned his family, it is something I never had the privilege of witnessing personally.

Chapter 25

The Killer Who Never Changed His Spots

No sooner had the hangover dissipated from my impromptu meeting with Jenny than another murder case meandered its way into my inbox. On the surface, I could fully appreciate how the layperson might be shocked by the case of Mr Elgin Smithson. The family of his victims would have every right to be incensed at the authorities. How could they release a man who had killed not once, but twice before going on to then do it a *third* time? Isn't this negligence? Shouldn't somebody be made to answer for it?

Elgin was a man in his sixties who was on remand at HMP Belmarsh, a category A prison in south-east London that houses the country's most dangerous criminals. Its distinguished alumni include the seventeen-year-old with autism who threw a six-year-old from the Tate Modern balcony, Jonty Bravery; the Captain Hook-inspired, one-eyed hatemonger Abu Hamza; and the worst man to ever share your intimate secrets with, Julian Assange.

Elgin was charged with the murder of his ex-partner in late 2019, about six months before we met. He had strangled her to death with a dressing-gown cord. He sustained critical injuries from an immediate suicide attempt, eerily mirroring Arnold's. He walked out of the apartment leaving his victim's limp body slumped in the kitchen and jumped straight in front of a bus.

Elgin's history was well established within the hundreds of pages of medical notes I was sent. He grew up in poverty as one of fourteen siblings in the Dominican Republic. Three of them had schizophrenia, which would have genetically predisposed him to mental illness. He described an unhappy childhood marred by regular physical chastisement from his oft-missing itinerant father. 'We all got the belt, but I got it most often and hardest,' he had reported to a psychologist years ago. There were even unconfirmed suspicions that his dad had another secret family. I cannot condone such deceitful behaviour, but I'm also flabbergasted by how somebody could manage so many offspring, when my two keep my hands so full and my wallet so light.

Elgin had numerous children and had a pattern of sowing his seeds and then leaving, seemingly modelling his father's philandering. He moved to the UK around the age of twenty-five. He had worked in a variety of manual-labour roles and in retail over the years, though struggled to keep a job down, often turning up late or calling in sick. To me, this all screamed commitment issues.

Elgin had convictions for two previous offences of

manslaughter, both of previous partners. The first was in 1984, following an argument with his then-wife. He pushed her from the eleventh storey of the tower block they lived in. According to the case papers, Elgin told police that he had a very tumultuous relationship with the victim and they would frequently physically tussle. He said that on that fateful day, they were both at home and he was reading the newspaper. She apparently started swearing at him, mocking him for being a jobless layabout and yelling about how much she hated him. She smacked him around the face with a shoe. The fight escalated and they both tumbled onto the balcony. He informed authorities that he pushed her by accident and she fell. She was pronounced dead in the hospital the next day. He was sentenced to eight years' imprisonment and served half of them. There does not appear to have been any contact with forensic psychiatric services at that point, although back then this was only a fledgling subspecialty (it only became a formal faculty within the Royal College of Psychiatrists in 1997). His mental health was not considered to be an issue. After leaving prison, Elgin moved back to his home area of Birmingham to look after his children, though they were eventually taken into care.

He then moved to London where he started a new relationship with a woman fifteen years his junior. He reported frequent verbal arguments, though denied any domestic violence within this relationship. The second killing was around a decade after the first. According to Elgin, the victim had an affair and when he confronted her about this, she kicked him out of the house. He apparently returned a few days later to collect the rest of his belongings and realised that his partner's new lover had just left the house as he could smell cigarette smoke. He and the woman had a row, then he grabbed a knife and stabbed her repeatedly in a rage before attempting to hang himself. A neighbour alerted the police to screams and officers kicked down the door to find Elgin dangling from a noose. According to the available prison notes, while he was on remand, Elgin developed severe depression. He barely left his cell, hardly spoke to anybody and was crying almost constantly. He slept minimally and stopped eating, to the point that he had to be force-fed via a nasogastric tube. The medical reports were not particularly thorough, as was often the case in this period; I think due to the litigious compensation culture of modern times and the resultant aforementioned 'cover your ass' retort, we have become a lot more detailed in what we document. Reading between the sparse lines, it appeared that Elgin's mental illness was felt to be too much of a risk to be managed behind bars, particularly with his self-starvation. He was therefore transferred to a secure psychiatric unit. Prison psychiatry services have massively progressed since then – including the proliferation of forensic psychiatrists such as me – and I think there would have been a more concerted effort to treat him behind bars nowadays. During his trial, he admitted manslaughter on the basis of diminished responsibility, which was accepted by the prosecution. Elgin was disposed of by way of a hospital order with a restriction order; hospital was deemed more suitable than prison, but he was so high risk that his progress and eventual discharge had to be overseen by the Ministry of Justice, just like Yasmin's. Elgin was sectioned to a medium secure forensic psychiatric unit for around five years, from 1993 to 1998. The same place, incidentally, where I was later punched in the face. Once he was in hospital, Elgin suffered from other symptoms of depression, including apathy and anhedonia, and he was also hearing voices telling him to kill himself. These assuaged after a few months of anti-depressant and anti-psychotic medication.

When I saw him at Belmarsh, Elgin presented as a frail, elderly, dishevelled, unkempt Black man in a wheelchair. Two consecutive perpetrators of murders in wheelchairs. What were the chances? I asked myself. Unlike the spacious room in the prison in Manchester, this one was not as accommodating for the less able-bodied killer. The visiting area consisted of a vast landing of small rooms with huge windows clumped together in a sea of dark green and mahogany. For prison assessments, I often brought along a pro forma for the defendant to sign, giving me permission to view their medical records, as some GP practices and psychiatric hospitals won't release them without this. With its heightened Category A security, Belmarsh stipulated that I had to read and sign their own (in my view, massively over-complicated) pro forma to declare that I was passing my one to Elgin. Not only was this a pain in the ass, but a perfect metaphor for the pointless bureaucracy that runs in the blood of all penitentiaries.

I could hear the clanking of the side of his chair against the narrow corridor corners and the cursing of the prison guard pushing him before I actually saw Elgin in the flesh. He had two very conspicuous stubs for arms, poking out of the sleeves of his loose light-blue T-shirt. His lips collapsed as he spoke, with a notable lack of teeth. Bad dentition or his rendezvous with the bus, I did not know. An anomaly that I was becoming accustomed to was that perpetrators of the most serious offences often do not look particularly deadly. Disfigurement aside, Elgin had a very slight frame and looked altogether unassuming. I remember asking myself if he radiated 'that vibe' that Jenny spoke of. He did not, at least not to my receptors.

He was taciturn and answered questions minimally. When I asked him about his psychiatric history, Elgin reported that he had suffered from depression since his mid-thirties and had been on various anti-depressants over the years. He would also have random panic attacks when surrounded by people. He was unable to relay the diagnosis that led him to the forensic unit or describe to me in any detail the rehabilitation he had undertaken during his five-year stint there. Not exactly a glowing endorsement for the effectiveness of this work. Elgin depicted a fairly stable and happy relationship with his most recent victim, Sabrina, whom he had met in the local library. I had no evidence to confirm or refute this. However, I did note that he failed to mention to me that when this relationship began, three years earlier, he did not inform the consultant forensic psy-chiatrist supervising him in the community, despite this being one of the specific conditions of his restriction order; all future partners needed to be warned of his previous offences, for their safety. According to the notes, the team social worker found out about this romance and Sabrina was invited to an appointment with the psychiatrist. A medical letter summarising this consultation stated that she 'was informed in detail about Elgin's previous discretions', which I thought was an overly polite way to put it. Sabrina seemed nonplussed and it obviously didn't hinder their relationship. The social worker kept tabs on the couple with occasional home visits, concerned with the possibility of domestic violence, though found no proof.

I asked Elgin to give me his account of the period leading up to the death of Sabrina. He reported that he had a generally irritable persona and was feeling particularly depressed. His psychiatrist had upped his anti-depressant dose with little effect. On the day before the incident, according to Elgin, Sabrina had agreed to come round to his house to help him sort out the paperwork for his benefits. She purportedly had changed her mind at the last minute, which annoyed Elgin. He convinced her to come the next morning instead, though she was more than three hours late, which incensed him further. A sarcastic comment escalated into an insult, then an argument, then a fight. He claimed that Sabrina had tried to hit him with a hammer. Elgin said that he had only a very patchy memory of what happened next, and 'came to', lying next to Sabrina's body, realising he had strangled her. I tried to get an insight into his thought process at the time, to ascertain whether he was acting in self-defence or anger or as a direct reaction to symptoms of mental illness. But he was unable to expand, answering 'I don't know' to further questions. He broke down in tears and said between his sobs, 'I don't know why I did this. I hate myself. She was good to me. I wish I was dead.' As a doctor, I felt an instinct to show sympathy to the patient in front of me and not to judge. As an assessor, I knew I had to keep the rapport strong to maintain the flow of conversation. However, given the circumstances, it wasn't easy. At one point, tears cascaded down his face and, without hands, the best he could do was dab at his cheek with his shoulder. I had an urge to get up and find a box of tissues, though I knew this would be forbidden under Belmarsh's strict security protocols (or alternatively, there would be an unnecessarily lengthy pro forma for me to fill). There was nothing I could do except shuffle uncomfortably in my chair and resist scratching my own face from sympathy itching.

Elgin also had only very vague memories of his suicide attempt. 'It was like I was trapped inside somebody else's body, looking through their eyes. It was like watching a scary movie. But I already knew the ending. I knew I had to give up my life because I took hers,' he rasped. He explained that he woke up in hospital about a month later, with all of his limbs amputated. He was carted off to prison, straight to the healthcare unit. He stated that he had been suffering from very low mood and had thoughts of suicide on a daily basis though, somewhat ironically, couldn't follow through due to his disability.

Naturally, with three separate yet morbidly similar killings, I had to question whether the system had failed Elgin, the public and, most importantly, his victims. Could this have been predicted? While analysing this, I tried to remain objective and eliminate any bias I might have had to defend my forensic psychiatrist peers. To all intents and purposes, since his discharge from hospital in 1998, Elgin had been in remission from his depression. He was monitored carefully in the community and despite the occasional dip in mood, there was nothing particularly risky about his behaviour. There were no known instances of aggression. And Sabrina *was* warned about his past. If there had been domestic violence, she had not reported this during the many check-ups with the social worker. Was she scared of the repercussions? Either punishment from Elgin, or external sources breaking up the relationship? It does seem that his depression was gradually relapsing in the month leading up to the killing, though was still in the early stages. The notes indicated a couple of instances when he met with his community psychiatrist and reported being tearful and lonely and he seemed to view his future through a pessimistic lens. From what I could tell, a thorough risk assessment was undertaken and he did convincingly deny thoughts and intentions to commit any violence. One could argue that given his murderous behaviours during previous relapses, maybe at that point there could have been a higher level of input and observation. However, it is hard to justify shifting more resources to monitor somebody like Elgin regularly if, in fact, there were far more overtly aggressive and directly threatening patients on the caseload. Even if this extra monitoring had occurred, would it have made a difference? There would have been no logical reason to admit him to a psychiatric unit at that time, because he wasn't ill enough to require hospitalisation. He was cooperating with medication, so treatment against his will, such as jabbing him with needles, was unnecessary. To me, his killing was impulsive, senseless and spontaneous. As opposed to being related to a gradually bubbling and potentially foreseeable build-up of rage or deterioration of his mental illness. Although I could not fault any individual decision, clinician or service, simply taking a step back and doing a basic 'eyeball test' would suggest that the system had to be flawed to allow one man to commit three similar devastating homicides. The nebulous, unaccountable *system*. The truth is that only a tiny proportion of killers go on to take life again (so tiny, it is hard to garner any meaningful statistics). This, combined with Elgin not telegraphing his future violence in the spaces between his horrific acts, meant that services were not sufficiently equipped.

Interestingly, Elgin was also assessed by two other psychiatrists on behalf of the court around the same time as me, and we all proffered disparate views. This is fairly common in forensic psychiatry and reflects the fact that, to a degree, all psychiatric constructs are man-made and arbitrary, as opposed to scientifically proven – a fact I am happy to admit. One doctor diagnosed him with no mental illness at all and the other with moderate depression. I thought he had mild depression, given that despite his symptoms he had been functioning to a reasonable degree, such as attending work two days a week, shopping independently, using public transport and socialising down at the pub.

For my report, I examined the criteria for diminished responsibility vigilantly. I concluded that although there was some evidence to support that at the time of the incident Elgin was suffering from an abnormality of mental functioning in the form of low mood, the severity was not sufficient to have substantially impaired his mental ability to understand the nature of his conduct, form a rational judgement, or exercise self-control: the three relevant categories for this defence. He did, of course, lose his temper during the argument with Sabrina and this indicated both a lack of self-control and irrational judgement. However, vitally in my view, this was in the context of an argument, as opposed to being caused by his depression. It also appeared that anger and impatience played a role in the killing, which are not psychiatric symptoms. Therefore, I concluded that a defence of diminished responsibility was not open. I did not recommend a transfer to psychiatric hospital, though I stated that Elgin should be reviewed regularly by the prison psychiatry healthcare team. The court agreed. He was handed a minimum sentence of thirty years behind bars, making it very likely that he will die in prison.

Elgin's case made me reflect on how pertinent risk analysis is within forensic psychiatry. Often, we are hedging our bets on which subjects seem more dangerous than others, and rationing our resources appropriately. But we cannot read minds or predict the future. We will inevitably make the wrong call sometimes. Typing up Elgin's reports, I was curious to know what Jenny made of all this. I called her up, and as I had predicted, she had no sympathy. 'There are so many other people who are mentally unwell, and limited funding in mental health services. Frankly, I don't think he deserves any psych input at all,' she said. 'Let him suffer with his depression in jail. At least he gets to be alive. Not like those poor women.'

I could hear children's voices squabbling in the background. I felt a pang of guilt; we used to be close friends and we'd not even met each other's kids. We arranged a play date in an equidistant park for the following week. 'A leopard never changes its spots,' she said later, circling back to Elgin. Unsure of how to respond, I grunted, knowing that she wasn't entirely wrong.

Chapter 26

Darker Realities

As time passed, I noticed that slowly but surely, parenting became a little less stressful. Cautious optimism, I believe is the phrase a politician would use. The boys refused to eat less often, woke up in the middle of the night less often and left little presents in their nappies less often. In the mornings, aside from wiping the odd bum, cleaning up the odd stain, and wiping occasional tears (with different tissues, I hasten to add), I was able to leave them to their own devices. The purchase of two new iPads may have been a contributory factor. The kids' increasing self-sufficiency allowed me to focus on my work, particularly in the mornings, before my wife awoke. Of course, I still had to answer their inane questions.

'Yes, your tooth is wobbly.'

'No, you can't have any chocolate now.'

'Yes, you can have some later.'

'No, I don't know what time.'

'Yes, most dogs are brown.'

These extra nuggets of free time accumulated, often leaving me feeling fidgety and at a loss for what to do. While procrastinating one morning, I came across a click-bait celebrity depression story on some trashy website. An hour later, I found myself extending the boys' iPad time with a dismissive wave of my hand, so I could continue crawling down the rabbit hole of famous people airing their various diagnoses and struggles with mental illness. From Zayn Malik overcoming his crippling anxiety, to Jade from Little Mix's battle with anorexia, to Miley Cyrus's depression, to Lady Gaga's post-traumatic stress disorder. On the one hand, it was encouraging to see that the youngsters' idols were breaking the stigma of talking about mental illness. On the other hand, it was disheartening to see just how out of touch with youth culture I was, despite my edgy haircut. What the hell is a Troian Bellisario? Some new coffee blend I hadn't heard of?

However, as I read more 'inspirational' anecdotes something felt … off. Many of the stories appeared to be PR stunts. I'm not saying they were fake, but I noticed that an awful lot of them coincided with a book launch or a new album. I felt there was something cynical, calculated and disingenuous about only disclosing mental illness when it would happen to drive attention towards the sufferer and ultimately dollars towards their accounts. Another uncomfortable realisation was that all of the tales were about celebrities who had achieved recovery. All their vicissitudes were in their rear-view mirrors. Obviously, if they inspired other sufferers to open up about their experiences, this could lead to health catharsis, or better yet, might edge them over that hump of reluctance to finally seek treatment. I knew this could be a positive thing. But ever the cynic, I couldn't help wonder about those with more severe and pervasive mental illness. Those whose symptoms drove them in and out of hospital or prison, or both. Those who had the misfortune to require an assessment from me. Could celebrities' stories of overcoming alienate these people and make them feel even more marginalised? Also, what about those with less 'sexy' diagnoses, such as schizophrenia or delusional disorder? Where were their equivalent celebrity stories? I decided that I wanted to use my voice and my professional experience to give *them* some representation. I hoped by discussing and normalising the somewhat taboo world of forensic psychiatry, in my own tiny way, I could contribute to reducing stigma for those who experienced it the most.

It also hadn't escaped me that many people were fascinated with aspects of my job that had become routine and even mundane for me; it was evident from the multitude of enquiries from friends and neighbours and in the obligatory polite conversation during school pick-ups and drop-offs. People had a lot of questions and I had a lot of answers. Eventually this seed would sprout into this very book, but at that time I started writing a blog for the *Huffington Post* about a wide range of topics related to forensic psychiatry, from the experience and process of being admitted to a psychiatric ward, to the criminal code of prisoners, to what it feels like to work with psychopaths. I got some responses and comments, but typically, instead of enjoying the process, I became impatient, yearning to get more exposure. I

had a rare lull in cases for a few days and spent them fever-
ishly researching further media opportunities. Almost all
of my emails were ignored. But before I got the chance to
wallow in self-pity, life slapped me in the face with a harsh
distraction. It was a Sunday evening when I received an
ominous phone call from the court psychiatry team manager, Alicia. 'I need to tell you about Harry,' she said in an
uncharacteristically sombre voice.

Mr Harry Jackson was only nineteen years old. He had
been charged with assault on an emergency worker. He had
phoned the police claiming that his landlord had broken into
his flat when he was asleep and injected him with AIDS. He
also believed that the same man had installed radioactive
smoke alarms with the intention of giving Harry cancer.
When the police discredited him after examining the
alarms, he became agitated and started swearing and spitting at officers. Acknowledging his anguish, they gave him
a pass and managed to placate him. But as they were leaving, he ran outside his flat in his dressing gown and threw a
brick at their car. Pass revoked.

When I saw Harry in the court custody suite, he was
withdrawn and uncooperative. He lay down across the
bench in the interview room with his hoodie pulled
over him, neglecting his coffee. He refused to answer
any questions for the first twenty minutes. After some
gentle coaxing, he did engage to a degree but remained
very evasive and vague. He was convinced that this same
landlord had been trafficking children for prostitution. I
asked if he had any proof. He said he'd overheard a conversation that the culprit had had over the phone, though

would not elaborate on further details. Elements of what Harry said didn't make sense, such as the landlord being in a different building at the time, indicating to me that he had been experiencing a hallucination. My suspicions were confirmed when he also complained of hearing this man's voice whispering derogatory remarks when he tried to sleep, including calling him a paedophile and mocking him for having effeminate, wispy pubic hair. He reported that over time, these insults had chipped away at his confidence and mood. Harry let slip that he had specific plans for suicide, including wanting to jump in front of a Number 9 bus. His belief was this: 666 is the mark of Satan, and when the digits are added together you get 18, and the sum of those figures is 9. Although nonsense to the average person, in his delusional mind, this indicated that this vehicle was sent by the devil. Naturally, I thought of Elgin's gruesome accident. I pushed away the intrusive image of Harry in a wheelchair with his arms amputated to stumps. I couldn't let that happen.

I probed further, asking whether he had determined exactly where and when he would carry out the deed. Harry's countenance changed instantaneously. He went from his sedate, irritable and distant demeanour to paranoid and alert. 'Why are you asking me these stupid questions? It's none of your business. Any pact I make with the devil is private.' He threw his coffee at the glass panel between us. After a split second of panic, I and my crisp white shirt were grateful for the court staff who were sensible enough to have placed us in this interview room, rather than the open one down the corridor. Harry turned around, lay back down and pulled the drawstrings around his hood tightly, looking like a turtle retreating into its shell.

Alarm bells were ringing after a quick mental suicide risk assessment. First, the demographics. He was young, male, single and lived on his own with almost no social support: all factors that would nudge the probability of him taking his own life higher. Further, he had a mental illness with active symptoms which were causing him substantial distress; a monumental risk factor. In terms of current social stressors, Harry also had to deal with the consequences of his recent legal trouble, facing a potential prison sentence. Most disturbingly, Harry had distinct and well considered plans for suicide that he was trying to conceal (as opposed to vague thoughts, without any measured intentions). I started the long, drawn-out uphill process of organising a Mental Health Act assessment for him to be sectioned to a psychiatric unit from court. As previous violence is one of the strongest predictors of future violence, I chased down his solicitor to obtain Harry's Police National Computer record. This showed only one previous conviction for possession of cannabis years ago, but no assaults. Therefore, a normal locked unit seemed more appropriate than a forensic unit as the likelihood of violence seemed minimal (at least, to anybody that wasn't his landlord).

Unfortunately, as was increasingly becoming the norm, there was no space at the inn. No free hospital bed available in his geographical jurisdiction of Brent, in north-west London. So Harry had to be remanded to prison overnight while bed managers made frantic arrangements behind the scenes. To make room, it's often a matter of discharging the least unwell (though not necessarily well) patient from the unit or making a 'deal' with another hospital, to 'borrow' a bed.

When I saw him back in court the next day, Harry was irate that he was about to be hospitalised.

'How *dare* you section me? I'm not crazy, you're crazy!'

'I'm really sorry you feel that way but I'm very concerned about your safety and I think—'

'Fuck your concern! I never asked for your help. Leave me alone.'

I took a deep breath. 'Our priority is to keep you safe. Hopefully you won't need to be in hospital for too long. With the right support and medication—'

'I should never have trusted you,' he seethed. 'Shouldn't have told you about the devil and his bus. You are so sneaky, pretending to be concerned. You were just looking for any excuse to lock me up. The judge couldn't make anything stick so you so-called psychiatrists have a go. You're all in cahoots.'

'I'm sorry you feel that way,' I stated, repeating myself as I couldn't think of anything else to say.

'And what about that child-molesting bastard that gave me AIDS? Did you section him?'

'No.'

'Why not?'

I twiddled with my pen and looked away.

'And what about those fire alarms,' he asked, 'did you put a Geiger counter to them?'

I had learnt very early on in my psychiatric career

that arguments against delusions are not winnable. I said nothing.

'What about patient confidentiality?' Harry snapped. 'You're breaking the law by telling other people about my pact. I could sue you.'

'I felt your risk of suicide superseded confidentiality. I think hospital is the best and safest place for you,' I said, trying to strike a balance between empathy and authority.

'Oh, yeah? Why don't *you* go there, if it's so fucking amazing?'

Harry didn't have a drink on him during this interaction. But if he did, I'm pretty sure I know where it would have ended up. I must admit, I left that consultation with minimal concerns. I appreciated why he was so vexed. If I genuinely didn't believe I was mentally ill, I would be furious if some smug stranger used my personal secret about my deal with the devil against me to lock me up. And in my line of work, disgruntled patients are hardly a rarity. Plus, I was confident in my clinical decision to section him. I barely gave Harry a second thought. Heck, he wasn't even the most challenging patient I had seen that day.

Fast forward around three months and I got the gloomy call from my team manager, Alicia. She never calls me on a Sunday evening, so I knew it was something serious even before her ominous words. Harry had taken his life. Not by jumping in front of the Number 9 bus, but via a paracetamol overdose. He wasn't the first patient I had worked with who had died, but the others had passed away years after our interactions and so this case felt personal. I knew we did everything by the book, but that was little consolation.

I found myself pondering his future life, had it not been prematurely extinguished. What would he have done for a living? Would he have had a family? Would he have found peace?

The next week, our team had a debrief and of course we cogitated carefully about whether there was anything else we could have done. We scoured for any gaps in our care. I had recognised Harry's suicide risk on the day and acted on it accordingly. From the medical notes, it seemed that he was admitted from our court to a psychiatric hospital for two months. Although he was aloof and evasive on the ward, he had seemingly gained a level of insight and could convincingly guarantee his own safety at the point of discharge. If this was accurate, it would have been unnecessary and even cruel to keep him hospitalised longer.

So, what went wrong? Unfortunately, I don't think I'll ever know. Harry could have genuinely improved during his hospital stay. He could have become non-compliant with his medication after discharge (we know that he collected his tablets from the pharmacy, but that's no guarantee that he actually took them). He could have had the intention all along to end his life and been biding his time to do this in peace, away from all these pesky interfering professionals. I couldn't help but wonder if I had inadvertently 'coached' Harry in what not to say, to stop doctors meddling with his freedom. Another possibility is that the hospital may have discharged him prematurely. They may have taken his reassurances at face value and not dug deep enough to really test them. Once again, I saw potential cracks in the system, which raised more questions than answers. Uncomfortable questions.

I found myself thinking again about those 'inspirational' celebrity stories of recovery and how far removed they are from the tragedy of some patients' darker realities, like Harry's. Obviously, suicides are, and should be, a time for reflection. That also goes for other tragedies, such as our patients going on to commit serious violence after apparently being cleansed by our car wash of rehabilitation: variously called 'never events' or 'serious untoward incidents' in management speak. These occurrences are part and parcel of dealing with the high-risk patients ubiquitous within forensic psychiatry. When I am faced with one, while deliberating over any potential shortcomings in the care provided by me and my colleagues, I can fully appreciate why some of my psychiatrist peers like Jenny might want to give them a wide berth, by choosing a less complicated category of clientele.

Chapter 27

Funny Bones

As the months passed and fatherhood continued becoming marginally less taxing, I once again found myself not sitting comfortably with random pockets of free time. Not only could I not relax, but worse, I didn't *want* to. I wanted to be creating something, regaling the public about the world of forensic psychiatry somehow. My *Huffington Post* blog helped, but it didn't feel like the platform was big enough to get my message across. My wife would shake her head and tease me, not incorrectly, about needing to find a suitable mid-life crisis.

I took on a series of hobbies. Within the space of eighteen months, I tried my hand at poker, amateur boxing and writing short stories. Typically, instead of easing in gently, I dived head-first into all of these pastimes. For poker, I bought several strategy books and woke up at 5.30 a.m. to cram them in before work. For boxing, I pushed the coach to let me spar before I was ready. For short stories, as well as devouring several texts on the craft, I attended a *Guardian* literary course for a few months. I have been asked in interviews and by concerned relatives if these distractions are to balance the tragedy and intensity that I'm exposed to in my professional life. The honest answer is no. At least, not consciously. I just like doing stuff. I think I would probably cycle through pastimes if I was an accountant or if I stacked shelves. My low threshold for boredom, and my misguided sense of always assuming things look easier than they actually are, drive me.

I achieved varying levels of success (not great at boxing or poker, pretty good at writing). Each hobby brought some mild distraction. But I needed something bigger. More intense. Something to wake up whatever lay dormant inside me. A mid-life crisis to match my overinflated ambition.

Full disclosure: this foray into stand-up comedy was not my first. I initially dabbled in my mid-twenties when I was newly qualified as a doctor. I did around forty gigs over the space of three years. Within that time, I moved from Newcastle to Sydney to Edinburgh to Essex. I didn't have much discipline and I didn't 'train' properly in the form of developing my material. I gigged randomly and erratically, committing myself for a few weeks, then giving up for months at a time. I eventually threw in the comedic towel around the age of twenty-seven. More than a decade later, in 2019, out of the blue, a very strong impulse to give it another try came over me. I was driving home from work one day when the epiphany struck me. I conjured up a realistic target timescale: two weeks to write a five-minute set and another fortnight to book my first return gig. On the rest of the drive, joke ideas kept popping into my head. As soon as I got through the door, I sprinted upstairs to grab a pen and jot everything down. An hour later, my wife called me down for dinner. I yelled over my shoulder that I was busy and that I would warm it up later. Two hours later, I had written the entire set. The next morning, I had booked a gig for a few days later.

Around this time, my little one graduated from nursery to join my big one at school, drastically cutting down our daily journeys. As my life had eased up over the preceding few months, I figured I would be able to fit in my new old hobby. How naive I was. The London scene was saturated with hundreds of fresh wannabe comics. Most were in their twenties and weren't blessed with the burden of children. They gigged four or five evenings per week at open mic events and some gigged every single night. This meant, for me to stay visible to promoters and not be diluted in the pool, I had to commit to a minimum of two shows per week. Gigs usually started around 8 p.m. and open mic-ers were expected there at least an hour early. The etiquette was to stay for the headliner. Typically, I would leave the house at 6.30 p.m. and get home after midnight. I soon realised that my pastime was unsustainable. I was banking on the outside chance that I was a precocious comedy genius and could somehow jump up the hierarchy and establish myself within months, rather than years.

Like anybody trying stand-up who isn't a clinical psychopath, I would feel utter terror before a gig, at least for the first dozen or so. However, after a couple of months, I subconsciously developed an ability to contain my fear with Zen-like focus. This type of scenario is akin to 'flooding', a psychotherapeutic technique and form of exposure therapy that is used to treat phobia and anxiety disorders including post-traumatic stress disorder. The sufferer is repeatedly confronted with the same situation that caused the original trauma. (I'm not flippant enough to think that facing a room full of expectant strangers, demanding I make them guffaw, is an actual trauma, but it is at least a stressor.) Patients are encouraged to use relaxation techniques in order to dissipate panic. The theory is that the adrenaline and fear response has a time limit, so the patient eventually calms down and realises that their phobia is unwarranted. It is the psychological equivalent of pushing somebody into the deep end and forcing them to swim (assuming that they don't drown). I rapidly came to the realisation that my sense of dread was superfluous. I 'bombed' a couple of gigs and also 'killed' a couple of gigs, with the majority being somewhere in the middle. In the former scenario, audience members would awkwardly avoid eye contact for the remainder of the show. For the latter, I might get a pat on the back or an encouraging comment during the smoke break (the nerves led to a full-blown relapse of daily smoking). But I understood that none of it mattered. I mean, *really* mattered. A terrible gig didn't lead to the audience throwing rotten fruit and jeering. A triumphant gig didn't lead to Dara Ó Briain inviting me on to *Mock the Week* (Dara, if you're reading this, I'm still available).

And then I noticed an odd thing. My skill at giving evidence as an expert witness improved. I was already reasonably comfortable on the witness stand. However, I would still occasionally get flustered, usually when I was asked to comment on a psychiatric issue from an angle I hadn't considered previously. With stand-up, thinking on your feet and adapting to the environment while keeping your cool is vital. From bantering with the audience to forgetting one's material, to responding to a heckle. And what is cross-examination in court, if not a polite heckle, peppered with legal jargon, from someone in a wig and gown? Arguably, freestyling from the witness stand is easier than from the stage, as your response only has to be correct, not witty. When asked a tricky question in court, I found myself formulating coherent, clever arguments with equanimity under the gaze of the judge and jury, instead of blurting out cobbled-together snippets of facts. My stand-up experience allowed me to solidify other elements of giving oral evidence. I videoed every gig I did on my phone, and when I watched the footage back, I noticed that I would talk too fast and not enunciate words when anxious (such as when tumbleweed rolled in after a punchline that I had assumed was sidesplittingly hilarious). After I had defeated (or at least diminished) my anxiety, I would recognise this problem as it was happening during my routine and had the presence of mind to slow down. Other nervous tics that I had been unaware of became apparent, including slouching forwards and blinking excessively. Again, with practice, I conquered these on stage and, to my surprise, I could transfer this to the courtroom. Not emphasising punchlines is another common mistake for the rookie comedian, which I corrected. I found myself slowing down and emphasising my conclusions when giving evidence: consciously at first, but soon automatically. And it worked. I could sense barristers retreating after I sidestepped their many traps. I could hear deference and defeat settle into their tones during cross-examination.

It wouldn't be long until my new-found skills as a comedian-cum-expert witness were put to the test, with one of the most bizarre cases I've ever worked on.

Chapter 28

Containing Histrionics

One morning in mid-2019, having slept poorly after the adrenaline rush from a victorious gig, I tanked myself full of coffee before attending Crown Court to see what would turn out to be a surreal assessment for a fitness to plead case. Mr Denzel Choo was in his sixties, of Chinese origin and faced charges related to possession of a weapon and persistent misuse of public telecommunications.

The case papers alleged that Denzel had grabbed a hammer in his garage and held it above his head in front of his wife. He then phoned the emergency services, threatening a messy suicide. I'm not sure if it's logistically possible to kill oneself with a hammer, but there was at the very least a risk of a monumental headache. The solicitors stated that they found it difficult to obtain clear instructions from him due to his tremendously anxious and histrionic presentation. They said that Denzel and his wife claimed that he had a diagnosis of post-traumatic stress disorder. They also emphasised that he was an educated man. He had a PhD in mathematics and had worked successfully as a university lecturer for many years.

The case papers also showed that Denzel was a nuisance. The police described him as an alcoholic who frequently made similar dramatic threats to hurt himself. Every couple of months, he would make such phone calls incessantly for a period of several hours, usually into the early morning. Despite a huge drain on their resources and a huge waste of their time, the emergency services had to take each call seriously. We all know the fable of the boy who cried wolf. On this particular evening in June, when services arrived, they found him lying in his bed groaning, with the hammer ominously lying on the pillow next to him. They spoke to him for a while and, once satisfied that he was intoxicated and did not require any intervention from mental health services, they left. Denzel called another ambulance twenty minutes later. When they arrived, they did a very cursory physical health check, and unsurprisingly didn't stick around. This incensed Denzel, who allegedly chased them outside with the hammer and smashed their front windscreen. During the police interview and to his solicitors, he insisted that he had simply held the hammer above his own head with the intention of self-harming. He categorically denied that he had threatened anybody or broken anything.

The medical records outlined brief psychiatric assessments from multiple occasions when Denzel had presented to accident and emergency; the overriding opinion was that his challenging behaviour and claims of suicidality were related to him being drunk. There was no underlying mental illness and he had full capacity when he was sober.

When I saw Denzel in the custody cells of Isleworth Crown Court in west London, right from the outset I realised that I had my work cut out. He spoke over me and clearly had his own agenda, obstinately returning to certain topics. Much of his behaviour was nonsensical. For example, after my brief enquiries about his family, he kept telling me about his successful siblings, including his younger brother who was a barrister and had written several notable textbooks. Denzel brought seven or eight huge books along to the assessment, none of which his brother had authored. He repeatedly insisted on showing me paragraphs about the law, even though these were not relevant to his charges.

Denzel disclosed that he had had a number of traumas in his life that 'will haunt me to my last breath'. He incessantly ruminated about these, particularly when he had been drinking. These were, to say the least, peculiar. Over twenty years before, his wife had had an abortion. This was during a time of separation; she would periodically leave him, due to his difficult behaviour. Denzel had conceptualised this as him 'murdering that poor wretched foetus, my own flesh and blood growing inside her'. He would picture the child and imagine the life that he or she would have lived. Denzel also had a father with dementia whom he used to look after, before he passed away five years earlier. According to Denzel, there was a small scuffle; they fought over a cup of tea that his father didn't want and eventually threw at him. In anger, Denzel threw it back and caused a small bruise on his dad's forehead. Denzel's siblings saw this, accused him of physically abusing their father and called the police. However, nothing came of this, and Denzel wasn't even arrested. Despite it being a relatively minor incident which everybody else involved had moved on from, Denzel was absolutely obsessed with it; he frequently deliberated over the guilt of hurting his dad and of upsetting his siblings.

Denzel's pattern of behaviour was aberrant. He was always anxious and constantly preoccupied with shame stemming from these incidents. He would go on alcohol binges around once every two months, though would be completely sober in between. When this happened, he would become disinhibited and extremely agitated. This would lead to him undertaking attention-grabbing acts, such as phoning emergency services and wielding hammers. He had also purportedly run into traffic in the past and leaned out of his bedroom window, threatening to jump.

During my assessment, Denzel was immensely anxious and melodramatic. On at least six occasions in the middle of our conversation he lay on the floor and started praying at my feet, begging me to write a report that would prevent him going to prison. Each instance required several minutes of me reassuring him, pulling him up, calming him down and repeating my questions. The first couple of times I felt sorry for him, but as it kept happening it grew more frustrating and my patience wore thin. I could see how this man might end up having a cup of tea hurled at him. In addition, every few minutes he would become visibly agitated and start shaking and blubbering (though with no actual tears). Despite my growing irritation, I tried to remember that Denzel was a damaged man. There was deep-rooted dejection in this version of him, far removed from his stable, intelligent and driven former incarnation as a university lecturer with a PhD.

When it came to assessing his fitness to plead, Denzel was able to outline the evidence in his case, including relaying relevant information from the witness statements from the aggrieved paramedics. Although it was a struggle to get him to actually focus on the relevant aspects of the case, when I was eventually able to do so, Denzel was able to answer questions appropriately and sensibly. To ascertain his understanding of the court process, I asked him about the roles of different people in the courtroom, such as the judge, jury and barrister. He answered eloquently and was clued up on legal terminology.

'OK, so now you've told me the role of the solicitor, Mr Choo, can you explain how a barrister's role differs?'

'In some countries they don't even have an adversarial legal system, you know. In France, it's an inquisitorial system. If I could just show you this book, it says—'

'Mr Choo, please just focus on answering my specific questions. What does a barrister *do*?'

'They specialise in courtroom advocacy and representing their clients in court by liaising directly with the judge, unlike solicitors. Did I mention that my brother is a renowned barrister? He has undertaken tremendous research. If you can just take a look at this chapter . . . '

After an excruciating hour and a half, I asked his wife to join us so I could obtain some collateral history from her. In the end, I had to tell Denzel to leave the room as he constantly trespassed into our conversation. At the time, my younger son, a mummy's boy, seemed incapable of allowing my wife to speak to another adult without constantly interrupting and pulling on her skirt. Unfortunately, Denzel could not be fobbed off with an iPad.

Mrs Choo was around the same age as her husband and also of East Asian origin. However, her demeanour struck me as the absolute antithesis of Denzel's. Sombre, serious, quiet and, above all, calm. I could not picture them together as a couple, but as the great philosopher Paula Abdul once said, opposites attract. This might also explain why they periodically separated. To be fair, considering how swiftly the end of my tether had been reached, living with his histrionics over the years must have tested her immensely. Mrs Choo ignored his churlish antics during the assessment. I should not be surprised that she had become inured to a degree, blocking him out like the noise of an incessantly buzzing fridge.

Mrs Choo gave some very helpful background information, which helped me put Denzel's personality into perspective. His mother had a biblical fear of being left alone and would make threats to kill herself or to run away, even when family members were popping out to the shops. Mrs Choo described Denzel's dramatic behaviour, which permeated most aspects of his life, even when sober. The previous week, he had seen a mechanic for an MOT. He didn't get the reassurance that he sought about the thread of his tyres. He apparently lay down on the ground, grabbed the man's feet and started praying. This was, understandably, embarrassing for his wife. She relayed that when he drank, his theatrics intensified exponentially. She confirmed that he actually drank fairly infrequently. There was some light at the end of the tunnel in that after his arrest, Denzel had agreed to engage with alcohol services for the first time ever. They had requested an assessment and Mrs Choo showed me an appointment letter for the following month.

At the end of the interview, we both walked out of the room into the lobby in front of the huge looming court-rooms. Like a scared puppy being left alone outside a shop, Denzel jumped at us and started yapping. He badgered me, incessantly asking what was going to happen next and whether he would go to prison. I answered as best I could; I would write a report suggesting that he had support from the alcohol rehabilitation team in the form of a community order instead of prison, though ultimately it was the judge's decision. I explained that having an appointment scheduled for the following month would curry favour. Despite this, Denzel kept repeating the same question. He was becom-ing progressively agitated, to the degree that he became quite threatening. He barged into me with his shoulder and grabbed on to my arm. He would not let go, demand-ing reassurances that I had already given him. I felt more annoyed than threatened (I had about twenty years and twenty kilos on him). I prised his fingers off me and pushed him away. A couple of the court security guards murmured, peeled themselves off the wall, and drifted towards us, but I waved them back. There was no need to make a scene.

In my court report, I outlined a number of very strong personality traits for Denzel. He was extremely fragile, emotional, dramatic and histrionic. He also ruminated about certain traumas and the associated guilt, and this was all catastrophically exacerbated by his drinking, leading to his inappropriate actions.

Despite the solicitor's suggestions, I rejected the diagnosis of post-traumatic stress disorder. To guide the court, I pointed out that in *ICD-10* (*The International Classification of Mental and Behavioural Disorders*, a commonly used classification system in psychiatry in England, soon to be usurped by the *ICD-11*), PTSD 'arises as a delayed and/or protracted response to a stressful event or situation of an exceptionally threatening or catastrophic nature, which is likely to cause pervasive distress in almost anyone, such as a natural or man-made disaster, combat, serious accident, witnessing the violent death of others, or being the victim of torture, terrorism, rape, or other crime.' This did not fit Denzel's upsetting experiences. Furthermore, despite his guilty ruminations, he didn't suffer actual flashbacks (reliving or re-enactment of the trauma). In my view, this all negated a diagnosis of PTSD.

Instead, I proposed that Denzel's presentation indicated a chronic anxiety disorder, on the background of a potential personality disorder: when the sufferer experiences difficulties in how they think and feel about themselves and others. These difficulties are ongoing and problematic, negatively affecting their well-being, mental health and relationships with others. I felt he had features of borderline personality disorder, a serious mental disorder that causes unstable moods, behaviour, and relationships; it is the diagnosis shared by Stella, my screaming dirty protester, and also Pamela, my prolific horrific self-harmer in prison. I also identified several features of histrionic personality disorder in Denzel, which is characterised by a pattern of excessive attention-seeking behaviours, usually beginning in early childhood, including inappropriate seduction and an excessive desire for approval or reassurance. Although it cropped up with relative frequency in my earlier training, it is a very rare diagnosis in the offender population. Probably because dramatic attention-seeking individuals are terrible at keeping a low profile and evading police, resulting in short-lived criminal careers. Although I knew that ultimately Denzel would eventually need intense long-term psychotherapy to address his emotional issues, I did not make this recommendation in my report as he was clearly not in the right headspace to engage in this at that time.

I also concluded that Denzel's pattern of drinking was unusual in that he was not alcohol dependent; he did not suffer any withdrawal symptoms nor any compulsion to drink on his sober days. Nevertheless, he probably had a diagnosis of 'harmful use of alcohol'; also listed in *ICD-10*, this is a pattern of continued imbibing that is causing damage to physical or mental health. This was reflected in his destructive actions during his index offences.

So far, so straightforward. What was less clear to me was Denzel's fitness to plead. Generally speaking, I do not suffer fools kindly; if I feel that somebody is intentionally not cooperating or trying to sabotage an assessment by feigning debilitation, I call them out. After all, I resisted the tears of Daryna, the pretty Ukrainian fraudster. However, this felt different. I noted that Denzel became so distressed and he was so distracted with begging me to write a favourable report that he struggled to focus long enough to meaningfully engage in the conversation.

After some deliberation, in the end, I did find Denzel fit to plead. However, I warned the court that it was very likely that he would become agitated and this would make the process quite challenging. I recommended a high level of support for the trial, including an intermediary (a neutral go-between who facilitates communication between the defendant and the legal professionals) and regular breaks. I did feel, however, that the judgement about his fitness to plead was what is known as a 'coin flip' in poker terminology. Fifty-fifty. I even acknowledged in my report that if another independent psychiatrist felt he was unfit to plead, I could fully support this difference of opinion.

The prosecution barrister took umbrage with my stance. Accusing me of 'dillydallying' (his choice of vocabulary – I don't think I've ever said that word out loud) and sitting on the fence. He seemed to misinterpret my recognition that Denzel's fitness to plead was near the cusp as indecisiveness and suggested that my assessment was clinically unsound. Under his cross-examination, I channelled the spirit of my stand-up. I spoke calmly and slowly, exuding confidence and over-enunciating my words. I made sure not to slouch or over-blink. I emphasised my punchlines.

'How can you guarantee that Mr Choo won't start crying and lying on the floor during his trial, if that's exactly what he did with you, Dr Das?'

'I cannot. My understanding is that the court is not asking me to make any guarantees, but to give my opinion on the balance of probabilities. As I said in my report, there is a real risk that Mr Choo will decompensate. But, *on balance*, I believe that this behaviour can be contained if the court follows my recommendations to support him.' Heckler shot down, I thought to myself.

On the strength of my evidence, the judge agreed with the community order. However, sadly, I heard from a colleague that several months later, despite only just dodging the bullet of a custodial sentence, and despite engaging with rehabilitation services, Denzel got drunk and repeated his demanding phone calls to emergency services. Apparently, the end of the judge's tether had also been reached and he was imprisoned, though only for four weeks. I dread to think how he would've coped with incarceration, given his astronomic anxiety levels. I only hope that the experience forced him to re-evaluate the error of his ways, and dampened down his future drama.

Chapter 29

Flummoxed

In my time working in hospital, I was used to repeatedly discussing individual patients in ward rounds and the myriad of other professional meetings. A range of different perspectives were sought, from other doctors, nurses, occupational therapists, social workers and psychologists. Multiple heads were better than one. But with my medico-legal reports, this lone wolf had no backup. To be fair, the majority of the time I felt confident in my conclusions. However, with tricky 'coin-flip' cases like Denzel leaving me flummoxed occasionally, I felt that I needed a platform to discuss my assignments with other expert psychiatrists.

I reached out to a couple of peers and founded the North London Medico-Legal Forum. Before we met every couple of months, we would send each other copies of a report on a particularly challenging case we had taken on, blanking out the clients' names to keep them anonymised. We would then take it in turns to critically analyse each other's documents. The parameters of the game were simple: be polite but be brutal. No echo chamber here. The purpose was to challenge each other's thinking, thus exercising our medico-legal muscles, to ultimately improve the quality of our evidence for the future. Although there were no gaping holes in my reports, my peers pointed out a number of areas for improvement, which I have since adopted. This included writing a summary of my conclusions at the beginning of each report, in case the judge only wanted to skim read it, and also delving more into the emotional impact of specific traumas, rather than merely robotically eliciting the details. The very first report I sacrificed to the feedback slaughterhouse was the baffling case of Mr Barry Mulligan. The diagnosis was relatively obvious, though the legal issues were contentious.

I have known of other experts occasionally failing to submit reports on time, forcing the court to adjourn the case for a couple of weeks. To me, this is discourteous to the criminal justice system and unjust to the defendant and the victim. I am minded of the aforementioned tragedy of Sarah Reed; she was waiting indefinitely for a fitness to plead assessment when she committed suicide in Holloway Prison in January 2016. To this day, I have never missed a deadline for a court report, though I came uncomfortably close in Barry Mulligan's case. The week before, I had seen another man, Brian Caragan, who had assaulted his wife. This was a relatively straightforward and bland evaluation (once again, with alcohol driving his misdemeanours, not mental illness). I was distracted by numerous cases, playing with my kids at home, and answering their inane questions;

Kamran, then five, had developed an obsession with dinosaurs and kept asking me who would win in a fight between two species (I made up the answers, and he didn't have the cynicism or the resources to challenge me). Although I didn't want to admit it at the time, I was also preoccupied by comedy. Not just the drain on my time attending gigs, but reviewing my videos and honing my material (perhaps, retrospectively, a tad too zealously). I had mixed up the two clients' names, believing them to be the same man. I only realised this when I was fortuitously sent additional medical notes for Barry Mulligan from the solicitor. I was about to reply telling them they had missed the boat as I had already submitted the report. Looking through my emails, I suddenly realised my mistake. It was a Thursday morning and the report was due by close-of-play the next day. And I had a gig that night and I was loath to cancel it. As well as being poor etiquette, I had been on a four-month waiting list for the new comedian slot of the fairly prestigious Downstairs at the King's Head show, in Crouch End, north London. In a frenzy of phone calls, I managed to arrange a last-minute appointment with Barry that afternoon.

Barry was a gay man in his mid-twenties with HIV, originally from South Wales. He had previously been diagnosed with bipolar affective disorder and attention deficit hyperactivity disorder. With the clock ticking, I read through his medical notes with some urgency in the hours leading up to our meeting. They depicted a troubled childhood, I think it is fair to say. Barry used to set fires and would purposely swallow Lego bricks when he wanted attention from his mother. He once killed his pet guinea pig with a rock. He grew up in an environment tarnished by addiction, violence, gangs and poverty. He was one of five siblings, two of whom had died from drug overdoses. He moved to London in his mid-teens with his mother to escape his abusive stepfather. Barry started taking illicit drugs regularly around this time, including on a daily basis for an entire year around the age of twenty-one. Crystal meth, GHB and mephedrone were his poisons of choice. He engaged with community drug rehabilitation services, on and off, though still suffered from occasional relapses. 'When I'm sad, angry or bored, which is pretty much always,' he had reported to his last psychiatrist.

Barry had a rather tepid offending history with one caution for driving under the influence in 2012. When I saw him, he was facing a charge of assault occasioning actual bodily harm. Just after Christmas 2019, he was kicked out of his grandparents' house after an argument and found himself wandering the streets of Soho. He met a random man and went back to this person's house for sex and drugs (though purportedly no rock 'n' roll). They did a 'booty bump'. I had to admit that naive little me had never heard of this before and it sounded quite intriguing. I Googled it and discovered that it involved mixing a cocktail of drugs, usually crystal meth or cocaine, with water and squirting it into one's anus through a syringe. I thought, no thanks, I'll stick to my skinny hazelnut cappuccino through my mouth-hole.

When I assessed him in the slightly grotty, cramped office at the back of the library (the best I could do on such short notice), Barry explained that after taking the booty bump, he became increasingly paranoid that the police were going to raid the flat for drugs. He also started to hallucinate; he

was seeing dragons and hearing roars. His new lover unsurprisingly asked him to leave. So Barry went to the house
of another man who, according to the case papers, was a
suspected drug dealer. His psychosis deepened. His cousin,
Clarice, received a text message from Barry begging for
help. He asked her to attend the address and also claimed
that his insides were burning. Clarice sprinted the mile to
the flat in Central London and could hear screaming from
the street outside. She followed it to a locked bathroom in
the flat. She forced her way in and kicked open the door to
find Barry naked in the bathtub in a very disturbed state,
repeatedly stating that he was on fire. In his sheer agitation,
he had completely forgotten that he had sent the text and
was very suspicious that Clarice had magically appeared.
He assumed that she was there to collude with the police
and get him arrested. He was holding a pair of scissors
and stabbed them into his own cheek. Flabbergasted, and
wanting to get the hell out of there, Clarice took her eye off
Barry for a second to grab his clothes from the floor. She felt
a sharp pain in the side of her head. She didn't even realise
he had stabbed her until she felt blood trickle across her ear.
Clarice called the police, ironically fulfilling his delusional
concerns. The drug dealer, who had been smoking weed
all day and had fallen asleep, didn't even know Clarice was
in his flat. He woke up to the noises of the skirmish which
had by then tumbled into his kitchen. He hurriedly bundled
them both out. As well as the potential unwanted attention
from the authorities, I imagine a bleeding naked man and a
bleeding stranger must have perked him up from his stoned
phlegmatic stupor. The police promptly arrested Barry on

the street and took them both to the hospital. Clarice's cut was relatively superficial and only needed gluing. Barry needed twelve stitches.

After he sobered up, Barry had patchy memories of the incident. He was aware of hurting himself, though he said that if he had struck Clarice then it must have been unintentional, lashing out in his frenetic state. His cousin later dropped the charges, though the Crown Prosecution Service pursued the case. I suspect that his reluctance to disclose the source of the drugs would have goaded them.

Despite being evasive and defensive during my assessment, Barry reluctantly answered all my Pritchard Criteria enquiries. Therefore, I found him fit to plead. He kept emphasising that he couldn't remember his actions during the offence, seeming to insinuate that he could not be found guilty for this reason, which was obviously incorrect.

The evaluation went smoothly, as did my gig in Crouch End a few hours later. I bantered a bit with a noisy drunk couple who sat at the front. However, I couldn't fully enjoy it, knowing I had this mammoth report looming over me. I had to pull an all-nighter, though I did manage to complete it in time. My ever-sacrificing wife, Rizma, even did my scheduled school runs the next morning for me.

In forming my opinion for the report, I recognised that Barry had suffered a drug-induced psychosis after taking a 'booty bump' for the first time. My differential diagnosis (the most likely alternative explanation) was a relapse of his bipolar affective disorder, though this was unlikely as it should not come on so suddenly. I highlighted that the exact details of the alleged assault appeared to be unknown.

If the court accepted that Barry accidentally stabbed his cousin, then he had not committed the alleged offence (which required basic intent). However, I also considered the defence of not guilty by reason of insanity if the court accepted the prosecution's version. As per the specific legal criteria (the M'Naghten rules) I suggested that Barry was suffering from a defect of reason from a disease of the mind at the time of the alleged offence (i.e. he was floridly psychotic). Although he did know the nature and the quality of the act, as he was in fear for his life and he was seemingly acting in self-defence, he likely would not have known it was wrong. While writing up my conclusions, I considered that in many cases the court might not accept the insanity plea if the defendant's behaviour was as a direct consequence of voluntary drug intoxication. But this case was trickier. Barry's actions were related to actual psychosis (his delusional beliefs) rather than pure inebriation. I realised I needed to do more research before finalising my report. The more I read into this (finally opening my huge forensic psychiatry textbook almost five years after purchasing it), the more confused I became. There seemed to be multiple possibilities and different ways to interpret the law. Did this mean Barry was open to the insanity defence? I hedged my bets that he wasn't, painstakingly giving the details of my reasoning.

I presented this case to my colleagues at the very first meeting of the North London Medico-Legal Forum a couple of weeks later. Three other psychiatrists attended that day (though our number has since grown). We gathered in the outhouse of Marjorie, a lovely Scottish lady in her fifties.

One of my peers, a smart, newly qualified consultant with floppy hair called James, backed up my views about the lack of validity for the insanity plea. Marjorie suggested I should ignore Barry's account because he had obviously been extremely intoxicated at the time and was therefore unreliable. She thought that the defence was not even on the table. Although she reached the same conclusion as me, I disagreed with her logic. I felt it was the court's prerogative, not mine, to decide upon Barry's dependability. The third psychiatrist abstained.

For this assignment, I had only been asked about Barry's fitness to plead. I had not been instructed to give an opinion on disposal for the case, that is, whether he should go to hospital, to prison or serve his punishment in the community. This could simply have been an oversight by the solicitor or perhaps they were worried that my recommendation might not have been favourable for their client and therefore didn't want me to raise it. My instinct was to state in my report that, although I had not been instructed to comment, I believed that I had relevant recommendations. I suggested a community order with a requirement for psychiatric treatment and drug rehabilitation; conditions could include Barry having to attend regular appointments with a Community Mental Health Team, taking the medication for his bipolar affective disorder consistently instead of sporadically, staying abstinent from illicit drugs (which could be reinforced by regular urine drug screens) and attending drug rehabilitation service appointments. I felt this was fair, given Barry's lack of previous violent offending, and considering that his assault seemed directly related to drug use.

This time, James felt that I was overstepping my boundaries by commenting on an issue outside of my instructions. However, Marjorie agreed with me, believing that regardless of the solicitors instructing me, my obligations were to the court.

Even though the dissection of my report led to little consensus amongst my peers, it was, in a way, reassuring to see that there was a range of opinions and viewpoints. I appreciated that psychiatry, and in particular expert witness medico-legal work, was full of grey areas and disparate interpretations. I was allowed to have doubts. As long as I was being honest, neutral and objective, and as long as I detailed all my cerebral dilemmas and conflicting perspectives within my evidence, sometimes there were no overriding correct answers.

Unfortunately, around this time, the novelty of the excitement of stand-up was fading. With it, so did my overall enjoyment, reflecting my other hobbies, and perhaps exposing one of my character flaws. The occasional highs from 'crushing' shows was massively overshadowed by the overwhelming disappointment I felt from the rare lead balloon gigs, which I would ruminate over for many days afterwards. I wasn't built for stand-up. I was way too impatient to progress, took failure too much to heart and put too much pressure on myself to succeed. Frequent dire audience attendance was also a huge turn-off for me. There is nothing more awkward than a comic trying to amuse a dribble of paying punters (I presume that is the collective noun) in an almost empty room, and nothing more desperate than a bunch of wannabe comedians rehearsing their material to each other, in an utterly empty room. Ultimately though, *time* was the salient factor that ended my short-lived second attempt at a comedy career. The near miss with Barry Mulligan's report was a wake-up call for me. I reluctantly admitted to myself that late-night gigs inevitably resulted in groggy early mornings. My consumption of caffeine and nicotine had insidiously increased. I couldn't afford to be sloppy at work, so something had to give. Of course, there was the option of only dabbling in stand-up occasionally. However, I knew my ego couldn't take seeing other open mic-ers around me progress to more high-profile shows, leaving me at the bottom of the overcrowded hierarchy.

I did around forty gigs in six months. My wife was very supportive and never put pressure on me to stop, though my absence for so many evenings and dodging so many bedtimes must have taken its toll on her. It was an enlightening experience (four stars). Not only did it give me closure, having given the art form the respect it deserved this time around, but it had made me a better expert witness (admittedly, unwittingly). And I felt some comfort in knowing with absolute certainty that I was *not* some unpolished comedy genius, destined for super-stardom. I was fairly decent though. Footage on YouTube is available for any doubters.

Chapter 30

A Psych for Sore Minds

With stand-up comedy out of my life, I needed a new fix of stimulation. I did love hanging out with Rizma and the boys. There was also a mini resurgence of socialising now that the kids were lower maintenance and could stay over at their grandparents' every once in a while. The occasional rave, rap or comedy gig (as a punter, not wannabe comic) was definitely doable. I continued to exercise religiously. I was well into my forties by now, even if I did try to hide it with an edgy haircut. Although I felt sharp in my mind, my body wasn't having it. I sprained my ankle in the summer of 2019, which took months to heal and, shortly afterwards, I developed severely herniated cervical discs in my neck from lifting weights that were far too heavy (once again, reflecting my naivety in assuming things look easier than they actually are). I also had regular nasty flare-ups of gout. Although I had no qualms taking colchicine for acute attacks, I was initially reluctant to take the prophylactic allopurinol, which I was prescribed by my GP. I felt like taking a daily medication for the rest of my life would be admitting defeat: ironic, I know, considering that I medicated patients and strongly encouraged them to accept their diagnoses. But I still felt young in my own mind. My right big toe cared not for my ageing-denial issues and would cause me excruciating agony for a week or so every couple of months. Even on the odd occasion when I could barely walk, I was too embarrassed to call in sick at my NHS court job. To me, gout sounded like the lamest excuse, both literally and figuratively. So, I would waddle in, walking slowly to disguise my limp. During periods that I was denied exercises by gout, my mood plummeted and I would feel sluggish. After the ninth or tenth attack, I conceded and took the pills. Touché, toe, touché.

Family, socialising, exercising and occasional hobbling aside, I needed an activity for myself. I had come to learn that I was at my most fulfilled when I was either obsessed by or striding towards something. My *Huffington Post* blog had led to some media work over the years, though this was somewhat sporadic. I appeared on a couple of episodes of *Murder, Mystery and my Family*, a daytime TV show on BBC One which investigates infamous old murder cases from the perspective of two renowned barristers, utilising current legal frameworks. I gave my opinions on some of the perpetrators' mental health issues, and whether or not psychiatric defences which didn't exist back then might apply in present times and vice versa. I covered the fatal shooting of Albert Baker in October 1937 by Walter Smith, his supposed best friend (who needs enemies?) on a boat. Smith was hanged at Norwich Prison. *Mania a potu* (literal translation: madness from a potion), a now defunct psychiatric defence, was attempted by him at trial. However, this is characterised by very frenzied, random inexplicable behaviour, which in my view contrasted with Smith's cold and calculated acts; he shot Baker three times with a single-bullet gun, meaning he had to reload twice, and scarpered with his money. I also gave soundbites for a documentary on Channel 5 about Broadmoor Hospital, and carried out psychological autopsies on a number of their very high-profile historical patients, including Charles Bronson and Ronnie Kray.

Bronson is certainly a fascinatingly warped character. Possibly Britain's most notorious prisoner, he was convicted of armed robbery in 1974 and originally sentenced to seven years in prison. He has been detained in various penitentiaries and Broadmoor Hospital for over forty years for his errant behaviour. He has attacked guards and other convicts, damaged prison property and taken numerous hostages. This included one incident, and I'm not kidding, when he forced his captives to tickle his feet with a feather and to hit him over the head with a lunch tray. Violence is usually reactive (for explicit goals such as to acquire money or improve one's social position), or expressive (unplanned acts of rage or frustration). In my opinion, Bronson committed both. Additionally, he seemed to actually *enjoy* regular violence. Not as a release of anger, but almost as a lifestyle. It wasn't only a means to achieve his goal but actually the goal itself. In the documentary, I proposed that he used his aggression to uphold his image and to gain notoriety and attention. He and Ronnie Kray became friends in Broadmoor. A film was made about Bronson, featuring Tom Hardy (who coincidentally also played the Kray twins in another movie). Bronson somehow managed to thump his way into popular culture. He even got married while in prison, which to me is more impressive than his eighteen-day hunger strike. None of this would have happened without his reputation. And he earned this with his fists. Part of me would have revelled in the opportunity to evaluate Bronson in person. But then again, there is a reasonable risk that he would've taken me hostage and possibly even forced me to do unfathomable things with a feather.

In addition to the documentaries, I was interviewed for the occasional newspaper article and appeared as a guest on a few podcasts and the odd radio programme, including Matthew Wright's show and on Radio 4. My most surreal media foray has to be when I went on a modern hip-hop-themed gameshow called *Don't Hate the Playaz*. I had to battle rap against another doctor in a huge warehouse with a live audience in a mosh pit, most of whom were half my age. It was as awkward and surreal as it sounds.

Even though I very much enjoyed my media appearances, something didn't sit right with me. The majority of the time I was being asked about issues that weren't quite within my area of expertise. Matthew Wright, for example, who was very welcoming and friendly, was focused on what drives serial killers. He wanted to know if I believed Anders Breivik (the Norwegian right-wing extremist who killed eight people with a bomb then shot dead sixty-nine more on 22 July 2011) was inherently evil and if he could ever be rehabilitated. While I was happy to answer his enquiries, they were more philosophical and judgemental than professional. 'Inherently evil' is not a clinical concept. Additionally, his questions didn't feel very representative of my patient group. In fact, the only person with whom I had been involved who had committed multiple killings was Elgin, who had taken the lives of his three partners. However, by the most widely accepted definition, a serial killer is a person who murders three or more random victims, usually for abnormal psychological gratification, as opposed to in a fit of anger towards people they know. Similarly, other interviewers seemed to be asking sensationalist questions, wanting to know the gruesome details of various assaults and murders. Sure, this scrutiny was an aspect of my work that was necessary for medico-legal opinions in a criminal case. And in all fairness, I could relate to the fascination of the macabre; it is, after all, what drove me towards my line of work. Nevertheless, it made me uncomfortable that there were no questions forthcoming about how certain symptoms of established mental illness could cause offending. Crucially, there was also very little enquiry about the rehabilitation process. This is ultimately the goal of the system I worked in, and I wanted to promulgate the success stories and educate the public. If I only discussed the gory details of my subjects' crimes, but not how they overcame their mental illnesses and reintegrated themselves into society, wouldn't I be contributing to the stigma instead of tackling it? I felt like my patients were not given a voice. Much like their lack of representation when celebrities with common mental health issues seemed to have stories when they had recovered, just in time to promote their new book or album.

The solution was obvious. I would have to make my own material. I started my YouTube channel, 'A Psych for Sore Minds', in September 2020. I dissected a whole range of topics related to mental health. Some episodes focused on individual symptoms and diagnoses such as hearing voices and drug-induced psychosis, and I even used Barry's story as a case example (keeping him anonymised, of course, as I have done in this book). In others, I disentangled complex psychiatric issues within high-profile cases, including Britney Spears' conservatorship; her father made all financial decisions on her behalf after her breakdown, even though she clearly had the capacity to record albums and go on tours, which he made money from. I answered questions about mental illness from the internet: 'Can a cat have schizophrenia?' was one of my favourites. I also interviewed people who had suffered from a range of disorders, including post-traumatic stress disorder and psychosis, and I talked to individuals who had been sectioned. I wanted to know about *their* experience in hospital. I thought it would be enlightening to hear both perspectives: psychiatrist and patient. Detainer and detainee. Enforcer and enforced. I wasn't afraid to ask them uncomfortable questions about my profession, such as whether they found their psychiatrist to be approachable, knowledgeable and helpful. Although I did speak about cases that I had personally assessed, I kept them unidentifiable and would change demographic details (again, as I have done here). I quickly learnt that it was much easier to comment on high-profile criminal cases that were already in the public domain as I was less restricted in terms of what I could say. I did this, focusing on discussing the psychiatric issues through my professional lens, rather than just outlining the juicy details as many YouTube true crime channels were already doing far more effectively.

The case that moved me the most, which I covered on my channel fairly early on, was that of Andrea Yates. She was a nurse who killed her five children on 20 June 2001 in Houston, Texas. That fateful morning, her husband got up and went to his job at NASA. Yates methodically drowned her children one by one, while they were eating breakfast. They were six months old, two, three, five and seven. Tragically, her seven-year-old boy apparently realised what was going on and tried to escape, though he was caught and suffered the same horrendous fate as his siblings. My elder boy was seven at the time I made the video, and the image of Yates's son running away stung my calloused heart. She phoned the emergency services herself to confess what she had done and also called her husband. She later reported that she had been considering killing them for two years as she believed they were not developing correctly and had been marked by Satan. She felt that the only way to save her children from hell was to end their lives. Yates also experienced other clearly psychotic symptoms, such as the belief that television cartoon characters were telling her she was a bad mother and auditory hallucinations in the form of a voice ordering her to grab a knife. She saw satanic teddy bears and ducks on the walls in prison.

I delved with fascination into Yates's background. She worked as a nurse in a cancer centre for eight years. She and her husband had strong religious beliefs and she hosted a

Bible-study night three times a week. They sought spiritual guidance from a fundamentalist preacher who sermonised hell, brimstone and damnation. I don't think that religion in itself was instrumental in Yates's mental illness, but I do wonder whether the fearmongering seeped into her consciousness and aggravated her delusions.

Interestingly, in the mid-nineties, seven years before the killings, after the birth of her first child, Yates started having hallucinations involving stabbing. She also appeared to have had a number of psychotic episodes after the birth of her other children, and an attempted suicide by overdose after her fourth child. She was taken to hospital but shockingly was discharged before she fully recovered because her insurance company would not pay for her to stay for longer.

After the death of her father a few months before the killings in early 2001, Yates deteriorated. She stopped talking, stopped drinking and was neglecting her baby. She also began pulling out her own hair. She spoke of video cameras watching her. She was taken to hospital for a third time and discharged ten days later, despite being depressed and mute, apparently because her sleeping and eating had improved. In my opinion, this was ridiculously early to discharge her. Yates was taken to hospital again after discharge and, amazingly, her psychiatrist began to wean her off her anti-psychotic drugs. To me, this sounded like another alarming mistake. Given the potential risks to the children, I would keep any patient with this presentation on anti-psychotics for an absolute minimum of six months before considering decreasing the dose, which, even then, I would do very gradually and with extreme caution.

Yates was diagnosed with major depression, schizophrenia, schizoaffective disorder, bipolar disorder and postnatal psychosis. The last, also known as postpartum psychosis or puerperal psychosis, is rare, occurring in one or two out of every thousand new mothers. This type of psychosis comes on faster and more intensely than other forms and is associated with a risk of suicide and harm to the baby. It is characterised by manic symptoms, stupor or catatonia, as well as delusions, hallucinations and confusion. Full recovery can be expected within six to ten weeks. Anti-psychotic medications or electroconvulsive therapy are the usual forms of remedy. The latter treatment is often vilified, not least because it was carried out in barbaric conditions (with no anaesthetic) in the distant past. But contrary to popular belief, it's actually very effective in specific circumstances, such as postpartum psychosis.

According to my research, Yates's psychiatrist told her two days before the killing that she had to 'think positive thoughts' which, in my view, was completely useless advice. He might as well have suggested trying homeopathy or visiting a witch doctor.

As it happens, the state of Texas uses the same 'not guilty by reason of insanity' laws as England: the M'Naghten rules. During Yates's trial almost a year later, she attempted this defence, though it was initially rejected and she was sentenced to prison. This confused me as the evidence appeared to suggest that this was a clear-cut case for the insanity plea. Apparently, the lawyer hired by Yates's family stated 'If this woman doesn't meet the test of insanity in this state then nobody does. We might as well wipe it from the books'.* I agreed. Perhaps her crimes were so unpalatable that the jury didn't care whether she was mentally unwell and just wanted her to suffer, like her children did.

However, Yates was granted a new trial in 2006, because of the dodgy expert witness testimony of one of my brethren, Dr Dietz, a forensic psychiatrist who had been hired by the prosecution. Firstly, he had no particular expertise in postnatal mental illness. Even more startlingly, he hadn't treated a patient since 1982. He appears to have been quite famous in his field, having given evidence in some high-profile cases such as that of Jeffrey Dahmer (the 'Milwaukee Cannibal', a convicted American serial killer and sex offender who murdered and dismembered seventeen men and boys between 1978 and 1991). Dr Dietz worked as a private consultant to popular television shows, including *Law and Order*, and he testified that just before the killing there had been an episode about a mother with postnatal depression who had drowned her children and was found not guilty by reason of insanity. I think he was insinuating that Yates had got the idea from the programme. However, after he gave his testimony, it turned out that no such episode had aired.

As I stated in my video, I personally thought that postnatal mental illness was quite niche and did not feel that an expert in this particular diagnosis was necessary as long as the doctor was confident about diagnosing psychosis in general and had a good understanding of psychiatric defences. It was also not unreasonable that some experts are retired

---

* https://www.thelancet.com/journals/lancet/article/PIIS0140-6736(06)69789-4/fulltext

from clinical practice, but having said that, twenty years is a long time for one's skills to rust. Dr Dietz apparently opined that Yates must have known what she was doing was wrong because she expressed the belief that it was Satan and not God that ordered her children's homicides. He acknowledged that she was mentally unwell but did not think her illness was that severe. As I said in the episode, this flagrantly contradicted the evidence. She purportedly felt compelled to listen to Satan and believed that the only way to save her children from hell was to kill them. So, in her deluded mind, she thought what she was doing was right. On a simpler level, it didn't make sense to me; he seemed to be arguing that if somebody is floridly psychotic and listens to a voice from God, they should go to hospital for treatment, but if it was a voice from Satan, they should go to prison (or could even be executed, given that it was the United States).

Covering this case, of course I drew parallels in my mind to Yasmin, who suffocated her nephew believing that she was ridding him of demons. I felt a similar degree of pity. Hearing about the incompetence of the psychiatrists who treated her before the killings stunned and angered me in equal measure. Even writing about it now makes my blood boil. I might be naturally defensive about colleagues being criticised for their patients going on to commit violence, because I appreciate that many individuals are unpredictable and there are often minimal overtly telegraphed risk factors. However, according to my research, the professionals in charge of Yates's care were beyond inept, seemingly negligent. There is a huge chasm between a psychiatrist doing their utmost for a challenging and inherently dangerous patient cohort with occasional tragic outcomes, and those who don't even seem to be trying. It might sound dramatic, but I don't think it can be denied that at least some of the blood of Yates's children is on the hands of the insurance company that would not shell out for her ongoing treatment, and more so on those of the callous professionals, including Dr Dietz. I had no qualms about blasting these charlatans in my video for their abysmal treatment. I believe that all psychiatrists, myself included, should be held accountable for our actions.

Another aspect of intrigue in making my episode on Andrea Yates was the slew of vitriol expressed towards her in some of the comments. The internet, to be fair, is not renowned for being the voice of reason. Many viewers had completely missed the point and were blind to the devastating influence that her mental illness had had on her actions. They only saw her as an evil woman who had murdered her children and 'deserves to be boiled alive in hell's lava for eternity', as one commentator succinctly put it. Although I suspected that such attitudes existed, it took my YouTube channel to coax them out in black and white. These are exactly the types of attitudes and the stigma I had been tackling professionally as a psychiatrist and now personally as a fledgling YouTuber. For some reason, I couldn't help imagining Yasmin receiving these kinds of comments, either on internet news story websites about her case or potentially even in public if people knew who she was. I pictured how upsetting and utterly damaging it would be for her. This may or may not have happened to her in real life and I would never know. But it was an image that I could not shake out of my head, nonetheless.

Evidently, I had my work cut out in making my YouTube videos, but at least I had found a new calling. And one that felt less self-centred and narcissistic than stand-up.

Chapter 31

To Catch Some Predators

When I started my YouTube channel, 'A Psych for Sore Minds', I was concerned that I would run out of topics and cases. In fact, I encountered the opposite problem; I was coming up with ideas faster than I could make videos (and currently have a list of well over a hundred potential future episodes). A few months in, shortly before Christmas 2020, a contentious medico-legal assignment was sent my way. Reading the case papers, I was immediately tempted to make an episode about it. I knew that if the story of Andrea Yates tested the moralistic sensitivities of my viewers, then they would drool over this one.

Mr Kai Fletcher was twenty-nine and was on bail in Coventry, facing a charge connected to sexual grooming. Several months earlier, a paedophile hunting vigilante group who called themselves 'Unknown TV' contacted a number of men via Facebook, many of whom apparently had some form of mental impairment. Kai was one of their targets. A representative from this group, a middle-aged woman, pretended to be a fifteen-year-old girl named Kitty. She exchanged flirtatious messages with Kai and spoke to him over the phone. Their conversations became increasingly explicit in nature and they arranged to meet for sex at a service station. The case papers reported that Kai had taken an Uber there, and must have had a rude awakening when he was met by a mob of burly male Unknown TV reps, who accosted and physically restrained him until the police arrived. This process, I had discovered, was known as 'catfishing'.

According to Kai and his solicitors, he had a learning disability, although this was not formally diagnosed. These types of disorders are associated with significantly reduced ability to understand new or complex information, or to learn new skills, due to impaired intelligence. One eminent form is autism (which has its own unique characteristics); this was the disorder that Charlie Wedger suffered from, the man who sexually assaulted a woman who was waiting at a bus stop with her baby in a pram. Although Kai had not attended a special needs school, he was significantly behind his peers in his reading and writing abilities and needed remedial one-to-one tuition, which would support this diagnosis.

When I assessed him at his solicitor's office in Coventry one rainy afternoon, Kai, a gangly man with curly hair, looked very nervous. He had come out in a T-shirt and was utterly soaked, shivering and rubbing his hands throughout the assessment. His younger brother had driven him and accompanied him to the appointment, seemingly not by choice, as he only looked up from his phone twice, the first time being when I entered the large conference room.

Delving into Kai's background, there were certainly some indicators of deficits in his functioning, which might have further pointed towards a learning disability. He was deemed unfit to manage his own finances and therefore required an appointee from a finance protection team, which gave him a weekly budget to spend. These professionals offer legal protection, a form of Power of Attorney, for people who are unable to look after their own affairs and deemed vulnerable to financial abuse. When making the video for my channel on Britney Spears's conservatorship a few weeks earlier, I had compared the American and British frameworks, so I was aware of the legislation in this area. This safeguard had apparently been arranged for Kai after certain people, including his own mother, had taken advantage of him by withdrawing large amounts of money, though he was reluctant to discuss this with me. I only got a shrug from his brother, who looked up for the second and last time. According to the sparse documentation, Kai had reportedly struggled with budgeting himself, previously spending all his money on cigarettes and video games and not having enough for food. Kai was also incapable of learning to drive. However, despite this, there were other areas in which he had no problems functioning and had a degree of independence; he was able to travel all over his local area autonomously to meet family and friends, and could cook meals by himself, as well as doing basic shopping. People with significant learning disabilities generally struggle to hold down employment.

Kai worked as a carpenter, though this was through his father's business, so it was feasible that nepotism rather than competency had got him the job. I did wonder if his poor choice of apparel, dressing like it was the midst of summer, was also a reflection of a low IQ, noting that his brother wore a large mac, which glistened with raindrops and dripped rhythmically onto the carpet of the conference room for the first fifteen minutes. A decade earlier, when he was nineteen, Kai was apparently pressured into moving in with his seventeen-year-old girlfriend after she fell pregnant. They had a baby, then split up shortly afterwards, although Kai was still involved in the child's life. His previous offending history was pretty unremarkable: one drunk and disorderly charge and an attempted burglary as a young teen.

Kai gave what in my view was an implausible explanation for the allegations, again, indicating somewhat low intelligence. He claimed that his friend had used his phone to hack into his Facebook account and had sent all the sexualised messages (once again, who needs enemies?). When I asked why he had travelled to the service station, he replied that this same friend had asked him to buy a phone charger from a particular shop there. From my experience of service stations, they are hardly niche markets for specialist items (aside from perhaps overpriced Ginsters pasties). Kai maintained that he had no knowledge of the more graphic inappropriate Facebook messages until he was apprehended.

I noted that during my assessment, Kai made some odd statements and there were contradictions in his narrative.

This included some areas that there would seemingly be little reason to lie about: for example, he told me that he was living with an ex-girlfriend and then later on with some friends, despite having his own council flat. He said afterwards that he was living with his parents. Again, I wondered if a learning disability influenced this. When I enquired about his previous attempted burglary, Kai told me that he once 'borrowed' his father's boss's keys to get into his own house. I asked him why the boss's keys would open his front door and he shrugged and told me it was a coincidence.

From the medical records, it seemed that Kai had never had a formal IQ test, which would definitively diagnose a learning disability. This type of evaluation is outside of my area of expertise and is usually done by an experienced, qualified psychologist. I knew that the court would not adjourn the case for this purpose, as with current waiting lists it could take a year or longer to arrange. Some of my peers would shy away from committing to a diagnosis without the backup of this test. This would not be helpful for the court. Instead, I carefully weighed up the evidence, focusing on Kai's functioning, which was variable. I concluded that although I could not be absolutely certain, on the balance of probabilities, I believed that Kai had a mild learning disability. I ruled out any other diagnoses such as a personality disorder or drug and alcohol issues. I also decided that Kai was fit to plead, despite his frankly comically unfeasible version of events.

The instructing solicitors had asked me whether Kai had formed the *mens rea* for the offence. This refers to criminal intent, the literal translation from Latin being 'guilty mind', that is, the culprit intentionally and knowingly breaking the law. This applies to most crimes, though not all. Speeding, for example, doesn't require knowledge of the speed limit, so being unaware of this is not a defence (as I can attest to, having unsuccessfully appealed numerous fines by pleading ignorance). As I painstakingly pointed out in my report, as a psychiatrist I am not allowed to give an opinion on whether Kai actually *did* form the *mens rea* (as this is a legal matter, solely for the court) but rather whether his learning disability affected his ability to do so. This might sound pedantic, but I had heard scare stories of colleagues being ripped to shreds on the witness stand for going beyond the boundaries of their professional evidence, even though, as in this case, the lawyers had asked the wrong question in their instructions. In tackling this issue, one area that I specifically tested was Kai's understanding of the legal age of consent, which he acknowledged was sixteen. I also took into account that Kai was not sexually naive. He'd had a few different relationships and had fathered a child with a previous partner and lived with her for a while. I also considered the very fact that, according to the screenshots of the Facebook messages I was sent, Kai had overtly stated on a few occasions that he was worried about meeting up with Kitty because she was too young.

'Please don't tell ur mates about R relashunship,' he had written.

'That's OK hun. U can B my secret guy.'

'Not shore it cool. When U 16?'

'Only became 15 last month.'

'We cld wait and meat nxt yr. Just be online bf / gf.'

'But I want U now hun. I want 2 do it.'

This abysmal spelling could have been yet another indication of a learning disability. But then again, perhaps a middle-aged fuddy-duddy like me just couldn't relate to how the youth message each other nowadays.

Having weighed up all the evidence, I concluded that Kai's limited cognitive ability and intelligence level would not be severe enough to interfere with his ability to form the *mens rea*. In other words, his learning disability might hinder his understanding of some complicated concepts (such as his ability to manage his own finances) but there was no reason he would not be able to foresee and understand the consequences of his actions: that he was meeting an underage girl, with the intention to engage in sex, and that this was against the law.

The solicitors asked me to comment on whether Kai was vulnerable and suggestible. I found this issue a little ambiguous. He clearly was both of those things. He couldn't budget and had been financially exploited by members of his own family, necessitating an appointee. He'd also been apparently pressurised into moving in with his seventeen-year-old girlfriend when he impregnated her, as according to him, he was reluctant to do so. Therefore, I thought that on balance he would be more susceptible to being convinced to engage in sexual contact than the average person. Further, it did appear from the Facebook messages that Kitty had instigated flirtation and had initially propositioned sex.

As Kai had no additional acute mental illness (such as depression or psychosis) and already had an understanding of the concept of the age of consent, there did not seem to be any rationale to transfer him to a psychiatric hospital. There was nothing to treat, at least from a mental health perspective. I proposed that if he were to be incarcerated, specific rehabilitation courses could be considered in prison to potentially address some of his behaviour related to future risk of sexual offending. The previous Sex Offender Treatment Programme designed by the HM Prison and Probation Service for inmates in the UK had been a massive flop; research from 2012 showed that it did not decrease the chance of reoffending and might have even marginally increased it, yet it was not shelved until 2017. However, there were newer alternatives for Kai. Of course, this would require a level of acceptance and motivation from him, which he was not displaying at the time of my assessment, as he had denied the allegations with his, at best, tenuous phone-charger-related excuse.

Although I had answered the questions I was asked in my report to the best of my ability, I also felt that I was giving mixed messages; I was saying Kai was criminally culpable, yet he was also vulnerable and susceptible. Instead of just checking over my finished report once for typos and grammatical errors as I usually did, I ended up obsessing over it for a couple of days. No, I am right, I finally decided. Kai is all of those things, even if they seemed contradictory, at least on the surface.

The outcome was a short prison sentence. I am unaware if Kai did engage in sex offender therapy, but I doubt it, given the brevity of his incarceration. I felt an ambivalence about the whole situation. It could be argued that Kai had paedophiliac tendencies that were flushed out and he needed to be imprisoned for the safety of further potential victims. But then again, it did seem like he was catfished and his learning disability would leave him less able to resist and to think through the consequences of his actions. Was he actually a danger to society? I don't think anybody can answer that with any degree of certainty. Prior to this charge, as far as anybody knew, he had not been initiating sexual contact with underage girls or, in fact, anybody. It is very feasible that if not entrapped, he would never have offended. He certainly wasn't as risky as Charlie Wedger, who was going around groping strangers. I suppose the counter-argument would be that if Kai were ever in a compromising situation, say at a party with a young girl, he might be more likely than others to make an unwise decision. I had to tell myself to stop overthinking it and have faith in the judicial system.

It also made me feel uncomfortable that Unknown TV, according to Kai's solicitors, targeted vulnerable men (including a man in his thirties with chronic schizophrenia, who had been ensnared a couple of months earlier). Wasn't this discrimination? Or was it only the particularly susceptible people who responded as they were not savvy enough to realise that they were being catfished? Around this time, I had taken an interest in *To Catch a Predator*, an American TV show which had much the same premise. Police would set up sting operations to lure potential sex offenders with lewd, suggestive messages from minors on internet chat rooms. They would arrange a sexual rendezvous in a house, full of hidden cameras, where officers would be hiding. A bit like *Candid Camera*, but for paedophiles. However, these perpetrators were different to Kai. They were predators with malicious intentions who instigated the inappropriate chat. It was compelling television, but it was trashy and it was voyeuristic. I found the presenter, Chris Hansen, to be smarmy and smug. It was very obvious that his line of interrogation was purely to make the culprits squirm and scramble to make believable excuses on the spot, for the viewers' pleasure. It was just dressed up as psychological investigation. A tiny part of me felt that I was perhaps contributing to a version of this warped show.

I had actually written and recorded a twenty-minute video on Kai's case for my YouTube channel. This was no small feat with my crippling technological incompetence. At one point I accidentally deleted all the footage I had recorded to make space on my hard drive. The whole task took me about five hours. However, when it came to releasing it on my channel, I had a last-minute change of heart and decided not to. Even though, like all my episodes, I anonymised the defendant and I had included some educational information (the diagnostic features of learning disabilities and the concept of *mens rea*), I had a strong feeling that there would be an overwhelming tsunami of vitriol towards Kai in the comments section. Some viewers would discount his diagnosis and vulnerability and label him a predacious paedophile, judging by the bile aimed towards Andrea Yates and some of my other cases. Although educating the masses, opening up conversations about mental illness and reducing the stigma were the key ingredients for my channel, I had to admit that my own narcissism was the seasoning. Therefore, even though Kai would never know, I felt there would be something gratuitous and unethical about putting him in this position, for what was at least partially my own gain.

By a strange coincidence orchestrated by the catfishing gods, within a month of seeing Kai, another similar case from the same solicitors' firm in Coventry floated into my inbox. Mr Bradley Striker was on bail, facing two counts of attempting to engage a child in sexual communication and multiple other counts related to possession of indecent images. According to the case papers, Bradley had been duped by an undercover police officer who logged into an internet chat room, pretending to be a fourteen-year-old boy. Bradley messaged him privately, initially saying he was sixteen and then changing his age to nineteen. He was, in fact, twenty-nine, the same age as Kai. After some banal chat about gaming, Bradley propositioned the target (or should I say, the bait), asking for naked pictures and suggesting that they perform oral sex on each other. A warrant was obtained by the police and, after searching his house, they found nine indecent images on his hard drive.

In their letter of instruction to me, his defence team stated that he had been diagnosed with autism, though after some digging I found this was not accurate; this diagnosis was only suspected, not confirmed. Bradley had reported to his solicitors that he'd believed the communication was only role play and his past experience of using chat rooms was that people were older than they pretended to be, so he presumed the 'boy' was older and that he would've known that Bradley was older too. I was asked whether his autism could be relied upon as a psychiatric defence and also whether this made him more susceptible to engaging in role play with others online. According to the defence statement, Bradley flat out denied making the indecent images found on his computer, claiming that the hard drive came from a second-hand laptop that he had purchased years ago.

His medical records were minimal, numbering a few pages, and they noted that he was on a waiting list for assessments for both autism and attention deficit hyperactivity disorder. I found it suspicious that he presented to his GP querying these conditions only a week after his arrest, considering they are both lifelong disorders and would probably have impacted him the most during his school years. I approached the assessment with my detective hat on and my bullshit radar on high alert.

I saw Bradley in the same conference room, in the same solicitor's office where I had assessed Kai and eerily he had chosen the exact same seat as his predecessor. Bradley was a friendly, overweight man who was dressed very smartly. He attempted to engage with the assessment, though appeared nervous, often losing his train of thought or asking me to repeat the question. I noted that he made good eye contact, which is uncharacteristic for autistic people. He was also able to convey his ideas and opinions very clearly and communicate normally. He followed the conversation well, including not interrupting me: not behaviour that might be expected of someone with attention deficit hyperactivity disorder.

Bradley relayed his personal history, including struggling academically at school and being bullied badly, as a consequence of severe dyslexia and a lisp, respectively.

He was apparently a bit of a handful as a child and would become aggressive and distressed for little reason. He gave an example of slashing his neighbours' tyres after being told off for having his punk-rock music playing too loud at the age of fourteen. He'd had a number of menial jobs, such as working as a pizza delivery driver and at Burger King. He also had a history of misinterpreting other people's actions, which led him to be a social outcast and rejected by peers. As an example, he reported an incident the previous week when he had been speaking to a random group of strangers while drinking alone in a pub and then joined their table for a few pints. He had thought that he was welcome as everyone had been laughing and joking together, though apparently a few of them asked him to leave as he was encroaching on their personal space. Bradley also reported to me that he had youthful interests; he spent most of his time playing video games and chatting to teenagers – 'in a non-sexual way,' he hastened to add. When I asked him if he had friends, he replied, 'Of course, I've got loads,' though then explained that these were all online. He said, 'I don't really want to meet them in real life. We'd probably want to play *Call of Duty* anyway, so what's the point?'

There was, to be fair, some evidence of a limited level of functioning. Bradley lived with his mother and she did most of the cooking, shopping and washing. He had never had a romantic relationship, though he said, rather sheepishly, 'I'd go and see prostitutes once in a blue moon for my needs.' I do recall him rushing back through the door five minutes after the assessment had finished, apologising profusely for using the term 'prostitutes' and insisting that I specify in my report that he had said 'sex workers' instead. I did as he asked, but I remember thinking that that was the least of his problems.

To assist the court, I highlighted the common symptoms of autistic spectrum disorder in my report. In my opinion, Bradley did display some of these features, including difficulty regulating emotion, only participating in a restricted range of activities and specific interests, and limited social skills. He might also have difficulty interpreting what others were thinking or feeling. However, from my assessment, he did not seem to have some of the other features, including trouble keeping up a conversation, difficulty maintaining the natural give-and-take of a dialogue, or being prone to monologues on a favourite subject. I also noted that Bradley was able to make good eye contact with me and there was some social reciprocity in our interactions: factors which would be at odds with the proposed diagnosis. Much like Kai's potential learning disability, the evidence was mixed and convoluted. Having taken everything into account, I concluded that Bradley might have a mild form of autism. However, many of his issues, behaviours and difficulties seemed to be more attributable to anxiety, depression, and anger management problems. I also outlined the cardinal features of attention deficit hyperactivity disorder (such as impaired attention and over-activity) and refuted this diagnosis from Bradley's presentation during my assessment.

As regards the two counts of attempting to engage a child in sexual communication, I stated that, on balance, even if he had mild autism as I had suspected, there was no discernible psychiatric reason that would cause him to believe that his communication was role play with older people. Therefore, there was no prospect of a psychiatric defence. As per my instructions, I also considered whether Bradley's possible minor disorder may have made him more susceptible to engaging in role play with others online. I concluded that, on balance, yes it might. His restricted social circle, existence as a misfit, inability to mingle and seemingly poor distinction between online and real-life friendships would encourage his internet liaisons. I wondered why the solicitors asked this, as it was unrelated to Bradley's criminal culpability. I suspected because, like me, they weren't convinced by their client's explanations. They were fishing (routine, not the cat variety) in the hope that the judge might show some leniency due to mitigating circumstances.

As a professional, I of course refrained from making judgements on Bradley's guilt within my evidence. But personally, I felt a little more at ease about my involvement in his case than in Kai's. Yes, arguably Bradley would not have committed these offences without the entrapment. However, crucially, unlike Kai, he was an instigator: the exact type of perpetrator who could have had a starring role in *To Catch a Predator*. Whereas Kai seemed to me to be, at least partially, prey. Although they both denied the accusations (unconvincingly), Bradley's excuses seemed more devious and calculated. He even appeared to have dragged his GP and his solicitors into his deceit.

Bradley was found guilty, sentenced to three years' imprisonment and put on sex offence notification requirements. Colloquially known as the 'sex offenders' register', this involves the subject having to notify the police of certain activities, in order to curtail future potential abuse, such as foreign travel or moving into a new household with any minors.

Incidentally, I received no further instructions from that particular solicitors' firm. Perhaps all the criminals in the Coventry area had seen the error of their ways. Or perhaps the lawyers weren't getting a pass from me for their clients as they had hoped for and they went expert-shopping elsewhere. My honesty was losing me work. I was the opposite of a cowboy expert (fitting, as I am an Indian).

I had no qualms in making a YouTube episode dissecting Bradley's case, while keeping him unidentifiable. It was refreshingly cathartic to be able to convey insights within my videos that had no business in a formal court report, such as how certain defendants made me feel and the ethical dilemmas some assignments burdened me with. I also presented both cases to my colleagues at our medico-legal forum. They reassuringly echoed the many murky areas that I had been struggling with, even though by then I had more than three hundred criminal cases under my belt.

After philosophising with my psychiatrist peers and making content for my channel, it eventually dawned on me that my perspective was askew. Some cases would never feel less ethically messy, even if I did another three thousand. A degree of doubt would always plague me. That wasn't the point. I had to become *comfortable* with uncertainty. More tolerant of the inevitable flaws in the system. I assess complex, multi-faceted individuals whose diagnoses are sometimes not easily classifiable, and whose actions are sometimes not cogently understandable. If easy answers didn't exist, I shouldn't be trying to force them. Einstein once said, 'All things should be simplified as far as possible but no further.' I dug that.

I understood that my purpose was to be a pair of spectacles for the criminal justice system. To make the cases less blurry, to the best of my ability, for the *court*, not for *me*. Any moral dilemmas that reared their ugly heads were my duty to absorb. After that, I had to accept whatever decision the court reached.

Don't overthink it, Sohom. I told myself then, and I still have to tell myself once in a while now. You're blessed with a fascinating, variable, unpredictable, complex profession.

Just do it.

Epilogue

Writing this book has been a genuine eye opener. I had to scour through dozens of old reports to extract the particulars of patients' stories. I was shocked at what I'd forgotten; not just details, but entire cases. Not only does this reflect my disgracefully poor memory, but also the sheer number of assignments I have undertaken. It is slightly disconcerting that I have become inured to the degree that so many of my assessments (which would have impacted the individual's futures and their psychiatric care and their victims' sense of justice immensely) have eroded in my recollection or have merged together. However, thankfully, this process has helped rekindle their stories in my mind. It has also made me reflect on the intricacies of what a forensic psychiatrist *really* is. We assess and rehabilitate mentally disordered offenders – that's a given. But, as I've come to realise, we are so much more.

We are *detectives*. We sift through evidence and assess defendants to elicit proof (or lack thereof) of psychiatric symptomatology. We must ascertain if very serious offences, including murder, were directly driven by mental illness.

We are *mountain rescue workers*. We save the lives and the sanity of people like Adriana De Silva who are drowning in undetected psychosis, ignored in prison.

We are *relationship counsellors*. We mend fractured bonds for those perpetrators, like Yasmin Khan, who have often figuratively and literally damaged their loved ones.

We are *surrogate parents*. We set boundaries for grown men and women detained in hospital, who need to fix their ways to be re-integrated into the world. Many of these patients were not raised with discipline, boundaries or even love. Like Reggie Wallace, the drug dealer, whose own father broke his arm when he was only one year old. Who in a paranoid psychotic state, attacked a random stranger on a bus, and who struggled to comply with the rules on our ward.

We are also *agents of fate*. We ultimately decide (or at least strongly influence the judge's decision) on the destiny of the accused. In cases like Yasmin Khan's, where the killing has been committed in the context of acute symptoms of mental illness, we lead them down a path of long-term rehabilitation and an eventual future, amalgamated back into society. In cases like that of Arnold Davis, which are not compelled by mental illness but rather in the context of a breakdown of a relationship, feeling rejected, increasing loneliness, an escalation of drinking, and jealous rage, we make sure that offenders are dealt with appropriately by the strong arm of the criminal justice system.

We are *bullshit detectors*. We must voice our suspicions of people we think are trying to cheat the system, by feigning or exaggerating mental illness. Such as the Ukrainian ex-model who was accused of multi-million-pound fraud, Daryna Boyko. I believed she was intentionally turning on the waterworks and evading participation in her legal proceedings, to dodge prison.

We are *punching bags* (ideally not literally, like I was). We absorb the anger and frustration of many who wish to lash out at society for marginalising and neglecting them. Like Jordan Dorian, who almost killed himself and his mother in a fire. Or Pamela Thorne, who needed thicker skin: both to prevent herself from being so easily provoked and to protect herself from her prolific self-harming when upset. On occasion, this can literally leave pools of blood to mop up.

We are *combat training students*. We regularly learn physical restraint techniques to contain aggressive patients, in order to keep ourselves and other residents safe. We must act swiftly and decisively to avoid injury, yet humanely and proportionately to avoid tragedies like the killing of Rocky Bennett, the patient with schizophrenia who died in October 1998 in a medium secure psychiatric unit in Norwich, after over-medication and a protracted restraint by staff.

We are *gamblers*. Sometimes, we are forced to hedge our bets, based on clinical decisions. Rarely, we must even go against the grain of our colleagues' opinions, risking professional embarrassment. Such as the case of Stella Lawrence, who I believed was too mentally ill to release from prison safely, though it seems was one amazingly convincing prankster.

We are *consiglieres*. We advise judges about extremely complex mental health issues and help guide them through the minefield of appropriate disposal options in criminal trials. Like the case of Barry Mulligan, the Welshman who stabbed himself in the cheek and his cousin on the head in a frenzy of drug-induced psychosis. I convinced the judge to utilise a community order with a requirement for psychiatric treatment and drug rehabilitation. This seemed justifiable in the circumstances, given Barry's lack of previous violent offending, and considering that his assault seemed directly related to drug use.

We are *barman at the last-chance saloon*. We rescue those heading towards prison who might be too vulnerable to cope. We give them an alternative and an opportunity to prove themselves. Like the case of Denzel Choo, who ruminated over historical guilt, and when drinking would threaten suicide in a profoundly histrionic and irritating manner, causing massive unnecessary inconvenience for emergency services. Instead of incarceration, he was given a disposal of a community order (though sadly, he later burnt his bridges and ultimately failed).

We are *diplomats and pacifiers*. In some situations, we need to use our voice of reason to calm down and de-escalate situations, such as when Jordan Dorian slammed me into his wardrobe after I was forced to stop his leave. We must negotiate and appease, like in the case of Johnny Benson, the semi-professional mixed martial artist who kept us hostage in his psychotic state after learning that his brother had died. At times we must use equanimity to elicit information from the incandescent. Like Ralph Reilley and his cantankerous fingerless-gloved father, whose assessment was arduous due to their incessant diatribes against the medical profession and inept psycho-babblists like me.

We are the *bearers of responsibility*. In our role of distributing limited resources, we must decide who will need high levels of ongoing observation and support in the community and, crucially, who will not. In this way, we are expected to be psychic; we must try to predict which of our flock will go on to injure or kill again and which will not. We are tasked with preventing tragic cases like Elgin Smithson, who killed three of his partners and attempted suicide, ending up with all of his limbs amputated.

We are sometimes *scapegoats*. Like Dr Danièle Canarelli, the French psychiatrist whose patient with paranoid schizophrenia killed his grandmother's partner. She was given a one-year suspended sentence and a €7,000 fine.

We are *critics*. We analyse our peers' evidence and occasionally we must oust 'cowboy experts' who, driven by greed, twist information and even the truth for the benefit of the party who instructs and pays them, rather than maintaining neutral objectivity for the court. I suspected this in the case of Jake Gove, the ex-soldier whose post-traumatic stress disorder supposedly caused him to racially attack a shopkeeper.

We are also *self-critics*. We can never be complacent or arrogant and we must be aware of our limits. We should take heed of cases like Professor Sir Roy Meadow, whose flawed evidence led to Sally Clark's unjust murder conviction. Professor Meadow claimed that her babies were smothered intentionally, though years later it was established that they had died from cot death.

We are *blind cogs in a system*. We assess, diagnose and heal dangerous patients, thereby protecting society and the safety of future potential victims. However, we often do not get to see the fruits of our labour unlike other types of psychiatrists.

We are *selective traitors*. In extreme cases, when life is at risk, we must break confidence. I had to reveal Harry Jackson's secret delusional thoughts about his deal with the devil and his suicidal intentions with the Number 9 bus, in order for him to be sectioned for his own safety.

We are *therapeutic leaders*. In calamity, like when Harry went on to commit suicide, it is our duty to absorb the emotions of each other and of our teams. We must reassure and we must heal. We also need to exercise introspection and humility to ascertain that our services are watertight. We must identify and plug any gaps in the system, to prevent future tragedies.

We are *students*. For those extremely convoluted, complex, nebulous cases where there are many different valid perspectives, we are obliged to research and to educate ourselves. This might include reading up on the minutiae of case law and seeking second opinions from our peers. Like in the case of Barry Mulligan, whose drug-induced psychosis and its relationship with the insanity plea befuddled me and my colleagues.

We are many things.

I qualified as a doctor almost two decades before writing this book. I specialised in psychiatry around fifteen years ago. I have worked exclusively with offenders for around a decade. It is only in the last couple of years of my career that I have come to realise that we forensic psychiatrists have an obligation to be more.

We need to be *teachers and reporters*. We must open those large, escape-proof, fingerprint-scanner-activated, industrial-strength, magnetic doors to reveal the clandestine world behind them. People fear what they do not know. We need to demystify forensic psychiatry to truly tackle the stigma attached to the individuals in its system. Celebrity stories are not enough. We should inform people about the vicissitudes and horrific backgrounds that most of our patients have suffered, to explain why they have hurt others and taken what was not theirs. In doing so, we must apply caution. We should resist the temptation of sensationalism in only relaying the gory details of the crimes. We must promulgate the success stories, to show that against all odds, our patients can turn their lives around.

I have made it my mission to be a voice for those who are seriously damaged by mental illness, which often leads directly or indirectly to repeated offending. To be a representative for those who spend much of their adult lives sectioned in hospital or locked up in prison. To tackle the many lurid, often media-driven, misconceptions. I started this process around a year ago via my YouTube channel, 'A Psych for Sore Minds', which has gradually been going from strength to strength. Now, I can add this book to my arsenal.

I only hope reading it has been as enlightening as writing it was.

Acknowledgements

Gratitude goes to my literary agent, Katie Fulford from Bell Lomax Morton, for going above and beyond, and having my back. To my editors, Nicky Crane and Rhiannon Smith, from Sphere, for their brutal honesty and taking out all the tasteless jokes that didn't make the final cut for this book. And to all of their colleagues for their help in creating and shaping this prose. Love to my parents and sister for encouraging my many antics. To all the lovely staff at Knight Ayton for helping me reach out to the public through the TV screen.

Kudos to all my work colleagues past and previous; our many discussions about mentally disordered offenders have honed my skills at making me sound cleverer than I actually am.

Shout out to all my Edinburgh University homies, especially the ones who have not allowed life and parenthood to hinder the occasional party. An extra special gratitude to the few of you who have taken the time to watch and read my material, follow my media endeavours and give me feedback. A nod to my more recent friends, from NCT, the infamous Slades Rise Bin Boys and parents from Merryhills Primary School.

Special thanks to my true-crime colleagues and collaborators, especially Shaun Attwood, who has been gracious enough to use his podcast to promote me. Credit to the viewers of my YouTube channel, 'A Psych for Sore Minds', whose words of encouragement helped me through my earlier dark times of pitiful viewing numbers. Keep watching! A massive thank you to past and present staff, especially Dimitri Frixou, the dynamo behind the channel, for doing all the groundwork that I am too busy or incompetent to do myself.

Lastly, but definitely not least-ly, to my beautiful wife Rizma (aka Wij Woo), who has put up with all my relentless mid-life crises (from boxing to poker to stand-up to short stories to wannabe YouTuber) and now this very book. (And also for putting up with my chat about intermittent fasting.) I owe you at least a hundred bedtimes. My beautiful boys, Kamran and Rayaan, you have robbed me of sleep and eroded my previous partying days, but you have given me some of the most intense love, laughs, cuddles and wrestles that I've ever experienced.

About the Author

Dr Sohom Das is a Consultant Forensic Psychiatrist working in prisons, secure hospitals and criminal courts, assessing and rehabilitating mentally ill offenders. He works as an expert witness in criminal and civil court cases. On his YouTube channel, A Psych for Sore Minds (youtube.com/apsychforsoreminds), he dissects a multitude of criminal cases and mental-health topics, covering diagnoses such as schizophrenia and PTSD, and offences from arson to murder. In between work, creating YouTube videos and parenting his two young sons, he occasionally dabbles in stand-up comedy and battle-rapping on TV.